THE RULE OF LOGISTICS

THE
RULE
OF
LOGISTICS

Walmart and
the Architecture
of Fulfillment

JESSE LeCAVALIER

University of Minnesota Press
MINNEAPOLIS • LONDON

This book was made possible through a grant from the Department of Architecture of ETH Zurich and the Future Cities Laboratory in Singapore.

ETHzürich
Eidgenössische Technische Hochschule Zürich
Swiss Federal Institute of Technology Zurich

(SEC) **SINGAPORE-ETH** 新加坡－ETH
CENTRE 研究中心

D**ARCH**
Faculty of Architecture

(FCL) FUTURE 未来
CITIES 城市
LABORATORY 实验室

This book is supported by a grant from the Graham Foundation for Advanced Studies in the Fine Arts.

Every effort has been made to obtain permission to reproduce the illustrations in this book. If any proper acknowledgment has not been made, we encourage copyright holders to notify the publisher.

Published by the University of Minnesota Press
111 Third Avenue South, Suite 290
Minneapolis, MN 55401-2520
http://www.upress.umn.edu

Printed in the United States of America on acid-free paper

The University of Minnesota is an equal-opportunity educator and employer.

22 21 20 19 18 17 16   10 9 8 7 6 5 4 3 2 1

Library of Congress Cataloging-in-Publication Data
Names: LeCavalier, Jesse, author.
Title: The rule of logistics : Walmart and the architecture of fulfillment / Jesse LeCavalier.
Description: Minneapolis ; London : University of Minnesota Press, [2016] | Includes bibliographical references and index.
Identifiers: LCCN 2016011049| ISBN 978-0-8166-9331-3 (hc) | ISBN 978-0-8166-9332-0 (pb) | ISBN 978-1-4529-5153-9 (ebook)
Subjects: LCSH: Building sites—Planning. | Wal-Mart (Firm)—Buildings. | Building layout—Psychological aspects. | Stores, Retail—Design. | BISAC: ARCHITECTURE / Buildings / Public, Commercial & Industrial. | BUSINESS & ECONOMICS / Corporate & Business History. | BUSINESS & ECONOMICS / Industries / Retailing
Classification: LCC NA2540.5 .L44 2016 | DDC 690—dc23
LC record available at http://lccn.loc.gov/2016011049

CONTENTS

INTRODUCTION

All Those Numbers

EVERY YEAR, tens of thousands of real estate brokers, franchisers, property speculators, retail location experts, and practitioners in a host of other subfields related to retail, real estate, or some combination gather in Las Vegas for RECon, a retail real estate convention organized by the International Council of Shopping Centers (ICSC). For this gathering, the floor of the convention center is organized as an alphanumeric grid, and the resulting plan reads like a city map. Lettered streets run the length of the building and are crossed regularly by numbered avenues. The Central Hall runs from Ninth Avenue to Twenty-First Avenue and from D Street to M Street. The upper floor of the South Hall continues from Twenty-Second Avenue to Forty-Ninth Avenue and from N Street to S Street. The floor below includes avenues from Fiftieth to Sixty-Sixth and streets T to X. Each exhibitor is assigned an address. The City of Oakland's kiosk, for example, can be found at S595 Y Street. This vast gridiron is known as the Leasing Mall, and it is the space in which these thousands of realtors and retailers converge to make deals that will influence the future of the American built environment.

The ICSC, a professional association for the shopping center industry, organizes RECon as part of its larger mission to promote the trade. The convention is less concerned with merchandising and more with real estate insofar as the retailers participating are not promoting products as much as their businesses as a whole. They attend in the hope of convincing landholders to offer them positions in their shopping centers or to persuade possible franchisees to take the risk of investing in their businesses. The complements to these efforts are those of companies that have space to lease and are looking for tenants. Since many of the real estate holders run shopping centers with multiple tenants, they come to Las Vegas to fill their vacancies with successful businesses that will, in turn, bring customers to the rest of their centers. Seeking to attract both retail and real estate investment, more than fifty participants at RECon 2010 were representatives of cities, each of which promoted itself as a dynamic locale on the cusp of expansion and transformation. The cities described themselves in language familiar to global real estate executives, who are accustomed to assessing investments in terms demographic analytics, including considerations such as trade areas and market segmentation. Apple Valley, California, for example, asserted that "low costs, free technical assistance, streamlined processing led by a single point of contact make it the place to do business! Apple Valley's economic development staff is ready to assist you through every phase of the development process as well as identify sites for your tenants."[1] Some cities were even more direct in their acknowledgment of the terms in which growing cities are evaluated by and depend on private development. Murrieta, California, for example, described itself as a "young, on-the-go affluent community just North of San Diego. Murrieta boasts a population of over 100,000 and a trade area of over 663,000. With a median age of 32, a median household income of $90,000 and recently recognized as the 2nd safest city in the nation, Murrieta is the future of Southern California!"[2] Companies with land or retail space to lease or sell also have a large presence at RECon. Walmart, the discount retailer based in Bentonville, Arkansas, and the owner and manager of sizable real estate holdings, has one of the largest corporate presences at the convention each year, including one of the event's most visible booths. In Walmart's booth, both aspects of the convention, retail and real estate, are consolidated in one site and in one corporate actor.

At RECon's seminars and workshops, speculators can get advice on a range of topics, from broad trends in retail to the specifics of lease restructuring. At RECon 2010, in a seminar called "Think Outside the

Box to Fill the Box," a presenter noted that the discount retail building whose image she was projecting on the screen behind her—a commercial shed building with cinder-block walls and light-gauge steel roof—was not adding any value to the parcel of land on which it was sitting if it was not in operation. In certain cases, she recommended retaining the land but "scraping" the site and starting fresh. In other words, the building on its own was unlikely to generate any revenue because the only way it could be productive was by performing the task for which it had been designed—that is, by actively enabling the movement of merchandise from supplier to warehouse to shelf to shopping cart. Otherwise, the bulky dimensions and large, undifferentiated interior volume would prove difficult to either inhabit or subdivide. So, according to the presenter, unless one wanted to use the building for its original purpose, a better bet would be to demolish the structure and start fresh on the land, the value of which would otherwise be diminished by the operation of such a building on it.

One hundred years earlier, Cass Gilbert, architect of the Woolworth Building, famously described the high-rise building as "merely the machine that makes the land pay."[3] What has changed in this long century so that buildings, once imagined as means of extracting value from the land itself (and thus more valuable if taller because of the increased amount of floors), are now seen, as suggested by the RECon seminar, as temporary situations built to enable the rapid circulation of consumer products? Gilbert's sentiment was directed toward building owners as he made the case that "architectural beauty, judged even from the economic standpoint, has an income-bearing value."[4] In the case of discount retail outlets like the one mentioned above, architecture is not a machine for making the land pay but instead pays the land to be part of a machine. William Cronon explains that pigs' "prodigious meat-making powers meant that once farmers had harvested their corn crop, pigs (along with whiskey) were generally the most compact and valuable way of bringing it to market."[5] In this example, the pig is recast as a medium within a network of exchange and as a solution to nineteenth-century ranchers' race against the tendencies of space and time to diminish the value of their livestock through weight loss, travel hardship, and even death. Likewise, the real estate parcel is a temporary housing for one switch of many in a long chain of circulation. Revenue is not extracted from real estate and rental agreements but through the availability of consumer products, themselves compact ways of transforming materials and bringing them to market. Because information can move incredibly fast but objects must still be moved physically, the processes of making such goods available are measured in terms both tangible and ethereal, spatial and temporal, in terms of weight and velocity but also in terms of anticipation and risk, calculation and information, concreteness and abstraction. Logistics is the industry associated with these concerns, and it is changing the world.

Logistics, according to a recent advertising campaign for the global package delivery company UPS, "makes the world work better." With this slogan, the company suggests that the services it provides help people to improve their businesses by enabling the exchange of goods in a timely, reliable, and transparent manner. In a TV advertisement, UPS touts logistics, to the tune of the Harry Warren song "That's Amore," as "a continuous link that is always in sync" and claims that with logistics, "technology knows right where everything goes."[6] Historically, logistics has been understood as the branch of military science that concerns the planning and coordination of operations, including provisions for movement, matériel, and maintenance.[7] The term is also used to describe contexts outside the military, especially those linked to global commerce, transportation, and coordination. The rise of logistics in this sense is coupled with neoliberal trade policies and the politics of globalization.[8] Because their aim is to improve efficiency, lower costs, increase profit, and so on, those involved in logistical practices may see things like national borders, labor laws, and certain trade policies as obstacles to their ambitions.[9] And because logistics has a distinctly spatial dimension, the sites of logistical practices are increasingly legible as spaces in which such obstacles are negotiated, reinforced, dismantled, or mutated.[10]

As both an area of work and a branch of knowledge, logistics takes its place next to similar categories such as economics, physics, politics, ethics, heuristics, and technics, to name a few. Logistics is also a process of transformation. In the same way that one might speak

The Walmart realty booth at the 2010 Retail Real Estate Convention (RECon) in Las Vegas, Nevada. Photograph by the author.

Stills from the UPS "We Love Logistics" advertising campaign in 2012 show a cross section of the company's distribution system, including technologies and infrastructures at a range of scales.

of the process of industrialization, mechanization, or automation, it is possible to speak of *logistification.* Industrialization concerned the systemization of production through the development of machines, mechanization represented the hybridization of human production with machinic processes and properties, and automation set about to literally make production machinic. Logistification, in turn, is an inclusive process that concerns the entire life of a product and works to flatten, connect, smooth, and lubricate as it organizes material in both space and time.

Logistics registers a number of trajectories that are relevant to questions of architecture, urbanization, and the built environment more generally, often reflecting what Zygmunt Bauman has identified as tendencies toward "liquefaction," including "the mind-boggling speed of circulation, of recycling, ageing, dumping and replacement which brings profit today" as well as the value of "travelling light" as an asset of power because "holding to the ground is not that important if the ground can be reached and abandoned at whim."[11] These images of things moving frenetically through space, of holdings freezing and thawing, appearing and disappearing in accelerated ways, as if viewed through a time-lapse camera, are precisely enabled by practices of logistics. Rather than encouraging congestion, logistics pursues unencumbered movement. Rather than seeking density, logistics aspires to coverage. It is a horizontalizing and externalizing industry, not a vertical and integrating one. It does not leave things to chance (e.g., the unplanned urban encounter is not accommodated in logistics regimes) but relies on calculation to reduce risk. And while logistics planners prefer to anticipate future concerns rather than react to them, when the unexpected occurs, the nimbleness of the industry allows it to make adjustments quickly. Instead of the friction of an earlier era in which things rubbed up against each other along their way (e.g., in the narrow streets of Manhattan), logistics tries to lubricate movement as much as possible. In the retail sector this is especially true because static merchandise is a liability. In this sense, the ideal condition for a retail logistics network is to have all of its merchandise suspended in a constant state of circulation, a humming network of movement with no backups, no bottlenecks, and no accumulation of storage.

All of these tendencies play out in the built environment. For example, the behaviors that Gilbert identified were the same ones that contributed to the development of the dense and congested twentieth-century metropolis. By many accounts, these outcomes have been positive from cultural, social, energetic, and architectural perspectives. The world, as is well known, is becoming increasingly urbanized as more and more people seek out cities for the expanded opportunities they promise. However, the networks of production and distribution on which the world's population depends are more and more attenuated, externalized, and otherwise obscured. Practically every item we encounter on a daily basis has come from somewhere else and is going somewhere else—sometimes quickly and sometimes slowly. The stuff of everyday life is also becoming the stuff of logistics. However, it is generally easy to remain ignorant of where a thing comes from and generally hard to find out. It is equally easy to disregard the specific built environment that attends and supports these logistical networks, partly because it occupies an externalized territory itself, and, if noticed at all, the built forms of this environment are themselves characterized by utilitarian neutrality. Moreover, the processes that govern the production, distribution, and consumption of goods increasingly operate at a global scale and introduce a set of demands and pressures that operate against the logic of the city of congestion, encounter, and adjacency. Instead, these processes privilege control, predictability, measurement, division, and management. They work to produce an overspecified version of the world that leaves as little room for chance as possible.

Logistical systems intertwine with and condition everyday life, with implications ranging from labor rights to national security to ideas of personal fulfillment. The tendencies and imperatives of logistics are actively transforming buildings, landscapes, and bodies, and these transformations are legible in the spaces, organizational forms, and technologies they generate. In this sense, individual consumption habits form part of a complex network of exchange among people, organizations, and production systems, mediated by a host of technologies that are constantly collecting and producing data. A single transaction—say, the purchase of a pack of chewing gum—is just one moment in an entire network of prediction, measurement, and calculation that is perpetuated by a collective willingness to sustain it through our habits, our desires, and the consumer data we generate.

Spatiotemporal by nature and imagined as the lubricant for global trade, logistics is an agent in the transformation of territory. In the words of another advertisement, more precisely targeted than the one mentioned above, UPS claims that logistics allows "crossing borders with ease" and makes "clearing customs a breeze" and that it can operate "overseas, over land, on the Web, on demand." If logistics is active in shaping territory, what means does it employ to define, produce, or otherwise transform space? What do these transformations look like, and what, if any, are the opportunities they might be freighting (or smuggling)? One point of entry to address these questions is through some of the very banal instruments of the logistical systems themselves: the things that enable the movement and switching of vast streams of capital and merchandise and the things that mediate among territory, technology, and bodies—the things called buildings.

In order to investigate the relationship between buildings and logistics, in this book I focus on one company, Walmart Stores, Inc., not only because it deploys a vast host of logistical services but also because its entire operation is fundamentally characterized by its obsession with logistics. For example, in an artifact from Walmart's corporate culture—a commemorative lapel pin depicting the planet Earth encircled by three communications satellites and superimposed with the words "WAL★MART 2000 AND BEYOND"—territory, technology, and the human body are all represented: the first two explicitly in the graphic content of the object and the last implied by the wearing of the pin. However, even though Walmart relies on buildings in fundamental ways, their absence in this depiction is noticeable, especially because it is the buildings that mediate among the other three. While it is true that Walmart's buildings are only one part of its larger logistical network, it makes sense that they might recede from view, given that they are more closely associated with infrastructure than with architecture. Indeed, logistical systems are often defined primarily in infrastructural terms, and seeing them as such suggests the expanded scope of their capacities. If infrastructure can condition the ways in which aspects

Commemorative lapel pins are popular
souvenirs of Walmart meetings and events.
This one, from 2000, depicts Earth encircled by three communications satellites.
Collection of the author.

of daily life unfold, and if Walmart's collection of built elements tends toward the infrastructural, then this collection of buildings becomes more active even as it disappears.

This book tells the story of these buildings and how they are designed, located, and inhabited. It covers the period from Walmart's founding in 1962 until roughly 2009, when the company's third CEO, Lee Scott, stepped down. I use Walmart to look at the ways in which logistics—as a branch of knowledge, an area of work, and a collection of processes—takes shape and how, in this case, logistics affects the built environment at the territorial, urban, architectural, and occupational levels. By understanding Walmart as a large technical system and by analyzing different parts of the company's organization in terms of related scales and technologies, I seek to offer an image of the fundamental features of one of the world's largest and most influential corporations while also identifying traits specific to a logistical approach to spatial, material, and experiential definition.[12] Underlying this investigation is also an interest in the future forms that architecture might take when confronted with systems that exceed its current capacities. As the built environment becomes increasingly overdetermined by technical systems and constrained by economic performance criteria— in other words, as it becomes a problem of management rather than of design—the ability to understand these dynamics better and subsequently imagine them otherwise becomes more urgent.[13]

For Walmart, logistics is a guiding principle, a rule that organizes all else. It is a rule not just for making decisions but also for generating models, defaults, and conventions. Similarly, just as rules contain formulas to be applied to different situations, the rule of logistics encapsulates a host of abstracting algorithms that allow ideas and information to be processed and optimized. To rule, as a verb, is to mark an area with lines, to demarcate, or to delineate. So too does logistics shape and define the territories it creates, but these definitions are elastic and their boundaries fugitive. To rule is also, of course, to govern and to control, even to dominate. Walmart has indeed created an empire of logistics. And yet, the ways in which logistics comes to control are not always the most obvious, the means by which it lays down its marks are not always the most legible, and the conduits through which it governs the thoughts and habits of its subjects are often buried.

Sam Walton opened Walton's 5–10 (or Walton's Five and Dime) in Bentonville, Arkansas, in 1952; ten years later, he opened the first Walmart store (its name styled as Wal-Mart) in nearby Rogers, Arkansas. As of January 2014, Walmart had 4,835 store locations in the United States and 6,107 international stores. The retailer earned almost $473 billion in fiscal year 2014 and employs more than 1.3 million people domestically.[14] The global retail sector as a whole took in almost $4.4 trillion in fiscal 2014, making Walmart responsible for roughly 10.75 percent of that. Altogether, the top five global retailers accounted for 21 percent of overall retail revenue, but Walmart's sales were greater than those of its next four competitors combined.[15]

From the company's outset, Walmart adopted unorthodox approaches to retail location and inventory management. Instead of looking to established settlement areas, it targeted rural communities. Instead of turning a profit with high markups, it reduced its margins to their minimum in the hope that sales volume would make up for it. And instead of relying on third parties for storing, shipping, and replenishing requirements, Walmart came do to almost everything itself. Walmart's logistics operations have also come to define the company. Its senior leaders identify logistics as an area of core competence to such a degree that one manager asserted, "The misconception is that we're in the retail business, [but really] we're in the distribution business."[16] This expertise has contributed to Walmart's growth and subsequent dominance in both the United States and the global marketplace.[17] Moreover, Walmart's logistical ascendance is linked to what has come to be recognized as the "revolution in logistics" that took place after World War II, when organizations began to consider not only aspects of physical distribution but also the "total cost" of their products, from sourcing to transportation.[18] The stages in these processes involve an entanglement of objects, people, buildings, infrastructure, money, information, and communication systems and are mediated by combinations of thresholds, zones, membranes, surfaces, and environments. These stages are especially evident in Walmart's operations.

Walton founded Walmart on a low-price/high-volume business model that anticipated the revolution in logistics. By selling things more cheaply, Walton could generate profit through high sales volume rather than high markups. This approach, while successful, relies on narrow margins that must be maintained and improved. As a result, Walmart strives constantly to reduce costs. The company has a reputation for negotiating relentlessly with suppliers, and its leadership puts tremendous pressure on store managers to achieve maximum profitability.[19] This pressure has its roots in Sam Walton's obsession with individual stores' weekly performance data. He would review these data every Saturday morning with his executives and managers in order to root out inefficiencies, either within their own operations or in those of suppliers. Through such scrutiny, Walmart's leaders concluded that they could handle most external operations better, cheaper, and faster than outside contractors could.[20]

This early realization led the company to develop its multilayered distribution system and to identify logistics as its primary expertise.[21] Because the company earns money through thin profit margins, it attempts to improve efficiency across all levels of its operation. To enable this complex coordination, Walmart devotes significant resources to the development, maintenance, refinement, and synchronization of its distribution and data networks, including the processing of large amounts of consumer data. Walmart uses this information to monitor shoppers' behavior and develop predictive purchasing and distribution models.[22] The company's large satellite network and Retail Link, the inventory management system that Walmart shares with its suppliers, enable the transmission of these data. Walmart was an early proponent of the Universal Product Code (UPC) and one of the first retailers to insist on compulsory adoption of the system by its suppliers; this enabled the company to substantially increase the amount and quality of the data it tracked.[23] For Walton, this logistical capacity was largely a means to an end. The founder remained focused only on how logistics affected performance—measured in profit. Discussing the company's extensive data network, he wrote: "What I like about it is the kind of information we can pull out of it on a moment's notice—all those numbers."[24]

To generate those numbers, Walmart has deployed a selection of predesigned, proprietary building types and adapted them to local requirements. Although Walmart directs few resources to its own corporate architecture, it has invested considerable amounts, along with substantial design intelligence, in its collection of retail outlets, distribution centers, and data centers. The retailer's generic buildings are the foundations of its empire, and the resulting environments have saturated the United States. As of 2015, this network comprised four domestic categories: 470 discount stores selling variety goods; 3,407 "supercenters" selling variety goods plus food; 639 neighborhood markets and other "small format" stores being tested; and 647 Sam's Clubs operating as members-only warehouses, similar to Costco (Plate 3). The total area of Walmart's retail locations is more than 848 million square feet, or about 19,500 acres. (Manhattan, by comparison, encompasses 14,694 acres. See Plate 4.) Each individual store is modeled on one of a collection of company prototypes and is then modified according to commercial considerations such as size, layout, and program and to meet the requirements of local conditions such as building codes, zoning ordinances, and traffic access. Regardless of the retail type, the Walmart environment includes not only the commercial venues themselves but also all the elements of the surrounding commercial landscape they produce: the parking lots, streetlights, traffic lanes, median strips, freeway exits, drainage systems, retaining walls, grass berms, gutters, sidewalks, curbs, fire lanes, and more.[25]

In fiscal year 2014, Walmart opened 198 locations in the United States, 72 of which were supercenters, the largest Walmart formats, with an average area of 182,000 square feet. Opening 198 new stores in a year meant that the company launched a new location roughly every two days, with a new supercenter almost every five days.[26] At each location, inventory typically cycles through several times a day. In this sense, Walmart designs stores to function more as valves regulating flow than as reservoirs capturing it; they are containers, but they are also conduits. And because the distribution system is so tightly coordinated, the store designs minimize areas for stock and maximize floor space for retail. Products are not the only things always on the move: Walmart's entire system is always transforming—at different scales and speeds—as new stores are built and (sometimes) existing ones are vacated or remodeled.[27] For Walmart, real estate, too, is a logistical practice in which the stores' spatial and temporal positions are critical to success. Strategically located to optimize the flow of goods, the stores and distribution centers form a dynamic and expanding network in which distances between locations are calculated in both miles and minutes. Walmart executives thus abstract territory in the same way their bar codes abstract merchandise. In other words, the nation's largest company perceives its territory as a data field over which "all those numbers" are monitored, tracked, allocated, and redirected in pursuit of market coverage.

Just as important as its stores, Walmart's distribution centers are hybrid structures—part architecture, part infrastructure—whose locations are determined by corporate growth strategies. By the end of 2008, Walmart's domestic distribution network consisted of more than 100,000 suppliers, 158 distribution centers, multiple data centers, the U.S. transportation infrastructure (mostly the publicly funded highway system), 6,500 tractors, 54,540 dry van trailers, 5,631 refrigerated trailers, 7,400 drivers, and roughly 80,000 other employees.[28] The largest distribution centers (DCs) constitute the core of this system and are highly automated. Goods are in constant motion, guided by electronically controlled actuators and conveyors, and monitored by employees wearing earpieces and scanners connected to central computers in Bentonville. The DCs are often the first structures built when Walmart enters new market areas—colonizers of sorts whose locations are timed to correspond with the construction of new retail centers. And just as one part of the network reaches capacity, a new distribution center opens to relieve the pressure and prepare the area for yet more stores.

The Walmart DC in the company's hometown, Bentonville, Arkansas, has an area of 1.2 million square feet. While limited public access makes it difficult to know precisely how the interior is configured, a conservative estimate might start with shelves that are roughly 12 feet high. If the shelves take up approximately 40 percent of the floor area, then they would hold some 5.76 million cubic feet of inventory, all of which, as recounted by the floor manager, is emptied and refilled—

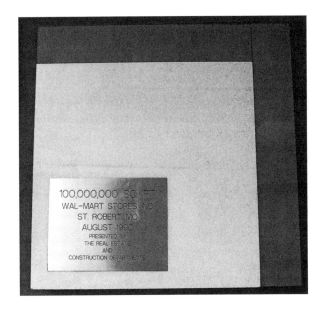

This floor tile in the former Walmart Visitor Center (now the Walmart Museum) commemorates the company's 100,000,000th square foot of floor area. This display was removed during the building's renovation. Photograph by the author.

Exterior of a Walmart distribution center in Bentonville, Arkansas. Photograph by the author.

or "turned"—every twenty-four hours.[29] A single twenty-foot equivalent unit (TEU), also known as a shipping container, is 8 feet wide, 8.5 feet tall, and 20 feet deep, which means it has a volume of 1,360 cubic feet. A Panamax container ship, currently the largest vessel capable of passing through the Panama Canal, can carry between 3,000 and 5,100 TEUs, depending on its size. The roughly 5.76 million cubic feet of inventory that the Walmart DC in Bentonville turns each day is the equivalent of 4,235 TEUs—that is, the capacity of one middle-sized Panamax container ship. Trucks deliver this inventory to a network of stores served by their local DC. For example, DC 6071, which occupies 1.7 million square feet near Tampa, Florida, serves 172 stores and has a fleet of 167 drivers. Once at the store location, merchandise is moved to the correct location on the shopping floor to await selection by Walmart customers.[30]

To anticipate what its shoppers might want to buy, Walmart keeps track of every customer transaction at every store and maintains two years' worth of those data by scanning the bar codes on all items sold. All of this information is stored in Walmart's network, enabled by the company's proprietary data centers, its extensive private communications network, and its custom inventory software. When the stock of an item dips below a preset limit, the network initiates a replenishment protocol and sends a command to the supporting DC, where the proper quantity of items is picked, packed, and loaded onto the next truck. Point of sale (POS) data also help Walmart monitor broader patterns and, ultimately, shape the corporation's larger inventory choices.

As Walmart has sought to expand its customer base, it has exhibited growth patterns that have differed from those of its competitors. Rather than seeking new markets in distant locations, the company at first grew steadily outward from Bentonville. It found locations on the edges of towns and close to transportation infrastructure, which, in turn, made it easier for the company to establish new distribution centers. However, Walmart has now nearly saturated its rural and suburban markets and has begun focusing on cities, where so far it has struggled to build successfully.[31] No single factor is responsible for this difficulty; rather, Walmart faces a combination of practical obstacles in terms of available lots and transport infrastructure. Cities also tend to have more active residents willing to mobilize in opposition to Walmart's efforts to enter their neighborhoods. Part of this opposition has been driven by the retailer's corporate practices, which have earned it a reputation as a ruthless negotiator, compassionless employer, and unfair competitor. For the first two decades of the company's existence, few within Walmart's leadership were overly concerned with these issues of public perception. However, as the retailer has become one of the world's dominant corporations, these problems have grown in significance. They are a reflection of both the very real difficulties posed by the company's practices and the ways in which it has tried to deal with them. These frictions present opportunities for an improved understanding of the mechanisms at work, as moments in which the workings of the system are exposed, and as moments to which the normal functioning of that system may be compared. This is especially the case concerning the peculiar forms of architectural intelligence that Walmart possesses and employs.

While it is convenient to refer to Walmart as if it were a single actor, it is important to remember that the corporation comprises an extensive network of agents, most of whom operate independently of one another, guided by local protocols. In the words of one review of Walmart scholarship, "The welter of ideas and interests surrounding this retail giant makes it virtually impossible to form blanket judgments regarding its overall impact." The authors go on to identify five "sociologically relevant themes" that preoccupy and divide the "social scientists, humanists, and nonacademics who are writing about" the company: "Wal-Mart's business model, its economic impact, its labor relations, its community mobilization, and its ties to the global economy."[32] The built environment that Walmart produces, both internally and collaterally, is absent from this list, even though all five of the categories identified are somehow mediated, reflected, and even transformed through Walmart's building efforts, real estate practices, and logistics operations.[33]

In 1960, in *Theory and Design in the First Machine Age*, Reyner Banham characterized the titular era of his book as one of mass production and competing ideologies. He suggested that the second machine age would be defined by the Cold War and computing technology.[34] If we accept Banham's progression, then contemporary conditions of neoliberal economics and globalized data have begun to define a third machine age, an age of logistics. Each of these defining periods has also had a corporate champion onto which its aspirations and reservations have been projected. Referring to these as "paradigmatic corporations," Daniel Bell writes: "One can say, without being overly facile, that U.S. Steel is the paradigmatic corporation of the first third of the twentieth century, General Motors of the second third of the century, and IBM of the final third. The contrasting attitudes of the corporations toward research and development are a measure of these changes."[35] The sequence of industrial development also follows this progression. U.S. Steel dealt in raw material, GM transformed that raw material into machines for personal mobility, and IBM extended mobility to the delivery and management of information, or even the production of information itself. Walmart—with its interest in collecting, distributing, and selling the world's things—can feasibly take its place after these three as the paradigmatic corporation of the turn from the twentieth century to the twenty-first.[36] In contrast with GM and IBM, which have actively cultivated high-profile—if suitably corporation-friendly—architects to develop their factories and work spaces, Walmart has made no effort to associate its corporate image with architecture (Plate 2).[37] Nonetheless, to be successful, Walmart depends on its buildings in fundamental ways—perhaps more than do companies such as GM and IBM. Because of Walmart's operations and reliance on logistics, the company imagines its architecture in increasingly infrastructural and temporal terms: redundant, repeatable, and abstract. While it has no corporate architectural emblems, Walmart uses the architecture of its store locations as a form of media through which it makes its merchandise available to shoppers and thus generates its income. Moreover, the corporate mascots that do emerge, even indirectly, are fundamentally associated with logistics. For example, the company's fleet of trucks (tractors and trailers) constitutes one of its most visible features in the landscape, a familiar symbol of Walmart's operations. This symbol is two-sided, in that the trucks' exteriors are legible as they move through various forms of transportation infrastructure and their interiors are linked with the organization's vast distribution network. Walmart's location maps guide the movement of these vehicles and become mascots themselves, triumphantly included in almost every annual report and prominently displayed in Sam Walton's office. The company's logo, the Spark, cheerfully signals combustion while also suggesting some distant motive force, giving form to power without giving it an image.[38]

In recent years Walmart's logistics strength—its expert use of "all those numbers"—has allowed it increasingly to influence areas beyond the typical concerns of a discount retailer, especially in environmental regulation and emergency response. It has also helped bolster the company's image in the eyes of critics and skeptics. In 2005, CEO Lee Scott laid out an ambitious plan to reduce the company's energy consumption. The goals were "to be supplied 100 percent by renewable energy," "to create zero waste," and "to sell products that sustain our resources and environment."[39] Walmart has approached this challenge with its characteristic rationalism, discipline, and zeal; it has understood that given the sheer size and scale of the enterprise, small improvements have big impacts. The company calculated, for example, that an increase in fuel efficiency of just one mile per gallon would save more than $7,000 in fuel costs for a single truck; multiply that across the entire fleet and the savings are significant.[40] As another example, the company started stocking milk in "case-less" plastic containers that require no crates or racks for shipping. With this modification of the packaging of one item, trucks carrying milk are able to hold 9 percent more volume. This means fewer trips, less gas, less packaging, and—most important to Walmart—a price reduction of up to twenty cents per jug.[41] Similarly, a few years ago Walmart decided to replace the fluorescent lights in its refrigerated cases with high-efficiency LEDs. When it found that no existing LEDs had the performance characteristics it sought, the company challenged lighting manufacturers to develop a better product—whoever designed the most efficient and least expensive fixture would get the contract.[42] Naturally, manufacturers devoted significant resources to meeting the challenge; only one got the job, but the competition ended up raising industry-wide standards. Since then, Walmart has expanded its LED program to include the produce and electronics departments and has awarded Cree, the company that produces the brightest and most efficient LED in the industry, an account for 650 stores.[43] These kinds of calculations and practices have led one columnist to suggest that Walmart "could drive the climate debate faster than years of congressional bloviation."[44]

Walmart's ability to communicate with suppliers quickly and directly and to implement new programs rigorously has been essential in its recent efforts to create a worldwide "Sustainable Product Index."[45] According to a 2009 press release, the program will have three phases. First, suppliers will assess their products in terms of energy, resources, efficiency, and social costs, using a standardized form generated by Walmart. Next, through a "consortium of universities that will collaborate with suppliers, retailers, NGOs and government," Walmart will develop a global database with life-cycle information for all its merchandise. Third, the company will use the database to generate a ratings system that will allow customers to access information about the sources and production of any item. Because Walmart is the largest customer for many of its suppliers, it can ensure cooperation for such an initiative. "It is not our goal to create or own this index," asserted Mike Duke, the CEO at the time. "We want to spur the development of a common database that will allow the consortium to collect and analyze the knowledge of the global supply chain. We think this shared database will generate opportunities to be more innovative and to improve the sustainability of products and processes."[46] Given the intent to create the index in the public eye and with the cooperation of nongovernmental organizations and universities, Walmart is positioning itself not simply as a discount retailer but also as a kind of de facto regulatory agency.[47]

Walmart's recent extracommercial activities underscore its logistics capacity. In the aftermath of Hurricane Katrina, the retailer mobilized its logistics expertise to facilitate relief efforts in the Gulf Coast region. Before the storm even made landfall, the company had anticipated supply shortages and had trailers loaded and ready in its Brookhaven, Mississippi, distribution center. After the storm moved north, Walmart dispatched trucks stocked with supplies to affected

Walmart changed its logo during a rebranding campaign led by the brand consultancy Lippincott.

Walmart's trucks and trailers constitute one of the most visible aspects of its operations. Source: Souvenir postcard from the Walmart Museum. Collection of the author.

areas in Louisiana and Mississippi—often ahead of the National Guard. As one local church official noted, "If the American government would have responded like Walmart has responded, we wouldn't be in this crisis."[48] Since then, the retailer has built nine "disaster distribution centers" modeled on its logistics network and stocked them with relief supplies and processing equipment in preparation for future calamities.[49]

These efforts are known as "business continuity" in retailer argot, and Walmart's emergency operations center (EOC) is part of the company's Office of Business Continuity. According to Jason Jackson, the Office's former director:

> Under normal circumstances, a six- to 10-person staff at the [emergency operations] center responds to everyday emergencies, such as a fire in a store or a shooting outside one. When disasters such as hurricanes threaten, the staff is joined by senior representatives from each of the company's functional areas [to coordinate tactics]. . . . The center is equipped with hurricane-tracking software, and on Aug. 24, days before Katrina made landfall, company managers were already planning their response.[50]

The subtext of Jackson's account is that Walmart's "just-in-time" ethos, coupled with its logistics expertise and clear communications channels, makes its private disaster response system more nimble and effective than the government's version.[51] Walmart's EOC and continuity operations are emblematic of the company's larger anticipatory disposition. According to Jackson, the Office of Business Continuity established a "watchdog" position "designed to do nothing more than identify business disruptions."[52] This employee "monitors a number of local and national news reports, e-mail reports from entities like the EPA, FDA, National Weather Service, and USGS, as well as bulletins from private sector security reporting companies. When the watchdog senses trouble, he alerts the team and then goes back to scanning."[53] Because Walmart's responsibilities are primarily internal, it can make decisions quickly. For example, Walmart used "reports from private weather companies and modeling software" to predict Hurricane Katrina's course before the National Weather Service made its similar announcement.[54] As a result, the company initiated its various hazard

Walmart tractor trailers deliver supplies after Hurricane Katrina. Source: *Wal-Mart 2006 Annual Report*, 10.

preparedness protocols in time to both avoid serious damage and provide extra relief supplies.

Walmart's efforts to improve product efficiency, supply chain transparency, and disaster response suggest that this large private organization can significantly influence public policy. These efforts also underscore how deeply Walmart has insinuated itself into the American cultural and economic landscape. However, just as the retailer's business practices differ from those of its corporate peers, so do its architectural practices. Walmart's incursions into affairs of state—whether they involve energy regulation, policy making, or disaster relief—recall a similar moment in the early 1950s. Charles Erwin Wilson, president of General Motors and President Dwight D. Eisenhower's nominee for secretary of defense, was asked if he would be able to make political decisions that might negatively affect GM—then the largest and most profitable corporation in the nation. Wilson answered affirmatively but added that he could not imagine such a scenario, because "for years I thought what was good for the country was good for General Motors and vice versa." In retrospect, this widely quoted sentiment—usually reduced to "What is good for GM is good for the country"—foreshadowed the increasingly intertwined relationship between the nation's interests and those of private corporations.[55]

In the cases of GM and IBM, corporate architecture was developed as an apparatus to support and promote the firms' respective products. From the "styling dome" of GM, in which the imagination of automobility was fueled, to the "white room" of IBM, in which the future of information was developed and promoted, specific architectural choices were linked to specific corporate agendas and fueled aspirational imaginations. Walmart, in contrast, uses its architecture to announce a different set of ambitions. Walmart's reliance on logistics has generated a far-reaching and ever-growing enterprise made up of information systems, landholdings, buildings, and infrastructure, yet Walmart's overall physical presence is more diffuse than the spatial manifestations of earlier corporations. This changing relationship to architecture might also suggest changing ideas regarding corporate representation. GM is a company concerned with technical innovation, and it could reinforce that pursuit through its corporate imagery and aspirational branding efforts. If the rising ubiquity of logistics brings with it both new opportunities and new kinds of exploitation and collateral implications, especially in terms of questions related to labor, resources, and the state of the public sphere, what then is the role of architecture within this? In the case of Walmart and its logistics operations, architecture's role as a tool has expanded significantly as it operates at different scales to orchestrate desire fulfillment, control territories, discipline bodies, and catalyze cultural growth.[56]

The different scales of Walmart's operations create a complex set of entanglements that reflect size but also organizational disposition and technological inflection. Thus, while it is true that humans can occupy buildings that are situated in a territory, some of the links between these scales bypass one another. Although scale is not a self-evident or stable category, it remains a useful organizational tool for investigating a large technical system like Walmart. Geographer Roderick Neumann cautions against a tendency to use the notion of scale to combine categories of size, level, and relation. For example, "households and cities are levels of social organization, not scales *per se,* and choices to study households or cities are epistemological moments."[57] This observation aligns with a broader understanding of scale as something "socially constructed, relational, contingent, and contested."[58] Others refer to scale as a "relational element in a complex mix that includes space, place, and environment."[59] Often omitted from such lists is the role that technology plays in constructing and complicating notions of scale through levels of entanglement and insinuation independent of size or level. As a result, elements operating at a certain "scale" are often distributed and mutable, just as the notion of scale itself is elastic and potentially fugitive or perishable.[60] Moreover, certain technologies and organizational impulses, while perhaps evident through an entire network's disposition, are more active at certain scales than at others. Historian of science Paul Edwards focuses not on scales of size but on scales of force, time, and social organization in order to develop a theory of infrastructure as it relates to technology. Doing so casts infrastructure in a much broader role and places it within a historical context that, in turn, highlights its role in "co-constructing" and "co-deconstructing" modernity at "macro, meso, and micro scales of time, space, and social organization."[61] These scales, moreover, are constructed simultaneously and rapidly. The links between the geographical and the technological illuminate the ensuing category of the logistical, in which space and time are combined, produced, transformed, and manipulated. The logistical mediates between the protocols of calculation and management and the contingencies of site, terrain, and locality. In order to develop these ideas, I have structured this book around scales of organization and their attendant technologies, with areas of investigation falling roughly into categories of buildings, locations, bodies, and territory.

In Walmart's network of buildings and infrastructure, the retailer employs three basic elements: the supercenter, the data center, and the distribution center. In the case of the supercenter, the interior layout of the shopping floor is defined by a strict set of protocols that pertain to inventory management, but it is ringed by a loosely formed band of ancillary programs like inventory storage, rentable space, and other service functions. While the interior of the store is inflexible, this outer crust is somewhat malleable. In the case of the data center, because of the intensive cooling requirements of the building-sized computers housed there, the perimeter is often quite rigid. However, because the contents of the facility require frequent updates (governed, as they are, by Moore's law), the interior of the building is often in flux, even if its exterior expression remains fixed. With the distribution center, the envelope of the building—the conventional means of delineating an architectural condition—is merely a necessary provision to keep the vast material handling system protected from the elements. Tightly wrapped but indifferent to form, here the envelope follows the interior configuration closely. Thus the supercenter has content but no form, the data center has form but constantly changing content, and the distribution center's content is directly reflected in its form.

Walmart has constructed thousands of these buildings, all precisely located, sometimes to reach specific demographics and at other times to evade political boundaries. Thus, while each type suggests specific attitudes toward architectural form, it also constitutes a fundamental element of a territorially ambitious and expanding network. Moreover, taken together, this collection of operational buildings suggests ways of thinking about architectural form as something much more contingent, a looser and lower-definition kind of architecture. Such questions are also related to the ways in which, in the case of Walmart, an international corporation accustomed to trading in the global and the generic collides with the local and the specific. Importantly and with good reason, qualities of locality have been mobilized in efforts to resist exactly the kinds of homogenizing effects that logistics brings. However, the parties involved in these struggles tend to talk past each other, as those defending their sites from incursion do so in terms of their own uniqueness while Walmart, in this case, sees each potential location not for what makes it unique but for what makes it equivalent. Locations must conform to Walmart's preestablished fitness criteria, themselves designed to be supple enough to be satisfied by a range of possible answers.

Walmart's collection of built forms is designed to be flexible and adaptable, which allows them to be, among other things, marshaled with particular territorial aims. As the company's initial intuitive understanding of territory was supplanted by imagination governed by measurement and prediction, Walmart found that it could use its precise location capabilities to operate at supralegislative levels, and thus imbue its architecture with political capacity capable of creating its own borders and undermining the political identity of constituents. In the same way that Walmart uses predictive market behavior models to find specific lots, it uses performance criteria to decide on strategic areas of expansion. The potential of these sites is calculated based on a host of considerations, many of which can be satisfied by multiple locations. In other words, Walmart's logistically informed perspective is indifferent to local configurations beyond the specific demographic criteria that mesh with the retailer's expansion goals. As a result, Walmart understands its sites as conceptually fungible conditions, decoupling, as it were, place from location.

Walmart's early adoption of the bar code allowed the retailer to imagine the objects of its network not just as inventory but also as information to be managed through both logistics protocols and facilities. Thus the corporation's collection of supercenters, data centers, and distribution centers must be understood in the context of its entanglement with the retailer's transmission circuits and information systems. By assessing locations in terms of performance characteristics, the company seeks equivalence in territory in order to satisfy its growth requirements. This allows it, in turn, to develop creative responses to constrained conditions as the company acts in a decidedly regional way, stressing elastic boundaries and fungible sites. At each stage, the physical locations in question become ever more abstract, until places, too, become data to be modeled and optimized.

At the human level, workers are asked to occupy spaces that are as much computers as they are buildings. Those who depend on jobs in Walmart's distribution system for their livelihoods are wired into one of the largest data networks anywhere. As consumer demand motivates the logistics of retail enterprise, Walmart sells products that reflect the things customers need to survive or the things they want. As a result, in many ways logistics networks are motivated by a range of emotions and desires that have financial, political, and personal consequences in terms of energy, labor, and money. Walmart distribution center employees make up only a very small portion of the world's population, but the environmental stresses they are asked to manage (such as speed, information density, and incomprehensible environments), while especially acute in the logistical environment, are similar to those faced by an increasingly large part of society. These large distribution centers invert imagined technologically mediated relations as they blur boundaries and produce seemingly paradoxical spatial conditions.

Walmart is both an index and an engine of globalization, yet it defies many of the truisms of a globalized and networked society. Large as it is, Walmart remains a family business of sorts. Far-flung as its networks are, it remains centrally headquartered in the somewhat remote city of Bentonville in northwest Arkansas. Logistics works to disaggregate multiple aspects of industrial capitalism, and a closer look at Bentonville helps to clarify the consequences of that dissolution because it registers the transformations being wrought by Walmart's logistical operations. The company's headquarters are not proximate to its sites of production, its customers, or its suppliers. However,

The Sam M. Walton Development
Complex in Bentonville houses
Walmart's real estate division, which
includes the architecture department.
Photograph by the author.

Walmart's sustained presence in Bentonville, the corresponding consolidation of capital in its managerial echelon, and the astonishing wealth of the heirs to the company (who make up one of the richest families in the world) have created a new kind of city, a city shaped by the rule of logistics. Rather than reflecting the creeping sprawl of some distant urban center, the Bentonville area has become a new metropolitan entity in its own right. While ostensibly a constellation of small towns, the Fayetteville–Springdale–Rogers Metropolitan Statistical Area, as the U.S. Census Bureau officially designates it, is an example of an emerging form of urbanism generated, in part, by logistics. The horizontal and programmatic congestion it generates, enabled by significant corporate patronage, suggests other forms of urban intensity as well as new forms of civic identity.

By looking at the buildings, locations, bodies, and cities of Walmart's logistics operations, I hope to improve understanding of one of the major social, political, and technological forces at work in the contemporary built environment. I do so in an effort to contribute to a greater awareness generally, but also to expand design repertoires by looking at something often residing just out of sight. At the root of this impulse is curiosity, in the sense used by Michel Foucault, who describes it as something that "evokes the care one takes of what exists and what might exist; a sharpened sense of reality, but one that is never immobilized before it; a readiness to find what surrounds us strange and odd; a certain determination to throw off familiar ways of thought and to look at the same things in a different way."[62] This appeal to engage the world while imagining it otherwise has motivated this study, a motivation I share with others who have scrutinized the social environment and the buildings, infrastructures, and technologies that support and shape it.[63] Bruno Latour echoes Foucault in his description of the "nonmodern" attitude that "deploys instead of unveiling, adds instead of subtracting, fraternizes instead of denouncing, sorts out instead of debunking."[64] Through deeper investigations into buildings, cities, and infrastructures, we can gain glimpses of their latent possibilities."[65]

1 LOGISTICS

The First with the Most

THE EMERGENCE OF LOGISTICS as a branch of management has brought with it new ways of seeing and imaging the world, propelled by a series of technological surges. Taken together, these new modes of perception and new technologies affect the ways in which architecture is imagined, sited, built, and inhabited. While the case study here is a retail corporation, the issues that emerge in the examination of Walmart's architecture are not isolated and are unlikely to remain historically contained.[1] Through the combination of the abstract and the concrete, through the conflation of time and distance, and through the deployment of elements both networked and discrete, logistics requires the creation of objects, systems, and environments that both mirror and reproduce these conditions. While military and managerial logistics might have emerged as discrete areas of concern, they are ever more entangled, as is evident in an illustration from an *Army Logistician* article titled "Modeling the Wholesale Logistics Base" (Plate 1). The image depicts an interior space as a monochromatic volume whose planes are inscribed with a square grid of white lines. In high-contrast black and white, a forklift operator uses his vehicle to transport a two-by-two cube rendered in the same manner as the surroundings. In this image, the objects that are being shuttled through the distribution center merge with the building itself, or vice versa.[2] Rendering objects and their surroundings in the same way conflates the two; they are united by the imagination of the logistician as elements that fit together perfectly and in which each element and each unit of volume and area can be accounted for and modeled. Treating environment and objects equally further erodes the boundary between figure and ground as they mutually evolve toward abstraction through the flattening tendencies of calculation.

The image from *Army Logistician* associates buildings, inventories, and data with the logic of computer models and simulations and subjects them to the protocols of prediction, measurement, and strategy. These are territorial concerns that trade in abstraction and are often visualized from an Archimedean point. However, the awkward presence of the human operator in the illustration is a reminder that these simulations only hint at a more sprawling set of circumstances, burdened by the contingencies of site, locality, and human frailty. Between these concerns of terrain, tactics, and making do and the aloof specificity of the simulation are buildings and their components, themselves part of a much larger, much messier network. It is at this intersection, a primary site for observing the habits and behaviors of the logistical, where the architectural work of Walmart sits.

Logistics Is a Spatial and Temporal Practice

Logistics is the science of managing things in space and time. This is true in both its military and its managerial contexts, whether it involves ensuring that a convoy arrives at just the right spot at the right moment or that the proper widget is available when the factory assembly system needs it. The military understanding of logistics is, in the words of one logistics historian, "the business of war preparation."[3] James Huston, writing under the auspices of the Office of the Chief of Military History of the U.S. Army, observes that "war is frequently likened to a game of chess, but chess is no strategic game, for there is no logistics."[4] In the version of logistics understood as the managerial science related to overseeing the entire "supply chain," this equally fraught metaphor is meant to encompass the "life span" of a product, from extraction of raw material to consumption and disposal by the end consumer. The chain image suggests fundamental linkages in a concatenation of global production, but the image of the chain fails to communicate adequately the complexity of a logistics network. In the same way that chess fails as a metaphor for battle because it addresses only strategy and tactics, with no account for logistics, the supply chain fails as a metaphor for logistics because it oversimplifies the approach.[5] The lack of acknowledgment of logistics and the dearth of language used to engage it are both indicators of opportunities for further exploration.

The origins of military logistics are connected to the growing complexity and bureaucratization of warfare. Armed conflict at its most fundamental—as a symmetrical struggle of two opponents with no planning and no required supplies—consists only of tactics. However, over the course of history, as the complexity and duration of campaigns expanded, not only was strategic planning necessary, but so was logistics. Waging war became an exercise in management, one that rewarded strategic thinking and calculation, both aided and enabled by logistics. As a result, the resolutions of many conflicts have turned on logistics, with outcomes often decided not by superior technology and cunning in battle but simply by miscalculation and mismanagement.[6]

While armies have always been concerned with questions of logistics, it was not until the Napoleonic campaigns of the early nineteenth century and the work of Carl von Clausewitz and Antoine-Henri Jomini that logistics was formally articulated as a specialized field of military knowledge. "Is logistics," asks Jomini in *The Art of War,* "simply a science of detail? Or, on the contrary, is it a general science, forming one of the most essential parts of the art of war? Or is it but a term, consecrated by long use, intended to designate collectively the different means of carrying out in practice, the theoretical combinations of the art?"[7] These lines open his entry titled "Logistics; or, The Practical Art of Moving Armies." Jomini first published his treatise in 1838 and is largely credited with establishing the tripartite structure of modern campaigns:

> Strategy is the art of making war upon the map, and comprehends the whole theater of operations. Grand Tactics is the art of posting troops upon the battlefield according to the accidents on the ground, of bringing them into action, and the art of fighting upon the ground, in contradistinction to planning upon a map. . . . Logistics comprises the means and arrangements which work out the plans of strategy and tactics.

> Strategy decides where to act; logistics brings the troops to this point; grand tactics decides the manner of execution and the employment of the troops.[8]

Following this summary of his theory of war craft, Jomini devotes an entire section of the book to questions of logistics. In his attempt to establish the contours of the field, he corrects an earlier position in which he stated that logistics was the name given to all those activities that in the past had been the responsibility of the quartermaster, namely, "to lodge and camp the troops, to give direction to the marches of columns, and to locate them upon the ground."[9] He goes on to assert that as warfare grew more complex, logistics became "nothing more nor less than the science of applying all possible military knowledge," in which "the functions of staff officers at the present day are intimately connected with the most important strategical combinations."[10] Jomini then proceeds to list eighteen key duties "relating to the movement of armies." These duties are characterized by anticipatory and managerial gerunds like *arranging, ordering, composing, prescribing, indicating, superintending, designating,* and, naturally, *organizing.*[11]

From this list of duties, it is clear that the quartermasters, or logisticians, are required to maintain a simultaneously tactical and strategic view of a given operation. For example, ensuring the proper pacing of a column of troops requires a quantitative assessment of the troops and a qualitative understanding of the conditions of the land they will be traversing. Additionally, both temporal and spatial requirements must be met, because, maintaining the example, a column of troops needs to arrive at a designated position at a designated time. This blend of organizational awareness and contextual attention is characteristic of the logistical imagination and has particular spatial consequences. Problems of coordination, of distances, and even of surfaces all become more acute as a campaign becomes longer or more attenuated.[12]

The term *logistics* reinforces these spatial dimensions, coming as it does from the French *loger,* meaning to lodge or house.[13] In order to make sense of the complex movement of troops and supplies, logisticians must, by necessity, employ diagrammatic and topological representations of the territory in question.[14] Rather than depicting every detail, these representations acknowledge only the aspects of the territory that pertain to the logistical processes in question, as is evident from the accompanying illustration showing supply movement from the United States to the European theater during World War II. This modeling process necessarily produces a distance between the ground and those logisticians charged with managing the movement of goods over it. It also further enables calculative tendencies to become dominant. As the stuff of the logistical process becomes measured, quantified, predicted, forecast, and simulated, this terrain is rendered in ever more abstract fashion.[15] This simultaneous encrustation of information and increasing dissociation signals a need for an expanded vocabulary with which to describe the condition. Geographer and historian Stuart Elden, for example, building on Foucault, uses the term *territory* to acknowledge the elusive complexity of the situation. According to Elden: "Territory is not simply land, in the political-economic sense of rights of use, appropriation, and possession attached to a place; nor is it a narrowly political-strategic question that is closer to a notion of terrain. Territory comprises techniques for measuring land and controlling terrain. Measure and control—the technical and the legal—need to be thought alongside land and terrain."[16] The technical, with its links to measurement and delineation, is also connected to questions of space, just as the legal, with its concerns about process and protocol, is connected to time; both reach together toward the logistical. Returning to the diagram tracking the movement of provisions during World War II, it is indeed a "territory" that it describes, including the depots, warehouses, and distribution centers that enable the movement of material in time and space.[17] These structures are the more overtly architectural features of logistics and also the sites in the system in which logisticians can actively modulate its parameters, often rehearsed in simulations and models. In early army warehouse models, for example, "if backlogs should develop, management intervenes. Any number of vital management decisions can be made to relieve choke points and increase outputs."[18] The logisticians' tasks, then, are both managerial and anticipatory. As they continually monitor these abstractions, they become trained to think forward temporally to the spatial consequences of their actions.

Jomini's expanded definition of logistics broadens the concept to such a degree that it becomes related to almost all aspects of a campaign. Perhaps in an effort to reclaim some specificity, Huston summarizes his sometimes-competing definition of logistics as

> the application of time and space factors to war. It is the economics of warfare, and it comprises, in the broadest sense, the three big M's of warfare—matériel, movement, and maintenance. If international politics is the "art of the possible," and war is its instrument, logistics is the art of defining and extending the possible. It provides the substance that physically permits an army to live and move and have its being.[19]

Huston calls logistics "the art of defining and extending the possible" for its capacities to overcome unexpected challenges and to push at the edges of feasibility.[20] Logistics, in this way, is a world-making enterprise that emphasizes awareness, foresight, and preparedness. At the same time, logistics requires a tactical mind-set that accepts that things rarely go according to plan.

If Jomini was concerned with the rules of war, Carl von Clausewitz was more interested in its nature. Clausewitz's formulations might be familiar, including the notion of the "fog of war" in reference to the uncertainty of events in spite of extensive strategic planning. Clausewitz also famously argues in his 1832 work *On War* that "war is not merely an act of policy but a true political instrument, a continuation of political intercourse, carried on with other means."[21] In describing war waged in "accordance with its essential spirit—the unbridled violence that lies at its core," Clausewitz suggests that provisioning the troops, the domain of the quartermaster, is only a secondary matter. However, "where a state of equilibrium has set in . . . subsistence is likely to become the principal concern. In that case, the quartermaster-general becomes the supreme commander."[22] When, as he describes it, "the conduct of war consists of organizing the wagon trains," war seems to become policy again, this time overseen and managed by logistics operations.

Logistics concretizes space and time through its material realities. As Manuel DeLanda notes, the movement of people, fuel, and resources is governed by the physical act of doing so and by the actual energy required. Thus "friction becomes the factor which makes or

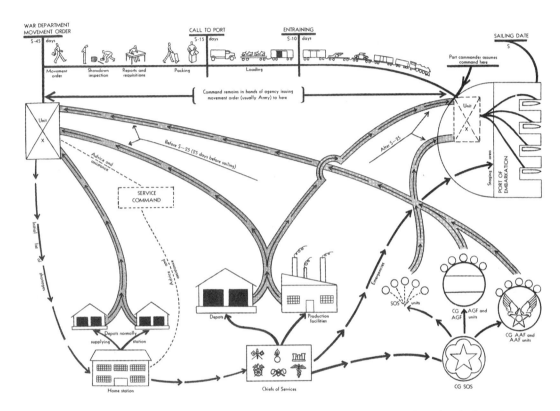

This diagram, "Procedure for Equipping a Typical AGF Unit for Overseas Movement: February 1943," presents a topological depiction of the space of military logistics. Source: James A. Huston, *The Sinews of War: Army Logistics 1775–1953* (Washington, D.C.: Office of the Chief of Military History, U.S. Army, 1970), 503.

breaks a logistics network."[23] This friction is evident at all scales of the logistics network, from the drag on vehicles to the gradual wear of mechanical parts bearing on each other for long periods of time. In this sense, De Landa rightly points out that logistics "has always been the major constraint on any war enterprise, even before ammunition and gasoline came to replace protein as the main fuel for armies."[24] The latter phrase is a reference to the saying, attributed to Napoleon, that an army "marches on its stomach." Thus, while military logistics governs operations over space and time, it can do so only if it receives a constant supply of fuel. Deborah Cowen links this trajectory to the industrialization of warfare, in which "logistics has come to lead strategy and tactics: it has gone from being the *practical afterthought* to the *calculative process that defines thought*. Changes in the material form and social organization of fuel saw logistics gradually become *the how that shapes the what*."[25] Once again logistics is cast as an active practice, concerned with repetitive efforts organized around specific techniques—that is, "the how." In this sense, the operations of logistics also condition the spaces they inhabit. In the case of the military, logistical demands transform the space of warfare into one of technology and infrastructure. Likewise, in sectors with less obvious martial origins, including commercial enterprises like Walmart, logistics is equally active and works at technological and infrastructural levels to shape the landscape.

Just as military campaigns were concerned with logistics even before the concept was named, the corporate world has always had to deal with the need to move goods through time and space. In Huston's words, if "the primary aim of logistics is 'to get there first with the most' (and the best), the question may be asked: Where is 'there'? The answer probably would be: The critical point."[26] In the case of real estate, Conrad Hilton's adage that the three most important elements in real estate are "location, location, and location" is a kind of shorthand summary of the demand, as cited by Huston, to be there "first with the most." Similarly, in both cases, *there* is a strategic position aimed at capturing a location or besting an adversary. In retail real estate, for example, companies like Walmart seek strategically and logistically optimal locations that reach the most potential customers while not competing internally with other locations. While companies do not frame their attempts to gain such locations as battles, in the sense that they are not amassing troops, they nonetheless gather intelligence, develop strategies, and operate tactically in order to secure the best possible positions. Such maneuvering echoes Huston's assessment that U.S. Army intelligence doctrine does not attempt to "guess what the enemy *will do,* but to determine what he *can do,* that is, to analyze enemy capabilities, and capabilities depend fundamentally on relative logistic positions." However, Huston is careful not to overstate the role of simulation, noting, "It is not to be suggested that the issue of battle necessarily turns on this calculation; if that were so, the whole process could be left to calculating machines."[27] Huston was writing in 1970, just at the threshold of large-scale automation of information, which presaged an increased reliance on calculating machines in both warfare and real estate. In fact, the trend toward greater affordability and availability of computing power in the 1970s—along with significant deregulation of transport policies—enabled what is often referred to as the "revolution" in logistics.[28] In the commercial theater battles are still fought, but most often they play out in computer simulations, zoning laws, and real estate negotiations. The stakes are high because a poor choice or ill-informed decision can result in a significant misdirection of resources. The process, thus, has come to include the handling of enormous quantities of information; increasingly dependent on and increasingly driven by "calculating machines." Battles for the city might, after all, "turn on calculation."

The contemporary management science known as business logistics combines branches of physical distribution, transportation planning, supply chain management, predictive analytics, and more into a field that adopts a comprehensive, systems-based approach to consider the entire extent of a firm's operations. In 1962, Peter Drucker, the influential management consultant and author of the groundbreaking book *Concept of the Corporation* (first published in 1946), identified distribution as "one of the most sadly neglected, most promising areas of American business."[29] In the decades that followed, the field became increasingly inclusive and also increasingly defined. Professional organizations such as the Council of Supply Chain Management

Professionals and the Logistics Management Institute formed, and new academic departments started to train systems managers to see operations in a comprehensive way. Drucker described this new breed of manager as someone who "points out that a proposed new packaging design will double freight costs, instead of having this come to light only after millions of the new packages have been made."[30] In Cowen's assessment, "A wide range of functions previously understood to be distinct from distribution were now part of its total cost."[31] She goes on to emphasize that "total cost analysis produced new sources of profit with very different kinds of effects on corporate strategy, and this strategy was inherently spatial."[32] This "inherently spatial" dimension has an attendant set of material and organizational forms that are increasingly evident in the built environment and especially evident in the logistical operations of Walmart.[33]

Managerial definitions of logistics remain equally focused on time and space but tend to cast logistics as a continuous process rather than as a goal-oriented sequence, as the military tends to do. For example, W. Bruce Allen quotes the Council of Logistics Management's definition of logistics:

> The process of planning, implementing, and controlling the efficient, effective flow and storage of goods, services, and related information from point of origin to point of consumption for the purpose of conforming to customer requirements. This definition includes inbound, outbound, internal, and external movements, and return of material for environmental purposes.[34]

Once again organizational verbs dominate, but in contrast to the military definitions concerned with timing and location, this definition of logistics focuses on flows and directions, on vectors and rates. This emphasis is evident in Paul Schönsleben's reference book *Integral Logistics Management,* in which logistics is defined as the "organization, planning, and realization of the total flow of goods, data, and control along the entire product life cycle."[35] The implications of the naturalist metaphors of flow and life cycle notwithstanding, the emphasis reinforces a view of logistics as a field fundamentally concerned with the coordination of objects' locations in space and in time. In the context of retail, for example, such an understanding is important because the process of the "turn" of merchandise—that is, its evacuation and replenishment over a given period of time—resists simple visualization.

In order to know what to stock and where to direct it, retail companies need to know what people will buy; thus they need to understand, predict, and condition consumer habits. In early explications of the logistics industry, this link between distribution and desire was already evident. For example, in 1967, Edward Smykay and Bernard La Londe noted: "Physical distribution is an offshoot of the marketing concept. The marketing concept focuses on delineation of markets through identification of consumer wants, resulting in product design, price, and promotional activities specifically tailored to sharply defined market segments."[36] As companies in turn aim to be as responsive as possible, knowing what to stock becomes critical, as does the constant presence of the right stock. In more recent studies, scholars such as Yossi Sheffi have observed that forecasting is crucial because it is exactly these models that determine demand for a product, which in turn triggers a whole set of subsequent decisions by all the various producers, procurers, and distributors. The more closely coordinated these links can be, the less inventory there is in the system, which dramatically reduces costs.[37]

These dynamics are linked to the emergence of so-called lean production (as opposed to mass production), in which placed orders are assembled "just in time."[38] A lean operation's primary goal is to have exactly as much inventory as needed. In the manufacturing world, this brings flexibility to changing demands, increases consumer choice, ensures faster delivery, and enables responsiveness in the face of disruptions. In logistics, lean, just-in-time production is often coupled with just-in-time delivery. Thus, rather than a supplier having an inert inventory of products that it needs to "push" onto consumers, consumers are able to "pull" products from the supplier's repertoire. A number of technological developments connect and enable these transformations, each of which contributes in some way to the spatial imagination of logistics.[39] These transmissive, topological, and abstracting tendencies of logistics have an architectural expression clearly evident in the buildings of Walmart, but they are also indicative of a broad set of tendencies toward spaces and environments that are increasingly automated, uncontainable, and illegible to humans.[40]

Logistics Mediates between Abstraction and Concreteness

Logistical architecture occupies the site of negotiation between tendencies toward the abstract and tendencies toward the concrete. As a result, buildings lose their status as isolated objects but become contingent sites of mediation within entangled systems. Implied in the image discussed at the beginning of this chapter (Plate 1), while inventory and data are conflated in the abstracted interior, the drawing still assigns the volumes substance and locates them in space. In fact the only elements "out of place" are those being engaged by human-operated vehicle. In the case of the image, the coordinate system enables an imagination of space capable of sustaining *both* understandings of these objects-cum-data. The drawing's use of single-point perspective further suggests that the inventory is part of the quantitative and calculative environment (the abstract) *and* part of the qualitative and impulsive/reactive environment (the concrete). Such an imagination is likewise not confined to an interior but blankets the landscape, so that these items may be distributed in the precise and timely manner that logistics companies promise. Thus imagining logistically requires the understanding of a given landscape as simultaneously terrain and territory, physical and abstract, material and informational. As Henri Lefebvre writes:

> The space of the commodity may thus be defined as a homogeneity made up of specificities. This is a paradox new to our present discussion: we are no longer concerned either with the representation of space or with a representational space, but rather with a practice. Exchange with its circulatory systems and networks may occupy space worldwide, but consumption occurs only in this or that particular place. . . . The paradigmatic (or "significant") opposition between exchange and use, between global networks and the determinate locations of production and consumption, is transformed here into a dialectical contradiction, and in the process it becomes spatial. Space thus understood is both *abstract* and *concrete* in character: abstract inasmuch as it has

no existence save by virtue of the exchangeability of all its component parts, and concrete inasmuch as it is socially real and as such localized.[41]

Logistics emerges as the mediating element between these two aspects of space. Capable of managing both the abstract and the concrete, logistics' specific material aspects and techniques allow it to occupy this intermediate position. This also underscores the spatial dimension of logistics: because the aim is not just to reach the right location but also to reach it at the right time, it is impossible to decouple the temporal from the spatial. Moreover, this intermediate position helps to illuminate the difficulties involved in attempting to visualize or map the form and extent of logistics. The space that logistics occupies, the space between the abstract and the concrete, conditions the ways that its material apparatus is understood and deployed, particularly the built forms that support its ostensible architectural components.[42]

Logistics' capacity to mediate between the opposing realms of abstraction and concreteness enables an imagination that focuses on action rather than on form and that measures distance in time. As a consequence, seemingly counterintuitive spatial manifestations appear and are increasingly normalized. These habits have one root in the manipulation of the relationship between time and territory during the standardization of time zones in the late nineteenth century as the result of pressure to standardize trade routes and schedules. While railroad companies shaped the mid-nineteenth-century urban and commercial forms of the United States, they also created a number of coordination problems, evident most noticeably in violent train collisions. For example, on October 5, 1841, two Western Railroad trains traveling in opposite directions but sharing the same track (as was common practice at that point in the railroad industry's history) collided, killing two passengers and greatly alarming the public. According to James Beniger, the public outcry that ensued "reflected the fact that people were not yet used to travel at the speed of inanimate energy—certainly not to the Western's operating speeds of up to thirty miles per hour."[43] Such accidents had many causes, but a primary one was the problem of coordinating schedules—that is, managing the times of the network and the locations of the trains. Even with the adoption of standard time in 1883, train companies still faced a number of unexpected challenges with synchronization. Another significant accident occurred on April 19, 1891, in Kipton, Ohio, when two trains of the Lake Shore and Michigan Southern Railway Company collided because one of the conductors was unaware that his watch had stopped for four minutes before restarting.[44] In response to the Great Kipton Train Wreck, as it became known, the railroad company commissioned a Cleveland watchmaker to develop a standard and reliable timepiece along with a system of inspections and enforcement protocols for these new "railroad chronometers." The name of this watchmaker was Webster C. Ball, and his design soon became the norm throughout the industry.[45] To get "on the Ball" meant both to have a standard timepiece and to be synchronized with the larger system of railroad traffic management.[46]

With increasingly reliable schedules and improved confidence in the rail system, planners could anticipate delivery times with greater accuracy and fewer expenses. Rather than measuring distances in miles and feet, managers could gauge the time needed to travel between locations. While such calculations are commonplace now, in the late nineteenth century the predictability of train travel and the currency of time opened new sites of value and competition that in turn enabled a liberated spatial imagination based on calculation and performance.[47] With increased speed of transit and the apparent shrinking of distance, the uncanniness of some of these spaces has intensified in recent decades. For example, Clearwater, a company that imports live lobsters to the United States from Nova Scotia, has figured out that it is most cost-effective to keep the lobsters alive as long as possible, and that doing so yields greater customer satisfaction. In order to satisfy the just-in-time expectations of those customers, Clearwater keeps a small building full of live lobsters, shipped directly from the subarctic waters of Nova Scotia, in the middle of the tarmac of Louisville International Airport, one of UPS's transshipment hubs. In the words of the company's website:

> Clearwater employs a team of biologists who apply biological science and technology to perfect handling and storage systems and maintain lobster quality and health. Once the lobsters reach shore, careful attention is of

Ball Watches Safeguard Millions

The public demand for speed in railway service necessitates untiring vigilance. Millions of passengers made the four track railroad with a train a minute a present-day reality, and "absolute accuracy" in the railroad man's timepiece is the first essential. You must have the protection of a safe watch when traveling. The

BALL
Twentieth Century Model
WATCH

is the culmination of years of building watches especially suited to the severe demands of railway service. It is a *Master among many—a standard of accuracy—tested and guaranteed*—embodying the best of the ideas and experience of Mr. Webb C. Ball, who began the "Safety First" movement twenty-two years ago when he worked out the original plan of time inspection for the Lake Shore Railway

The story of "Time Inspection on American Railroads" is told in our booklet which will be sent with a passholder free upon request

If your jeweler cannot show you the Ball "Twentieth Century Model" Watch, give us his name and we will arrange for you to see one

Ordinary care and cleaning once a year will preserve your Ball Watch accuracy for your Children's children

Webb C. Ball Watch Company, 2686 Heyworth Bldg., Chicago
Ball Bldg., Cleveland   Flood Bldg., San Francisco   Confederation Life Bldg., Winnipeg

Vintage advertisement for the Ball Twentieth Century Model Watch, a standardized railroad pocket watch that became part of the "untiring vigilance" necessary to keep the railroads running. Courtesy of Ball Watch Company SA Switzerland.

utmost importance. Clearwater is the inventor of the world's first lobster-friendly Dryland Pound Storage System, which has enabled Clearwater to supply premium hardshell lobster anywhere in the world, any time of year.[48]

Clearwater's Louisville building is the contemporary logistical imagination in practice, capable of reconciling the abstractness of miles of air transit, shipment manifests, purchase orders, and salinity levels with the need simply to keep lobsters from not dying so that people can eat them later. Because the requirements and behaviors of logistical conditions reflect a set of demands related to performance, prediction, speed, and delivery, the geopolitical landscape they map makes a number of less apparent dynamics more obvious, hence the small piece of the North Atlantic stranded in the middle of Kentucky. Such a condition is not only enabled by increasingly reliable and sophisticated data management systems but also actively produced by them.[49] Moreover, because the logics that generate such a configuration are often indifferent to the context in which they are established, the two systems rub against each other. It is at such sites of friction where logistical thinking is most frequently deployed, often in an effort to neutralize this friction and with particular emphasis on prediction, acceleration, and lubrication.

Logistics Makes Modules

The logistical imagination is characterized by an ability to render matter discrete and continuous simultaneously. The environment and the objects depicted in the World War II–era diagram discussed earlier in this chapter are mapped using the same coordinate system and thus made "mappable" in the sense that their future positions can be tracked and registered. This requires that the constituent elements be granular enough to be tracked with a useful degree of resolution. In the case of Walmart, as with most retailers, bar-coded products are designated as stock keeping units (SKUs) so that inventory can be monitored as closely as possible. However, more generally, it is at the "case" or "pallet" level that inventory is often managed. Thanks to ubiquitous but largely unnoticed technological innovations like the

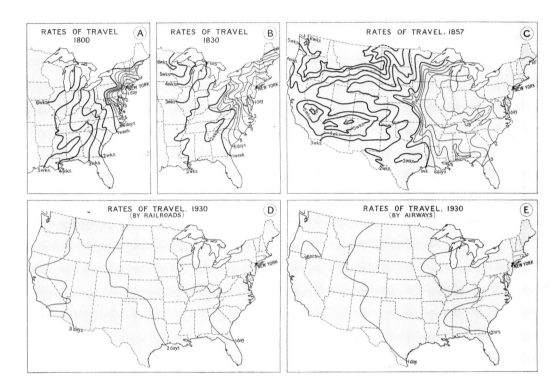

This series of maps shows changing rates of rail travel from New York to other points in the United States. In these images, distance is calculated and mapped in terms of time and implies the coordination efforts enabled by technologies like the Ball watch. Source: Charles O. Paullin, *Atlas of the Historical Geography of the United States* (Washington, D.C., and New York: Carnegie Institution and American Geographical Society, 1932), plate 138-D. Reprinted with permission by the American Geographical Society.

shipping container, the pallet, and the bar code, the ability to monitor the locations in time and space of the granular elements of logistics has increased significantly. These inventions are, in the words of Sigfried Giedion, "the humble objects . . . [that] have shaken our mode of living to its very roots. Modest things of daily life, they accumulate into forces acting upon whoever moves within the orbit of our civilization."[50] Before some of these transformations, the balance between the abstract and the concrete skewed decidedly toward the latter because few forms of media were capable of translating the world of objects into the world of information.[51] With the development of technologies that enabled data to be encrypted and displayed on objects, it was almost immediately possible to manage and measure products in new, faster, and more precise ways. The advent of such practices reflected mounting pressure on organizations to compete within a marketplace that placed a premium on efficiency and precision. The shipping pallet, for example, while still a predigital invention, allowed the bundling, moving, and tracking of diverse objects as if they were one. The shipping container then made it possible for these bundles to be further consolidated in order to be shipped at high densities, loaded and unloaded quickly, and, just as important, transferred from one mode of transit to another. In the words of Alexander Klose, "The container combines the ideas of computing time and space: workflows and storage capacities."[52] These developments came at the expense of labor, as they substantially reduced the amount of time, calculated in man-hours, that it took to load and unload cargo.

The pallet and container work together to ensure optimum packing of modules of merchandise. When parcels can be rendered as data, their positions can be monitored at increasingly high levels of resolution. The pallet, by providing a small piece of movable floor, allows a forklift or pallet jack to consolidate and maneuver merchandise into a container. Pallets are sized to fit into each container in a densely efficient manner.[53] In the sense that pallets become units that are packed into containers that themselves become units to be packed, monitored, and manipulated, logistical behavior tends to collapse object and field, figure and ground, as all of the elements in its scope become data to be attended to.

The interior drawing from *Army Logistician* discussed above (Plate 1), which is intended as an illustration of a military warehouse building, could be describing any number of logistics interiors and, in its diagrammatic relentlessness, the shipping container itself from both interior and exterior. As with the logistical imagination more generally, the container's logic oscillates between material stubbornness and informational dematerialization.[54] In his book *The Box,* Marc Levinson refers to the container as a "high-efficiency transportation machine."[55] He describes the process of unloading a container ship: "Almost every one of the intricate movements required to service a vessel is choreographed by a computer long before the ship arrives. Computers, and the vessel planners who use them, determine the order in which the containers are to be discharged, to speed the process without destabilizing the ship. The actions of the container cranes and the equipment in the yard all are programmed in advance."[56] This passage vividly evokes the actual sites of logistical exchange, as containers are transferred onto and off ships, to and from waiting tractor trailers, all by means of quickly moving gantry cranes. While these areas are the most visible sites of distribution, the effects of logistics are increasingly evident in more and more of the built environment, especially in the context of the United States. Klose extends the logic of the shipping container into what he calls the "container principle," in which the container as concept exists as an "epistemic object" that structures knowledge formation both in the physical world of distribution and the digital world of packet switching.[57] In both cases, some kind of transferable and interchangeable module enables exchange. To return to the *Army Logistician* illustration, while the discussion in this section has focused on the orange cubes of inventory/data, the next section looks at the grid that organizes the total environment of the space described by that image.

Logistics Is Infrastructural

Logistics does more than define a series of landscapes—it has an imaginary all its own that is capable of both transforming existing spaces and producing new ones in pursuit of better alignment with ever-larger logistical regimes. Using technical artifacts, protocols, standards, humans, and elements of the built environment to propagate themselves, logistical systems share features of infrastructure more generally. In a relatively short amount of time, logistics has gone from being a specialized branch of management to underpinning and conditioning almost every aspect of commerce and exchange, which in turn condition much of daily life. Logistics is, among other things, a "technological system," and such systems, in the words of Paul Edwards, "reside in a naturalized background, as ordinary and unremarkable to us as trees, daylight, and dirt. Our civilizations fundamentally depend on them, yet we notice them mainly when they fail, which they rarely do. They are the connective tissues and the circulatory systems of modernity. In short, these systems have become infrastructures."[58] Infrastructure is a conditioning force. It designs the game board and governs where the pieces may go. As Susan Leigh Star and Karen Ruhleder argue, the features of infrastructure expand beyond physical installations to include embeddedness, functional invisibility, and a role in the replication and reinforcing of standards and protocols.[59] This normalizing aspect of infrastructure reinforces the tendency for these systems to become virtually invisible while still acting upon us.[60]

Logistics attempts to exceed the limits of infrastructural systems while simultaneously relying on them (and being defined by them). Linking infrastructure with technological developments also tends to emphasize novelty over functional continuity and expansion. While specific technologies, like the gas lamp and the telegraph, are no longer used, electrical illumination and long-distance communication have only increased.[61] Furthermore, these technologies become intertwined with both people and practices and become part of what historians of science call a sociotechnical system.[62] But the technologies need not simply occupy a physical register. As Daniel Bell points out, "Technology . . . 'is the use of scientific knowledge to specify ways of doing things in a *reproducible* manner.' In this sense, the organization of a hospital or an international trade system is a *social* technology, as the automobile or a numerically controlled tool is a *machine* technology. An *intellectual* technology is the substitution of algorithms . . . for intuitive judgments."[63] If logistics is infrastructural and algorithmic, its assertions in the built environment index performance criteria of a vast range of decisions made independent of each other but with lasting collateral influence.[64]

Not only are infrastructures active while becoming increasingly invisible, their work is not ambient or indirect but can be actively bent toward specific goals. Stephen Graham and Simon Marvin identify embedded infrastructural networks as "implicated in the process of production, reproduction, and legitimation in a functioning capitalist economy."[65] For example, Deborah Cowen shows how the global economy's dependence on logistics networks has challenged the stability of national borders while also conflating border security with economic security. Thus increasingly larger groups of actors are potentially implicated as "threats" to security—that is, to the smooth flow of capital.[66] Graham and Marvin see this as evidence of infrastructure's "desire to produce a 'spaceless world.'"[67] This desire exists acutely in logistics as well, and yet the creaky stubbornness of materiality, with all its gravities and frictions, constantly frustrates that desire.

The logistical imagination builds around itself an attendant environment comprising informational systems, physical systems, and mediating systems. Since logistics must constantly keep track of things, it prioritizes awareness. To be aware of where things are in time and in space requires a reliable way of mapping those locations and agreed-upon methods for understanding both where and when. The former is made possible through a shared coordinate system in the form of latitude and longitude and increasingly made available through the ubiquity of devices that transmit their positions to be mapped and translated by larger systems. Time is a more recent site of coordination.[68] In the case of the railroads and the U.S. Naval Observatory, time needed to become standard, predictable, and measurable.[69] Through the implementation of time "zones," it also became geographical. To be in a certain location also meant to be at a certain time. With location in time and space accounted for, and with certain behaviors being highly predictable, many aspects of logistics could be measured, calculated, and predicted.[70] The physical systems that support logistics networks provide the most visible manifestations of these operations, even if the logics are hidden or otherwise illegible. Familiar transportation network systems remain fundamental to logistics, tethered as transport is to a terrestrial and fuel-based approach. Air and water play significant roles here too, the former providing faster and more expensive delivery, and the latter, while slower, offering markedly cheaper options.

Mediating elements sit between these physical networks and data networks and translate between the two. Beyond mediating, these intermediate elements work to overcome certain territorial or spatial obstacles. For wireless communication, one such problem is the shape of the planet. Without some form of relay, radio signals eventually leave the atmosphere. However, as Arthur C. Clarke proposed in 1945, in a piece for the magazine *Wireless World,* a network of geosynchronous satellites can solve this problem. Clarke succinctly summarized the possibilities: "A body in such an orbit, if its plane coincided with that of the earth's equator, would revolve with the earth and would thus be stationary above the same spot on the planet. It would remain fixed in the sky of a whole hemisphere and unlike all other heavenly bodies would neither rise nor set."[71] Clarke suggested that these bodies could be "space-stations," large, light buildings supporting a range of inhabitations and functions and capable of sending and receiving transmissions from the surface of the earth. As illustrated in a diagram that accompanied Clarke's article, "a single station could only provide coverage to half the globe, and for world service, three would be required, though more could be readily utilized."[72] While Clarke was addressing the challenges of global communication, the physical apparatus he posited has terrestrial echoes within logistics networks. Attenuated and multimodal, such networks also require relays. In Walmart's case, for example, rather than geostationary satellites, it uses a collection of buildings that serve as staging areas for the managing of inventory, including switching inventory from one transit network to another. In the same way that people looking at the night sky can find it difficult to distinguish between satellites and stars, most people find it hard to parse the retailer's distribution buildings from other structures that surround them. Walmart's buildings are hidden in plain sight while undergirding a global logistics network and operating as relays at a global scale.

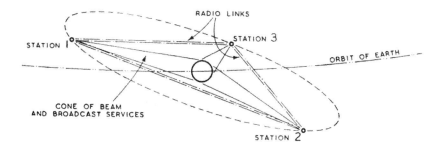

Arthur C. Clarke's proposal for a geosynchronous satellite communication system that
would allow instantaneous communication
to anywhere on the planet. Source: Arthur C.
Clarke, "Extra-terrestrial Relays: Can Rocket
Stations Give World-wide Radio Coverage?,"
Wireless World, October 1945, 305. Courtesy
of *Wireless World*.

Architecture for Logistics Supports, Architecture by Logistics Conditions

Industrial buildings designed to support production and distribution have a familiar lineage. From the Roman storehouses of Testaccio to Cass Gilbert's Brooklyn Army Terminal, these buildings occupy a significant place in architectural history for their apparent foregrounding of performance requirements over formal expression. Starting after World War II and maturing in the 1970s, the logistics revolution's host of new technologies and approaches—including the shipping container, the communications satellite, the bar code, and the computer—enabled coordination at new scales, speeds, and efficiencies with attendant new forms. These developments remain ascendant and are what allow a shipping company like UPS to claim, as it did in 2010, that logistics is not just what it loves and what it does, but what it *is*. While UPS operates a number of physical distribution centers that support the company's logistics endeavors, these buildings are more than simply housing for distribution systems. As they are fundamentally conditioned by the logics behind those distribution systems, their status as "buildings" merits some reconsideration.

The architecture related to logistics might be distributed along a spectrum, with buildings "for logistics" at one pole and buildings "by logistics" at the other. An architecture for logistics is designed to support functions or programs specifically associated with the movement and coordination of goods. For example, Gilbert's Brooklyn Army Terminal (1919) spatialized the replenishment and deployment operations of the U.S. military as it received matériel from all parts of the country in preparation for shipment across the Atlantic. The building's no-frills monumentality reflects the seriousness of its purpose, even though the consequences of its design, such as the offset balconies that index the array of gantries, produce dramatic spatial effects. The terminal is a more spectacular version of the many mundane buildings that support transport, consolidation, and distribution, including the stockyards, warehouses, and marketplaces of any given industrialized settlement.

Architecture for logistics expands outward to include larger landscapes, infrastructures, and territories. Manuel Castells argues that

Cass Gilbert's Brooklyn Army Terminal (1919) was built to support logistical operations as a node within a network. Photograph by Angela Co.

contemporary cities "are structured, and destructured simultaneously by the competing logics of the space of flows and the space of places. Cities do not disappear in the virtual networks. But they are transformed by the interface between electronic communication and physical interaction."[73] As identified by Susan Nigra Snyder and Alex Wall, as well as by Charles Waldheim and Alan Berger, the "space of flows" is fundamentally connected to logistics, forming part of a "logistics landscape."[74] Related investigations into logistics and urbanism identify surfaces and interfaces as primary sites of logistical agency because of their emphasis on performance and organization, "a composite that operates both as information receiver, infrastructure, and superstructure . . . [as] a subscape, a territory that structures/serves/ hosts multiple possibilities of interchange and occupation across its organization."[75] The development of a logistics landscape brings with it more fundamental realignments that suggest not just new forms of architecture but also new ways of understanding it as well as new ways of conceptualizing territory as it is increasingly abstracted in pursuit of optimization. Likewise, the humans who populate this new terrain are coupled with a broad array of technological developments that suggest new relationships to information and technology.[76] All these things together point to more than just configurations that precipitate from logistics; they suggest altogether new forms that are fundamentally conditioned by it.

Architecture developed "by" logistics reflects epistemological shifts brought about by new ways of seeing and thinking about information, space, time, and building. With the emergence of automated information management and machine-readable languages such as the bar code, logistics became more than a functional category— it became a conditioning way of both seeing the world and being in it. For example, Skidmore, Owings & Merrill's complex for the U.S. Air Force Academy in Colorado Springs was imagined and maintained as a recursive logistical enterprise in which the image of the building was constantly reinscribed in the machines designed to ensure its optimal functionality. All elements of the complex, from uniforms to building components, were marked with specific information that allowed their tracking and monitoring within the space of the academy.[77] This system also made virtually no distinctions among the kinds of objects it tracked, as if in anticipation of the indifferent attitude logistics displays toward the specific or the concrete. The IBM Corporate Headquarters, also designed by SOM, was, as John Harwood argues, "an experiment in the computerized management of space" in which "all of the office machines, furniture, and artwork for the building was organized according to a logistical system: each object was assigned a number, and its location, user, and use were tracked by the IBM 1460 computer installed on the first floor of the building."[78] Like the ambiguous orange object/environment of the forklift operator in the image discussed above (Plate 1), the building and its contents were imagined and managed as one system in which every element could be tracked and accounted for. In the case of IBM, such an approach to the building undermines the authority of the conventional methods for communicating architectural organization in the sense that "flow charts and diagrams were understood as just as, if not more, significant than the plan of a building, insofar as they promised the capacity of architecture to order, and make whole, a disparate and complex range of media and practices."[79] As suggested by SOM's experiments with IBM, buildings themselves begin to acquire new roles in architecture "by" logistics. Because logistical systems are constantly seeking to improve performance, they are also subject to constant feedback, which in turn requires input in order to guide subsequent decisions. The buildings become sources for this because they are used to process material, not just to store it. In this sequence, they also become sources of information, communicating the amounts of merchandise back to those coordinating the overall movement of goods.

This shift to an architecture conditioned by logistics also connects with other transformations in the United States after World War II, like investment in redundant communications systems and intermodal transport networks, including the development of the shipping container, the U.S. Interstate Highway System, and the Advanced Research Projects Agency Network (ARPANET).[80] If an architecture "for" logistics was primarily a serial condition, in which goods were moved from Point A to Point B, an architecture "by" logistics increasingly operates in parallel and overlapping ways in which the topological conditions drive the organization. The multinodal network of freeways, for example, mimics the network diagrams of engineer Paul Baran, who was hired by the RAND Corporation from the Hughes Aircraft Company to study the nation's communications networks.[81] While at RAND, Baran produced a series of papers for the think tank that argued for a decentralized and redundant communications network. In one paper, Baran presented the network diagram now widely recognized as an early model of dispersed digital communication and influential in the development of ARPANET. Such robust and multiply redundant systems have become part of the vocabulary of many branches of network management, including logistics and retail. Moreover, such diagrams promote images of territory that are fundamentally logistical because they suggest a topological understanding of it while also promoting form over image.

Logistical Architecture Is Territorial

Architecture by logistics, or logistical architecture, is so fundamentally entangled with the larger networks and territories in which it exists that it is difficult to distinguish logistical buildings from their surroundings, leading to the possibility of further reconfiguring the buildings themselves. Geographer Jon Goss points to the field of architectural geography as one that can help to "explain architecture as a social product, [and] as the spatial configuration of the built environment incorporating economic, political, and ideological dimensions."[82] This area of study nestles into the broader category of political geography, itself intertwined with geopolitics and the latter's concern with the machinations of power at state, regional, and global levels.[83] Power can also be consolidated and manipulated through less legibly political means and is often indexed through material and local instances. Rather than being seen as a precipitate of geopolitical maneuvering, architecture can be understood as a more active instigator—not something to be read at a local level but something that is deployed and coordinated at a larger scale, not as a text but as a tool. Such architecture, politically enmeshed and territorially dispersed, might be the inverse of an architectural geography—that is, a geographical

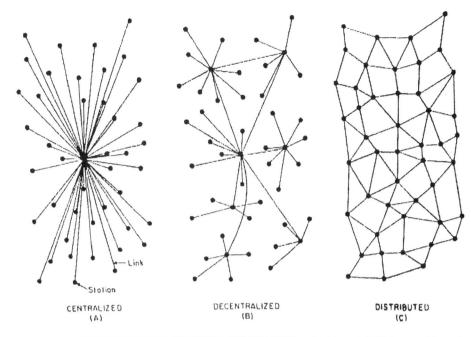

CENTRALIZED
(A)

DECENTRALIZED
(B)

DISTRIBUTED
(C)

Paul Baran's 1962 diagram "Centralized, Decentralized, and Distributed Connections" shows three network models to make a case for the last as the most resilient. Source: Paul Baran, *On Distributed Connections*, Document Number RM-3420-PR (Santa Monica: RAND Corporation, 1962), 2. Reprinted with permission from the RAND Corporation, Santa Monica, California.

Paul Baran's distributed network diagram, once developed for military research, now appears on the cover of a retail logistics publication. Source: Retail Industry Leaders Association, *Logistics Conference 2010,* cover. Collection of the author.

architecture.[84] This architecture possesses the capacity to act as a collective enterprise, beyond the single building and with a reach beyond its immediate context. Connected and separate, near and far, this geographical architecture is understood in terms of its position within a larger network and, as a result, frustrates conventional appraisals that tend to focus on the organization, form, enclosure, or symbolic content of a single instance. A geographical architecture, perforce, contends with expanded concerns around scale and agency while still not giving up its own disciplinary obligations.

It is increasingly clear that architecture is used by those in power as a means of leveraging control over territory.[85] These developments are frequently linked to the stubborn realities of physical geography and the beneficial aspects of some positions over others, especially within the activities of global capitalism.[86] In the United States, this clamoring for advantage—from range wars to conflicts over air rights to battles over eminent domain—highlights the links between land claims and political operations. While these actions are largely governed by national or state policy, there are instances where inventive moves supersede or work around the limits imposed by policy dictates. As the built environment is one of the tools for doing this, questions of architecture and urban design cannot be separated from questions of control and power. Architecture itself, when understood collectively, can acquire political valence through its ability to become a territorial instrument capable of securing space within the logic of the market.

The term *territory* can refer to relationships among the land, those living on it, and the political bodies that influence them. According to the geographer Roy Mellor, "The spatial pattern of mankind is molded by the interactive relationships within a tripartite association between nation, state, and territory, the core of the aspect of the discipline we term 'political geography.'"[87] In Mellor's sense, the concept of nation is connected to political associations (populations), and the concept of state is related to governmental and physical ones (terrain). Both population and physical land area can then be measured and rationalized, often under the banner of security.[88] Stuart Elden, drawing on Foucault, identifies this impulse of sovereignty to quantify and rationalize: "Just as the people become understood as both discrete individuals and their aggregated whole, the land they inhabit is also something that is understood in terms of its geometric, rational properties, or 'qualities.'"[89] But such qualities are quickly quantified in order to forecast future forms of both populations and the spaces they will occupy.

Questions of measure and control are fundamental to logistics and are linked to its tendencies to develop forecasting models and to establish tolerable ranges of error. In the service of this, logistical architecture is actively employed to control terrain. The boundaries of these lands are not fixed, and it is the logistical networks that enable some of this elasticity.[90] Elden suggests that "territory should be understood as a political technology, or perhaps better as a bundle of political technologies."[91] In this sense, logistical architecture—itself infrastructural and capable of acting as a territorial instrument—becomes a kind of political technology. As a result, its nature as architecture, in a conventional sense, begins to fragment and multiply as it becomes more elastic and fugitive. The dynamism that characterizes this logistical architecture seeps into an understanding of property, land use, jurisdiction, political boundaries, and regional designations. In the case of Walmart, the company's encompassing logistical vision is reflective of other practices (e.g., congressional redistricting) but at an accelerated pace and organized around specific growth ambitions. As the retailer's store locations are rendered as quantities to be optimized and exchanged, the external effects of such transactions are increasingly apparent in the urban development of the United States. If the industrial and historical city was "imageable" in Kevin Lynch's sense, how can one understand a city enabled, grown, and defined by logistics? In *The Image of the City*, Lynch, writing in 1960, points out that "the conscious remolding of the large-scale physical environment has been possible only recently, and so the problem of environmental imageability is a new one."[92] With large-scale urban transformations like the ones being wrought, in part, by logistics, the question is not one of typology (continuity and stable references) but one of topology (levels of organization and contingent relationships). It is not a question of *image* but one of *form*. Indeed, at such a scale, assembling any kind of image is impossible without some kind of mediating technology. Rather than fixing an image of territory, one encounters aspects of its form. This is often contingent and dynamic and ungraspable. It is what I am referring to as the logistical, and it negotiates between competing aspects of the territorial: between politics on one side and land on the other. It uses a range of instruments that can safely be adjusted to adapt to risks and to absorb uncertainties while buffering important operational protocols so that they can be enacted smoothly and without interruption.

2 BUILDINGS

A Moving System in Motion

JUNE 26 IS OFFICIALLY UPC BAR CODE DAY in the city of Troy, Ohio. On that day in 1974, a cashier at the local Marsh supermarket sold the world's first bar-coded product: a ten-pack of Wrigley's Juicy Fruit chewing gum.[1] In 2004, the town celebrated the event's thirtieth anniversary at the original site of the transaction by eating bar code–decorated cake in the presence of both the original cashier and the historic ten-pack (usually on display at the Smithsonian Institution). In the thirty years between the two events, the bar code found its way onto almost every single packaged product in the world, making it one of the most ubiquitous features of information and inventory management. Enabled by the increased speed and affordability of computing, the bar code transformed how objects were imagined because it not only encoded them with information but also allowed them to be treated like information. And while the bar code was indeed revolutionary, its debut in 1974 masked another revolution in shopping that was already normalized enough not to merit comment: self-service. While it is common today for a shopper to select items individually and bring them all at once to a single sales terminal near the store's exit, this form of shopping was not introduced until the beginning of the twentieth century and took decades to become a standard practice.

Self-service introduced a radical shift in the way shoppers interacted with merchandise because they acquired labor roles previously assigned to clerks, and, at the same time, they became sources of consumer data. Not only did self-service produce a new kind of shopping environment, but it also presented a host of inventory management challenges, including pricing, inventory, and distribution. In other words, self-service environments both generated and required the management of such large amounts of information that manual methods could not keep pace. The advent of the bar code solved these problems, but, because of the increases in speed and scale that it enabled, a new set of challenges ensued that had transformative effects on the nature of the retail spaces themselves. If self-service changed the relationships among customers, clerks, inventory, and the space of display (the shopping environment), the bar code changed the nature of the inventory by allowing physical material to be imagined and managed as data. This triggered a transformation in the buildings designed to support such systems. No longer isolated warehouses storing static and stable inventories of objects, the buildings of large-scale discount retail began to constitute an architecture of networked inventory and data *management*—an architecture of logistics.

Self-Service Turns Customers into Clerks

When Sam Walton opened his first store in Bentonville in 1950, it was, according to him, only the third self-service variety store in the country.[2] This was not a Walmart proper but a franchise of Ben Franklin stores that he called Walton's 5–10. Franchising was part of a larger shift in retail as general stores and specialty stores were superseded by mass merchandisers who took advantage of more efficient systems to reduce costs and eliminate price increases that could accumulate along their merchandise's path from production to consumption.[3] As a franchisee of the Ben Franklin chain, Walton had the support of a large company but also the freedom to experiment, hence his interest in self-service. The self-service model is intellectual property patented in 1917 by Clarence Saunders, founder of the Piggly Wiggly chain of grocery stores. Saunders opened his first location in 1916 in Memphis, Tennessee, and referred to its organization as "self-service" because customers could move freely through the shop once they passed through the controlled entrance turnstile. Customers would take a shopping basket, compare transparently priced merchandise, select

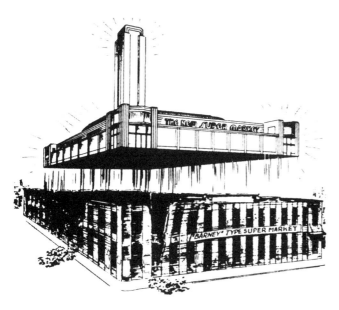

The supermarket emerged, in part, to meet new consumer demands after World War II. Source: Max Zimmerman, *The Super Market: A Revolution in Distribution* (New York: McGraw-Hill, 1995), 121.

Celebrating the bar code's thirty-fifth anniversary in Troy, Ohio, June 26, 2009. On the left, the original cashier holds a ten-pack of Juicy Fruit chewing gum, the first ever bar-coded product to be scanned and purchased. Photograph by Wes Jones. Courtesy of Troy Historical Society.

the desired items themselves, and pay for them all at once at a single point before exiting the store. The prevailing arrangement up to that time had store clerks choosing items for the customers or assisting them at multiple counters with cash registers. Saunders's new format gave shoppers more freedom to choose, and, even though the merchant was still responsible for selecting the products that would be displayed for sale, customers could assert their needs based on what they purchased.[4] In turn, the responsibility for marketing shifted to the manufacturers themselves, for they were now in direct competition with their rivals, whose products sat adjacent to theirs on the self-service stores' shelves. This new format intensified the need for manufacturers to brand products in legible and aggressive ways. Since the price was also marked on every item, customers could easily compare costs. Saunders was motivated by a desire to lower costs and increase profit; with self-service, under the guise of increased freedom and control, customers actually did the work of what would be paid clerks at his competitors' stores. With its overhead reduced, Piggly Wiggly could lower its prices in general based on the wager that customers would prefer to shop for themselves if they could save money. While early department stores were primarily urban and depended on a steady stream of pedestrian traffic, the more compact self-service stores lent themselves well to areas with smaller populations and proved to be especially compatible with rural, and later suburban, locations.[5]

In an effort to expand reach and revenue, Saunders also patented a system that would allow others to transform their existing stores into "self-serving" stores through his own franchise model. Through the use of a series of deployable components and standardized modules, the interior of a conventional retail space could quickly be updated to operate as a self-service store. In his 1917 patent application, Saunders described the system as well as the tenets of his self-service format:

> Furniture in the form of portable units adapted to be readily arranged for use or collapsed for shipping or closing purposes, the same being designed for use in a store room, or other place, and to be arranged in such a manner that the customers will be able to serve themselves and, in doing so, will be required to review the entire assortment of goods carried in stock, conveniently and attractively displayed, and after selecting

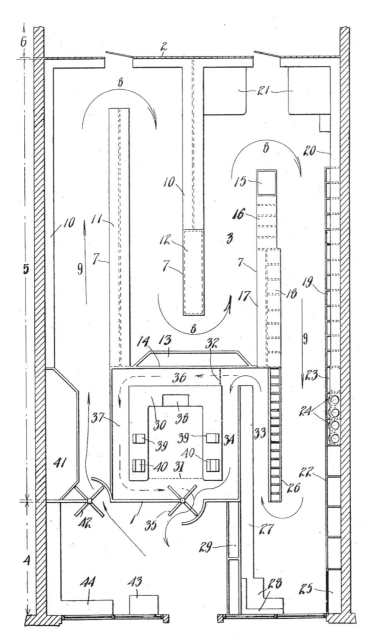

The floor plan of Clarence Saunders's patented layout for self-service shopping included some of the inventor's innovations, including turnstiles to control entry and exit, a prescribed path, and a single point of sale. Source: C. Saunders, "Self-Serving Store," U.S. Patent 1,357,521, 1920, 1.

the goods desired, will be required to pass a checking and paying station at which the goods selected may be billed, wrapped and settled for before leaving the premises. . . .

The store furniture disclosed in the present application is characterized in that the same is made up of standardized units, whereby stores adopting the system may be equipped with portable units readily set up for business and disassembled or collapsed as occasion requires, and wherein the units themselves may be constructed at a central point and all after the same pattern in construction and appearance, insuring a uniformity of stores employing my invention.[6]

The architectural aspects in this description characterize much of the ensuing discount retail architecture, including standardized systems of production, access, and display and the implicit temporariness of such installations. The standardization allows the interiors themselves to become effective copies of each other and to remain familiar to customers. Saunders was adamant about enforcing this equivalence. Beyond commonly describing Piggly Wiggly as a "system" and referring to the "Saunders apparatus," he produced *Whats and What Nots of Piggly Wiggly System,* which was distributed to managers of Piggly Wiggly branches. In this publication, part operating manual and part motivational tract, Saunders expounded at length about the importance of adhering to the system:

Each thing to do and each thing not to do is of equal importance one with the other. Failing to do anything that should be done in the conduction and operations of the stores is just as hurtful for the whole plan of merchandising as doing any particular thing that should not be done and vice versa. Therefore, the general good of these rules and regulations to each agency concerned is for him to know positively and without a doubt that each other Piggly Wiggly unit is doing and not doing the very same things that he is doing and not doing.[7]

For Saunders, and for many of the merchandisers and retailers who followed, store locations operated in concert and were conceptualized not so much as buildings but as components of a large and carefully coordinated system designed to enable the circulation of goods.[8]

The self-service model made inventory into display and systematized browsing to ensure that customers would pass by every item that was available. It required customers to absorb new labor roles

THE TURNSTILE

PIGGLY WIGGLY HOME OFFICE, Publishers

Vol. 1. WASHINGTON, D. C., SEPTEMBER 27th, 1919. No. 17

DEVOTED TO THE INTEREST

of

PIGGLY WIGGLY
All Over the World

Clarence Saunders insisted on coordinating all Piggly Wiggly operations and used the in-house publication *The Turnstile* to keep store managers and employees up-to-date on changes in policies and procedures. Courtesy of University of Memphis Library, Mississippi Valley Collection.

while also using their buying choices to generate information about preferences and habits. The space of self-service itself was not linked to a new building type but rather to a new organizational system, a means for formatting and structuring a set of experiences and processes designed in turn to generate both revenue and information that would make it easier to effectively generate still more revenue in the future. However, self-service's reduction in labor and simultaneous increase in merchandise produced new inventory management challenges. For example, at Piggly Wiggly, aside from regular and standardized inventory processes, there was also the requirement, stipulated in Saunders's Rule 26, that "each checker and stock-keeper of store must be furnished weekly by the operator in charge with a revised price schedule of those articles that have been changed in price."[9] With modest stores and limited merchandise, doing this manually was initially sufficient. However, self-service's ascendance in the United States was coupled with postwar prosperity, and increased consumer choice generated so many different kinds of products that managing them in a coordinated way (and thus a profitable one) became increasingly difficult. Furthermore, the format's capacity to generate consumer information at centralized points of sale produced new categories of information about shopping behavior, but without any simple way to consolidate or compare the data. The development of the bar code was a response to this bottleneck, and its adoption by and eventual ubiquity throughout the world of retail allowed inventory management to occur at dramatically new scales.

The Bar Code Turns Objects into Information

The bar code's most familiar form is the Universal Product Code, the implementation of which was set in motion at a meeting of retailers and engineers in 1970. They convened to develop a standard system of inventory management and, after examining various attempts, eventually helped to establish the UPC symbol. Within two years of the UPC symbol's 1974 inauguration, more than 75 percent of items in a typical supermarket bore the mark.[10] Of interest for purposes of this discussion is less the history of the technology than its significance for the built environment. The bar code's capacity to standardize data and enable the efficient management of information provided a foundational layer for today's logistical systems and their architecture.

The UPC is a means of encapsulating a product's pertinent information in an array of parallel bars that contain a one-dimensional data string. Each black bar is attached to its adjacent void to form a sequence of binary digits that can be read easily by a laser scanner. The combination of these digits is unique for each product, and the bar code is scanned at significant nodes along a product's journey. To visualize the structure of the bar code, one can separate it into smaller bundles of information, each containing one number and eight bits. Each number is composed of a sequence of ones and zeroes, represented as solid or as void. With practice, one might easily recognize the more solid "01111101" of the three or the lighter "10001000" of the eight. When the bar code is reduced to the size of a postage stamp, however, the difference between one number and the next is nearly impossible for the human eye to parse. The bar code is one of the first communication systems designed to be both written and read exclusively by computers and thus illegible to those human managers and operators who depend on it.

The machine literacy of the bar code provides an efficient, accurate, precise, and reliable way of managing information. With the semi-automatic process of scanning a code, opportunities for human error are reduced, formats are standardized, and inventory can be monitored with a significantly high degree of control and precision. Through this mechanization of inventory control, suppliers and shippers become more accountable for the manner in which they manage their goods. Likewise, various retail outlets can control and calibrate inventory levels to reduce the risks of overstocking or selling out of merchandise. Every item for sale is scanned when it is placed on display and then subsequently scanned to tabulate its price, its purchase, and its ultimate removal from the store. This information feeds into overall supply protocols and alerts the warehouses and distribution centers that more stock will be needed soon.[11]

The rise of the UPC demanded more extensive and responsive distribution networks. Once merchandisers had the ability to monitor their material stocks at a higher resolution, it became easier for them to calibrate their distribution requirements. The UPC's capacity to contain information allowed the material in question to be understood, and subsequently imagined, in abstract terms. In the early days of self-service, for example, inventory was logged manually, and its materiality was managed through physical manipulation. With contemporary inventory control needs and increasingly large areas of operation, it is both necessary and easier to conceptualize inventory as data. As corporate logisticians struggle to maintain the right balance of merchandise, the items' qualitative identities have become less important than their quantities. Although goods maintain their materiality and still need to be moved physically, they also acquire an additional informational register for this handling. In this sense, the bar code creates two versions of every item moving through a given distribution network, one borne physically by transporters and the other carried over the communications networks.

While the bar code is designed to be scanned easily and to reduce errors, its efficacy depends on its placement relative to the shape of the product it represents. This design consideration became acute when the symbol's rapid implementation required that placement of the bar code be folded into the front-end manufacturing processes of all manner of goods. To resolve this issue, the Universal Code Council (now GS1 US) established a set of guidelines to help producers figure out the best places on their products for the codes. A telling set of diagrams from a 1975 document about the UPC suggests ideal locations for bar codes on, for example, a six-pack of beer, an eight-pack of hot dogs, and a ten-pack of luncheon meat. In these diagrams, all the imagery relating to brand differentiation, the stuff that wins the hearts and minds of customers and that became necessary with self-service as the dominant retail model, is conspicuously absent. The only mark on the products is the bar code. In the eyes of those responsible for circulating these objects, this is the only mark that matters. It contains all the necessary information, including the manufacturer, the name of the product, its price, and—once the code is scanned—its location in time and space. While the bar code cannot communicate a product's specific location at any given moment, it narrows the options

Compositing a bar code for photography. Each digit is represented as an eight-bit sequence of black or white "bars." Source: Uniform Grocery Product Code Council, *UPC Symbol Specification* (Washington, D.C., 1973). Courtesy of Bill Selmeier.

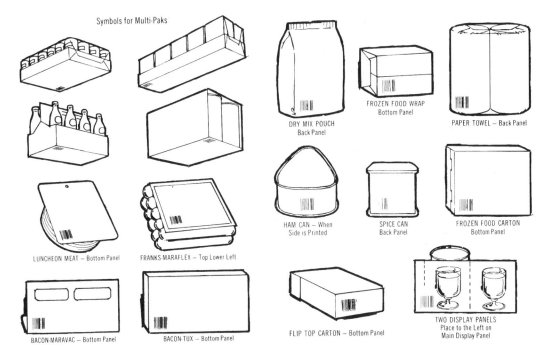

Symbols for Multi-Paks

DRY MIX POUCH
Back Panel

FROZEN FOOD WRAP
Bottom Panel

PAPER TOWEL — Back Panel

HAM CAN — When
Side is Printed

SPICE CAN
Back Panel

FROZEN FOOD CARTON
Bottom Panel

LUNCHEON MEAT — Bottom Panel

FRANKS-MARAFLEX — Top Lower Left

BACON-MARAVAC — Bottom Panel

BACON-TUX — Bottom Panel

FLIP TOP CARTON — Bottom Panel

TWO DISPLAY PANELS
Place to the Left on
Main Display Panel

Specifications for locating the bar code on product packaging. Source: Lawrence Hicks, *The Universal Product Code* (New York: Amacom, 1975). Courtesy of Amacom.

down to either a certain general location or between two of them. In this view, the physical aspects of these products, numerous as they are, start to matter less than their schedules and locations. Distribution, once concerned only with the physical handling of material, has increasingly become an exercise in information management as the objects themselves are reduced to and encapsulated by the bar codes on their surfaces. However, this spatiotemporal geography of objects is fleeting, because by the time any one thing is scanned, it is already on its way elsewhere.[12]

The bar code's introduction, like many of the logistical transformations to follow, was intended to increase the speed of transactions while reducing the likelihood of mistakes.[13] The bar code also has the added benefit of enabling the coordination of information and inventory. In addition to freeing the clerk of the task of manually inputting price information, it relieved stock keepers of having to inspect their inventory physically. They needed only look at the compiled data generated by the day's bar code scans. So while the bar code sped things up, it also further transferred labor to customers, a process already started by the shift to self-service. Simply by retrieving the items they desired and handing them to cashiers to be scanned and paid for, shoppers became a store's ersatz stockists and market analysts. Not only did they help manage and record inventory, but they also helped the store better understand what people were buying. Consumer desire, and the will to capitalize and manipulate that desire, is one of the primary forces behind the huge technospatial complex that constitutes retail logistics systems.

Consumer behavior is, of course, notoriously fickle, and the bar code helps to manage risk associated with unpredictable customer desire. On one hand, the bar code helps to generate large amounts of information about buying habits in fast and inexpensive ways, which in turn allows merchants to be more responsive.[14] The bar code also allows for multiple systems to interact with low entry barriers in what Karl Weick has termed a "loosely coupled" system (as discussed below). John Dunlop and Jan Rivkin, in an introduction to a history of the bar code, point to its "non-specific" character as one of its key features.[15] Both attributes of the bar code allow for further increases in responsive capacities to market risks. In the case of Walmart, a similar logic extends to the buildings themselves. Born from the combination of new organizational systems like self-service and new forms of information technology, Walmart's supercenters, data centers, and distribution centers operate collectively through a kind of architecture that, like the bar code, can absorb risk through its lack of specificity and its loose coupling between form and content.

Walmart Formats Formats and Prototypes Prototypes

A preoccupation of architectural discourse since the Industrial Revolution has been the relationship between the activities that a building supports (or contains) and the form that the building takes (i.e., function and expression, or form and content). Logistical architecture challenges the primacy of that preoccupation by further decoupling the two, by inverting their relationship, or by collapsing them onto each other. These relationships suggest a more contingent approach to architectural expression that allows certain aspects of a design to remain open-ended until forced to adapt to a local situation, an approach that is evident in Walmart's collection of buildings. Beyond that register, logistical architecture emphasizes horizontal organization over vertical expression, thereby associating these built elements with infrastructural systems (rather than reinforcing a given building's status as a discrete architectural object). While this renders the question of symbolism or expression more marginal, it also illuminates the ways in which architecture can act in concert and perhaps identifies a lacuna in current language for thinking through such configurations.

In Walmart's corporate lexicon, buildings are not referred to as *buildings* but as *formats* and as *prototypes*. Formats are the larger category and designate the kind of store, while prototypes are different configurations of given formats. The prototype designation is a reflection of the fact that Walmart's architecture division develops its plans without particular sites in mind but with certain performance constraints. New stores are designed for generic conditions but with highly specific interior organizations. The features of each new location, combined with Walmart's research about demographics and real estate, help determine what prototype is chosen. However, while the interior is highly specified, aspects such as the building's exterior, site orientation, and access to infrastructure all need to be modified in the field by a local architect or contractor. As a result, the task of design involves mainly developing an interface with an unknown condition and playing out scenarios of transformations for a given situation and its many contingencies.[16]

The term *format* itself is both a noun used to describe a generic condition and a verb for the process of creating that condition. The word originated in the preparation and production of books, in which *format* refers to both the size and the shape of a publication. Traditional book formats (e.g., folio, quarto, octavo, duodecimo) were differentiated by the number of times a single sheet of paper would need to be folded to form the individual leaves of the publication. Other forms of media have subsequently used the term to describe ways to store data beyond ink on paper. Examples include audio recording and, more recently, digital storage. In the latter category, the verb and noun often intersect as one is prompted to "format" a data storage device and thereby erase all previous data to make way for new input. A format is also "a defined structure for processing, storage, or display of data."[17] In the context of Walmart's use of the word to describe its buildings, this definition is revealing because it lays out three of the key roles the company expects its architecture to perform: processing, storage, and display. Significantly, a format's relationship to its form is somewhat slippery. In most cases, the form is in fact secondary to the performance of the artifact in question. Walmart emphasizes its buildings' *display* of information and symbols (primarily in the form of its applied facades), but such an emphasis hides the complex architectural machinations related to *processing* and *storage*.

The architectural prototype as deployed by Walmart is an incomplete condition, at times both overdetermined and underspecified. It is worth noting that the term *prototype* is not used here in the conventional sense, that is, to indicate an initial version of something that will later be copied repeatedly. Rather, the Walmart prototype is more of a contingent and relational condition sharing some of the features identified by Karl Weick in his study of loosely coupled systems. Weick examines the development of resilient forms of social and corporate organization and attempts to find potential in unpredictability, which he translates into the phrase "loose coupling." While his emphasis is organizational, given the overlap between form and organization that logistics buildings occupy, it is possible to claim some shared characteristics between the two. Primarily, the prototype for Walmart is capable of adapting to local conditions without modifying its core organization (Plate 5).[18] Similar to Weick's loosely coupled systems, this approach to building can "preserve more diversity in responding [to local conditions] than do tightly coupled systems, and therefore can adapt to a considerably wider range of changes in the environment."[19] In Weick's estimation, loosely coupled systems are also less vulnerable to minor environmental changes and can yield a greater number of "mutations or novel solutions."[20] In Walmart's case, there is a slack built into the design of the prototype that provides the architecture a role in mediating between the specific interior and the unknown exterior. As a result, the friction between the generic and the specific can produce surprising hybrids with specific, strange, and locally inflected expressions, as, for example, in Walmart's efforts to open stores in the New Urbanist town of Hercules, California. The architecture of retail logistics, constrained as it is by organizational protocols, tends to overdetermine cultural experience while simultaneously deploying techniques of underspecification. By allowing these loose and supple approaches to the built products that it deploys, Walmart can adapt to a wide range of unexpected circumstances and thereby use the buildings themselves to mitigate market risk.

Supercenters: Content but No Form

Walmart's most common building type, the supercenter, is a combination of a general merchandise discount store and a large discount food store. These buildings, the primary territorial instruments that Walmart uses as it expands its real estate holdings, are a collective manifestation of the retailer's vast infrastructural system of transmission. This system, formed in conjunction with Walmart's data centers and distribution centers, is a constantly transforming network of calibrated and interconnected interiors. However, while each type forms part of this system, it also exhibits specific architectural traits related to function and expression, or content and form.

The design of Walmart supercenter prototypes reflects the company's pursuit of expediency and cost reduction. By having only a small number of prototypes, Walmart can complete the processes of site selection and construction more quickly than if it were to design a store for each new location. This has been part of the company's approach even from its early days. According to Sam Walton, "We just started repeating what worked, stamping out stores cookie-cutter style. The only decision we had to make was what size format to put in what market. . . . I think our main real estate effort should be directed at getting out in front of expansion and letting the population build out to us."[21] Walton's emphasis on the stores' locations rather than their individual designs is not surprising, given his preoccupation with performance and quantities. For Walton, building a new store amounted simply to selecting the appropriate format and adapting to the location as quickly as possible. For this process, the Walmart real estate division and architects partner with local companies to transform prototype drawings through a process called "site adapt." They take the generic prototype drawings and modify them to ensure their compliance with local building codes and work through the specific interfaces between the new building and its context, including access roads, sidewalks, drainage, and fire safety.

The design of a Walmart building is secondary to its specific placement within a territory. However, it is on grounds of the former that local groups often challenge Walmart's crew of architects, real estate planners, and public relations specialists. For example, in Walmart's bid to enter Hercules, California, a small, affluent community north of Berkeley, community resistance obliged the retailer to modify the facade of its proposed building substantially to conform to the tenets established in the plan for the city. According to one account, Walmart prototypes come in eight styles—Main Street, Alpine, Industrial, Coastal, Ranch, Colonial, Mission, and Mediterranean—each designed to gesture toward visual appropriateness as determined by a given

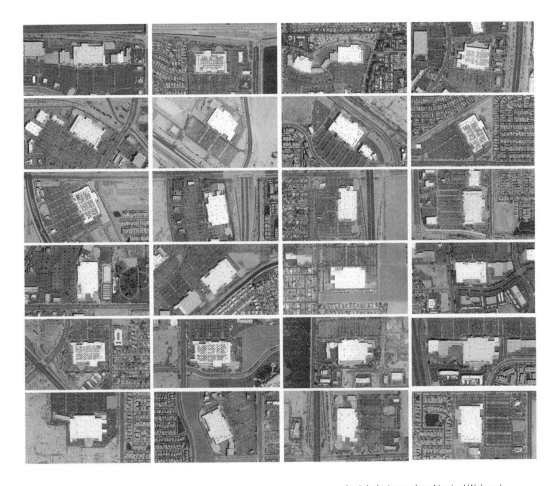

Aerial photographs of typical Walmart supercenters and land-use patterns in the Phoenix, Arizona, metropolitan area. Top row, left to right: Store 3360, Chandler; Store 5369, Goodyear; Store 1512, Chandler; Store 2766, Scottsdale. Second row: Store 5428, Mesa; Store 4430, Maricopa; Store 4451, Queen Creek; Store 4336, El Mirage. Third row: Store 3896, Peoria; Store 5186, Gilbert; Store 2112, Scottsdale; Store 2671, Chandler. Fourth row: Store 2768, Mesa; Store 2482, Mesa; Store 1218, Casa Grande; Store 1532, Glendale. Fifth row: Store 1533, Peoria; Store 2512, Phoenix; Store 2767, Mesa; Store 5190, Phoenix. Sixth row: Store 5331, Phoenix; Store 3861, Gilbert; Store 3465, Glendale; Store 3771, Phoenix. Source: Google Earth.

community.[22] The architecture of Walmart stores sits between the logistical demands that determine the organization of the shopping floor and varying degrees of populist demands, and this position suggests a version of architecture concerned primarily with surface and enclosure. Walmart's critics argue that "appeasing people's aesthetic sense will render them less likely to object to the real issue: the social, economic, and psychological impact of Walmart."[23] That is, by promoting the role of architecture as communicative surface, Walmart obscures design's utility as a territorial instrument. While this is perhaps not intentional on the part of Walmart, it is nonetheless a significant result of the company's approach. In an interview, William Correll, head of Walmart's architecture division at the time, reinforced this attitude:

> From a social and cultural standpoint, we deal with the buildings' exteriors all the time. That's literally a daily issue. Once folks know that a Walmart store is coming to their location, they ask, "Well, how's it going to look? How's it going to look when I drive up to it? I'll be driving back and forth from this place for years and years to come and my children will grow up walking in and out of its doors. Is there a way to make it feel like it fits in?" We have architects, engineers, and real estate people who are out looking at the surroundings and are working with local jurisdictions to build a consensus of what the exterior design should be.[24]

Although Correll did not say so, the exterior design is emphasized because the interior layouts of the prototypes are very rigid. These configurations are determined in part by the architects but mostly by the company's inventory and logistics experts, and they remain relatively inflexible. As a result, the architects are indeed left with little space for design. In response to this challenge, Correll went on to say:

> Productivity and efficiency are at the very center of what we're trying to accomplish in order to keep the prices low for customers. It all comes right back to that. However, when you are looking with an open mind, you start to see things that have been established over time that may not be so applicable anymore. . . . Some things must absolutely stay the way they are—and there are very serious reasons why they are the way they are—but other things have a little flexibility to them.[25]

In an effort to make buildings that "fit in," Walmart adapts its buildings to individual sites. From the company's point of view, this often

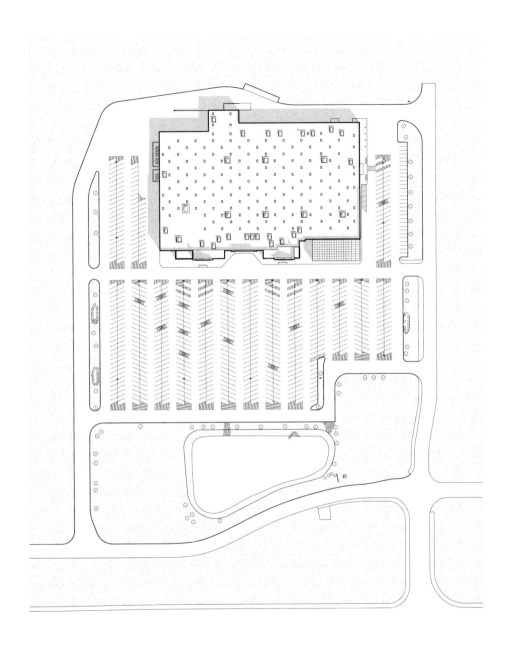

Typical site plan for Prototype 143. Redrawn
by the author. Not to scale.

amounts to modulating a building's surfaces to reflect some kind of abstracted or generalized architectural semantic of the region. The construction technology itself reinforces this bias toward surface because the buildings are often built of concrete masonry units and then clad with an exterior insulation finishing system. Such systems are superficial by definition and afford the kind of surface modifications that Walmart uses to mollify resistant publics.[26]

This kind of attention to local surroundings, however superficial, is costly and time-consuming for the company. In response, the architecture division has developed a new set of guidelines in an effort to streamline architectural production while raising the overall quality of Walmart's buildings.[27] Rather than offering the standard building and then only modifying that design when necessary to appease public concern, the plan aims to raise the standard of the common denominator so that customizing local outlets will no longer be necessary. In place of the diverse architectural responses produced by Walmart's previous design approach (referred to as "Store of the Community"), the new initiative, designed in part by New York–based Lippincott, is more standardized and sophisticated.[28] Lisa Spinks, then senior architecture manager at Walmart, summarized the company's goals in 2010: "We had to find a way to take what we stood for culturally, and what our customers wanted, and roll them into a consistent set of brand filters, so we don't track off into any extreme or any element that can bring you away from your brand message and your value proposition."[29] This design imperative aims at increasing the definition of each store through the elements of its new "brand filter": "Caring (compassionate, not cold)," "Real (approachable, not phony)," "Innovative (smart, not complacent)," "Straightforward (simple, not complicated)," "Positive (motivating, not pessimistic)."[30] This removal of ambiguity and increased resolution is reinforced by the program's acronym: CRISP. As evidence, consider Walmart's proposal for a new supercenter in Warrenton, Oregon. During the design review process, government officials and members of the community expressed frustration at Walmart's one-size-fits-all design approach. The company acknowledged these concerns and revised its proposal to be more sensitive to the local context through modifications to the site plan,

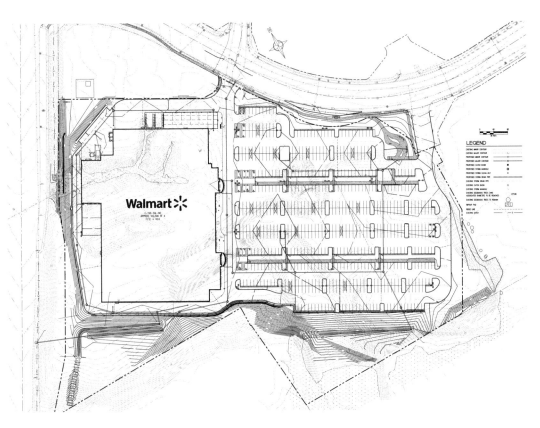

Preliminary grading and drainage plan, Walmart 5861, Warrenton, Oregon, 2012. As is often the case, this site needs to be regraded to be compatible with the prototype. Public document courtesy of the City of Warrenton, Oregon.

reduced visibility, the addition of stone veneer at entries, and new awnings over windows and "window-like" features. These revisions, reflected in a resubmitted design proposal to the city, were approved, and, at the time of writing, the proposal is moving forward.

While these guidelines are general, an examination of the construction documents of a specific design, Supercenter Prototype 143, reveals the company's focus on the surface treatment of its buildings (Plate 6). This emphasis on surface also supports certain prevailing discursive trajectories linked to architecture, especially those promoted by the work of Robert Venturi and Denise Scott Brown concerning the development of the "decorated shed." According to Venturi and Scott Brown's formulation, a decorated shed occurs when "systems of space and structure are directly at the service of program, and ornament is applied independently of them."[31] In many respects, Walmart's buildings conform to this definition. However, the emphasis placed on the design of enclosure by the company, the architects, and an attendant theoretical apparatus has obscured another set of characteristics demonstrated by these buildings—namely, the characteristics of an infrastructural network deployed to secure territory. Describing these buildings as "big boxes" further perpetuates an understanding of their architecture as one concerned with surface instead of interface, and with form instead of performance, thereby locating architectural agency primarily in the communicative possibilities of ornamentation.[32]

Within the corporate description of Walmart's architecture, the emphasis is clearly placed on surfaces—more specifically, on the *front vertical* surface. The other three vertical surfaces often perform service roles, as they receive delivery trucks and cars to be repaired and are punctuated with numerous fire exits. However, focusing on only the four vertical surfaces of a typical Walmart supercenter (as the company itself does in its own guidelines) fails to account for the other two surfaces crucial to the building's operation: the roof and the floor. These surfaces are significant because they have no symbolic obligations. As they are effectively invisible, there is no opportunity for them to communicate through architectural symbols (e.g., pediment, dormer, pilaster, materials). However, these surfaces are communicative in a literal sense because Walmart receives much of its essential

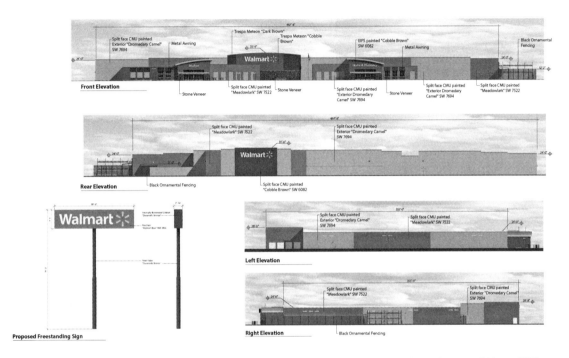

Proposed building elevations, Walmart 5861, Warrenton, Oregon, 2012. Public document courtesy of the City of Warrenton, Oregon.

Exterior view of Walmart 5861, Warrenton, Oregon, original proposal. Rejected by City of Warrenton Planning Commission for failure to comply with the city's Development Code. Source: PacLand, "North Coast Retail Center, Walmart Store #5861-01; Warrenton, Oregon; Revised Site Design Review Submittal, November 1, 2012." Public document courtesy of the City of Warrenton, Oregon.

Exterior view of Walmart 5861, Warrenton, Oregon, revised proposal, including variations in siting, visual screening, parking configuration, and facade enhancements. Approved by Design Review Board. Source: PacLand, "North Coast Retail Center, Walmart Store #5861-01; Warrenton, Oregon; Revised Site Design Review Submittal, November 1, 2012." Public document courtesy of the City of Warrenton, Oregon.

material through them. A closer inspection of the roof plan, for example, indicates that the surface's duties include more than letting light in, exhausting air, and keeping water out. The roof also plays host to the communications infrastructure, including several banks of security cameras and the store's satellite dish. The dish is the primary link to Walmart's satellite network and connects the store with the company's headquarters. On the ground, the floor slab is one of the key steps to formatting a site for a new store and a significant interface between the store and larger infrastructural systems such as electrical, plumbing, and drainage. While the vertical surfaces act as membranes for people passing in and out of the building, the horizontal surfaces enable the store's infrastructural connectivity and perform as membranes through which water, power, light, heat, and—most important—information pass.

Buildings like this accommodate significant material flows, including a constant stream of inventory. Products are delivered by trucks from the local distribution center, brought to the shelves, and then transported out of the stores by customers. The plan of a representative supercenter prototype, Prototype 143 (Plate 6), reveals a layout designed to minimize merchandise lag and optimize "throughput." Compared to warehouse-based models, Prototype 143 has only a very small amount of space for storage, but it has a maximized area available for merchandise display. The Walmart distribution system is responsive enough that a significant inventory supply is not required. As a result of its information management system's command and control of inventory, Walmart is able to replenish its shelves quickly with a minimum of storage space at each location. The floor plan of Prototype 143 indicates a large receiving area but only two relatively small stockrooms. Including all the areas off the sales floor, they account for roughly 25 percent of the total area of the store. By comparison, a prototypical supermarket layout from the 1955 manual *The Super Market* has 45 percent of its total area allocated to "non-sales" space and 55 percent for the sales floor.[33] In the past, retail outlets were designed to receive goods for sale in excess of what they could sell each day. These outlets served as both stores and warehouses, with stock replenished by distributors or suppliers on a regular, if infrequent, basis. By contrast, Walmart's supercenter is designed to evacuate its goods as quickly as possible.

In this light, referring to the supercenters as stores—that is, as places where items are "stored"—is in fact misleading, because they are designed to do the opposite. However, the etymology of the term *store* is telling: it originates in the Old French *estorer* and in turn from the Latin *instaurare*—"to renew." These buildings are designed not to accumulate material but to amass and dispense it cyclically. To manage this material, the typical supercenter's sales area has a highly specific and constrained layout. In this sense, Walmart supercenters operate in an infrastructural register as conduits and valves, capable of renewing and modulating the "flow" of material.

As both conduits and containers, these installations are simultaneously enclosures and passageways in which an exterior is both reinforced and undermined. The prototype approach demands that certain performance configurations remain tautly preserved while other elements, the exterior "crust" of the building, for example, have greater flexibility. Thus the layout of the racks and aisles is sacrosanct while this thick perimeter zone is more malleable and establishes an intermediate layer of slack program that mediates between the fixed layout of the interior and the exigencies of the local site conditions. The outermost layer of this crust, an architectural mantle, while only a small part of Walmart's building program, is the feature that is often the subject of public and architectural engagement. In light of this, it is possible to say that the content of the store is set but it has a loose relationship to the eventual form. Moreover, that form is highly contingent across multiple iterations, even if each one carries the exact same interior content (Plate 5). This approach to design, exemplified by Walmart, undermines the singular characteristics of architecture in order to foreground each instance's role in a larger hybrid system. It is an infrastructural version of architecture in which prototypes are deployed and updated, and it offers designers a model for preserving the core of a project while adapting to unforeseen local circumstances. It presents a number of opportunities to think through design in terms of what a context might be, what an inside might be (e.g., when there are two facades, an exterior and an interior), and what form might be.

As anonymous and bureaucratic buildings are increasingly the mode of choice for builders (and often responsible for shaping urban and civic spaces), designers are presented with an opportunity to engage such projects not as sheds to decorate but as the complex formal and spatial configurations they are.

Data Centers: Form but No Content

In order to manage its inventory and identify new locations, Walmart relies on an expansive network of data management systems that provide the "intelligence" for the company's logistical operations. The centralization of the corporate headquarters in Bentonville, Arkansas, has demanded that the retailer find ways to ensure the constant openness of transmission channels. Walmart has also developed proprietary software to record and process consumer and supplier information. With the bar code's ability to generate inventory statistics effectively, and with the company's vast network of stores, Walmart records huge amounts of data that it keeps in and relays through its own collection of data centers, one of which is just over the Missouri border from the Bentonville headquarters (Plate 7).[34] This data center is connected to the company's infrastructure network, but it has been built to disappear. Buried in the ground and hidden from view, the highly secured building is more legible as a node in a network of transmission than as a physical building. Its location, form, program, and use all present a version of architecture characterized and determined by its crucial role in the logistical system. As an automated structure that serves primarily as a relay station, it makes few provisions for its human occupants. Instead, its design is aimed at optimization and the seamless merging of building, infrastructure, and information.

Roughly the size of a standard supercenter, the anonymous data center is located in McDonald County, Missouri, and serves as part of the region's strategic plan for making more high-speed communications infrastructure available. From Walmart's point of view, the location is advantageous because property taxes in McDonald County are almost 85 percent lower than those in the retailer's neighboring home county, Benton County, Arkansas.[35] The installation is surrounded by

Aerial view of Walmart data center, McDonald County, Missouri. The building site is sealed by two layers of security fencing. Photograph by Max McCoy. Courtesy of the *Joplin Globe*.

Aerial view of Walmart data center, McDonald County, Missouri. The depth of the earth embankment that surrounds the building is most evident at the loading dock in the lower right portion of the image. Photograph by Max McCoy. Courtesy of the *Joplin Globe*.

the rolling hills of the Ozarks, but the pastoral image is at odds with the center's heavy security and fortification. Four security cameras cover its manned entry gate, two layers of chain-link fence capped with razor wire encircle the entire complex, and the grounds are patrolled by the McDonald County Sheriff's Department.[36] The building is fortified by earthen berms (which also help to offset the immense heat load of the data center) and bookended by two large HVAC arrays that are level with the low, flat roof. Viewed from outside the fence, the building has no discernible entrance; humans enter somewhere out of sight from the road. Data enter the building through a series of subterranean conduits connected to the large satellite enclosure in one corner of the site.

Compared to another large data center, the one belonging to Google, Inc., outside Portland, Oregon, Walmart's version is considerably more discreet. Because of the peculiar geographies of information storage and retrieval, the relatively remote Google data center has little impact on most of its users. It reflects the company's desire for cheap and reliable power as well as access to major telecom infrastructure.[37] Unlike Walmart's version of a data center, the design of the Google center emphasizes the assembly of metal-clad cooling components atop a mute container of servers. While the two corporations' versions of the data center conform to similar requirements, the differences between them illuminate certain features of Walmart's spatial operations. The Google complex is rendered discrete and autonomous, legible as a building in a very conventional sense. It is even possible to say that its mechanical features are decoratively positioned as celebrated features of the building. Conversely, the Walmart data center has been designed to disappear through camouflage and fortification, to become absorbed into the network to which it is connected. It is difficult to understand the Walmart data center using visual criteria. In fact, Walmart's data center, though a "big box," is designed outside of a visual regime.

The Walmart data center is an automatic building whose physical limits are ambiguous because of its integration with a larger infrastructural system. The building acts as information pathway because, even though it houses Walmart's collection of servers, it also stores

Walmart data center, McDonald
County, Missouri. Layers of security
and protective berms help to obscure
the building. Photograph by the author.

Google's data center complex outside
The Dalles, Oregon. Photograph by
the author.

and transmits the company's constant stream of proprietary data. Since any Walmart building, whether data center, supercenter, or distribution center, is also a local manifestation of the company's vast organizational network, this architecture is not only an information receptacle but also an information conduit. Information is applied *to* the building, but information also moves *through* the building in the form of material and data. This is especially evident in a building like the data center because the former category—that is, the symbolic function of the building—is eliminated completely.[38]

Like the supercenter, the data center is an interface in Walmart's network, and its various surfaces engage a range of transmission channels: the floor connects the building to a satellite while the vertical surfaces mediate human and vehicular access. Data centers are increasingly visible aspects of contemporary life, and their architecture varies. In the case of Walmart's data center, as the contents belong solely to Walmart, there is no requirement, from the company's point of view, to entice users through its architecture. The building is largely the result of a series of decisions aimed at yielding the most expedient result. In Walmart's overall logistics operations, the data center is the most spatially peripheral while still indispensable to the operations as a whole. This relationship hints at transforming intra-architectural relationships in the sense that the "interior" of the data center is relevant only for the data it contains. However, this building could be described in terms similar to those used by Luiz André Barroso and Urs Hölzle, two engineers at Google, who refer to that company's new Finnish data center as "one massive computer whose chassis happens to look like a warehouse—architecture as computer case."[39] Walmart's computer building on the Missouri border is connected to the retailer's other buildings but remains physically discrete. In this sense, data centers can span a seemingly insurmountable divide through their capacity to receive, store, and retransmit packets of information. Compared to the thick crust of the supercenter, in which restricted access forms a band along the outer envelope, the data center is a series of nested volumes that increase in both pristineness and security clearance as one moves toward the center. However, in the case of the supercenter, the contents of each location are known in

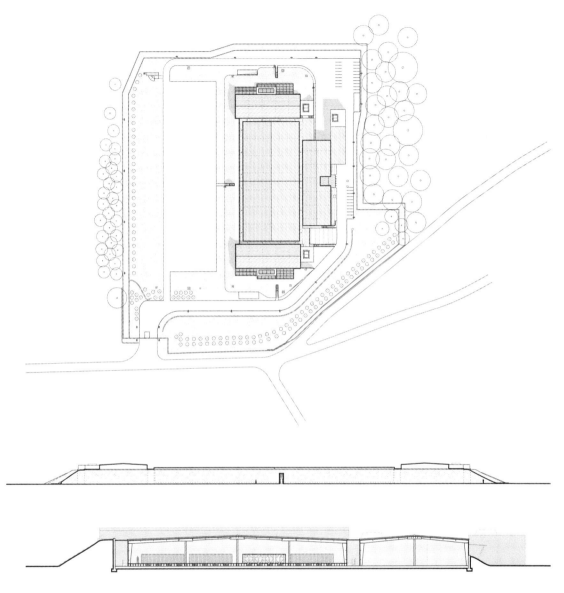

Site plan, elevation, and section of Walmart data center, McDonald County, Missouri. Drawing by the author with information extrapolated from aerial photographs, site visits, and descriptions of data centers in Luiz Barroso and Urs Hölzle, *The Datacenter as a Computer: An Introduction to the Design of Warehouse-Scale Machines* (San Rafael, Calif.: Morgan & Claypool, 2009). Not to scale.

advance and drive the outer form. With the data center, the physical contents are not known or installed until the building is completed because data management technology changes so rapidly that if more precise specifications were put in place at an earlier stage, they would be incorrect by the time construction was finished.[40] In other words, in this case, the building has a form, but its content is ever changing. Indeed, the data center is not a building full of computers but rather a computer with architectural qualities.

Distribution Centers: The Content Is the Form

Walmart's distribution centers are the linchpins of the company's logistics regime (Plate 8). These buildings are automatic sorting and storage facilities that route suppliers' merchandise to the supercenters in their regions. Not only are these large processors crucial to the company's physical distribution needs, but they are also used to establish new market centers and are key to the company's expansion efforts. While the supercenters are the most legible of Walmart's built artifacts, the distribution centers are the most important. As buildings, their relationships between form and content and between interior and exterior are more tightly coupled. DCs lack the constraints of function and image that characterize the supercenter (and thus have greater formal and organizational freedom). And while, like data centers, they prioritize their technical components, DCs have different functional needs and are more flexible as a result. In fact, conceptually, the edge of the DC building, that which distinguishes interior from exterior, only obscures the more active process of connecting one interior to another. The DC is a complex machine, and its form is reflected in the taut skin surrounding the conveyance mechanisms inside.[41]

DC 6094, for example, has an area of more than 1.2 million square feet and turns over more than 90 percent of its contents every day. The building, situated outside Bentonville, was built to serve the region, and the company uses it as a demonstration of its expertise in logistics and distribution technology. Its rural location (although it is gradually being surrounded by new housing developments) places no constraints on the building's size. Trucks, the fundamental links

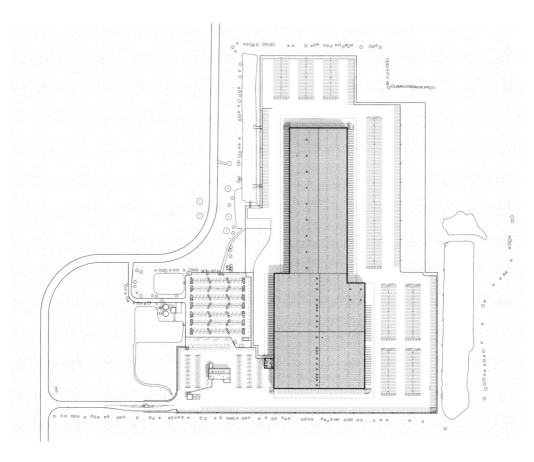

Site plan of a generic distribution center.
Drawing by the author, extrapolated from
aerial photography, site visits, and information from Dematic.com. Not to scale.

between DCs and individual stores, have a dedicated entrance and exit controlled by staffed checkpoints. In this sense, DCs act as regional hubs for the retailer's network of discount stores. As veteran Walmart executive Don Soderquist notes:

> The development of a warehouse system to receive, store, and ship merchandise to our stores was basically a necessity. Our stores were in small, rural markets, and the store managers could order only limited quantities of thousands of items of merchandise. . . . It was almost impossible to maintain a continuous flow of merchandise to our stores.[42]

As the company matured, this warehouse system developed into a distribution system whose primary purpose was to move goods as quickly as possible to where the company needed them.

The site of DC 6094 was chosen as much for the trucks as for the building's warehousing and distributing functions. Almost half the center's area is dedicated to trucks and trailers unloading their contents, receiving new shipments, or waiting for pickup or delivery. One of Walmart's logistics innovations is a practice know as "back-hauling," in which trucks that have dropped off shipments are reloaded with new shipments for their return journeys. Soderquist describes this process:

> Computers are a vital link in dispatching trucks to the stores and add to our efficiency in moving freight. Onboard computers are used for communications with all drivers while they are on the road. Since we already have so many outbound trucks driving down the highway and delivering merchandise to our stores, it didn't make sense to haul empty trailers back to the distribution centers on the return trip. Since we drive right by many of our suppliers' manufacturing plants, we decided to have our truckers stop and pick up that merchandise and bring it back with them, which saved significant costs on inbound freight. The onboard computers made this possible. . . . Today, our own trucks deliver over 50 percent of our inbound merchandise to our distribution centers.[43]

The successful implementation of this seemingly commonsense practice relies on Walmart's extensive communication systems. Since a significant portion of the company's merchandise is held in the trailers of its own trucking fleet at any given time, the vehicles themselves

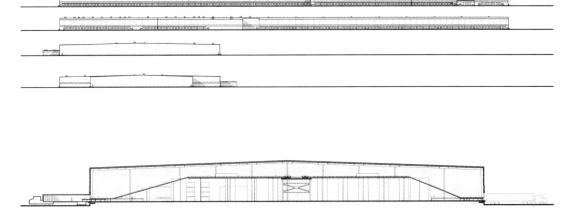

Elevations and section of a generic distribution center. Drawing by the author, extrapolated from aerial photography, site visits, and information from Dematic.com. Not to scale.

become part of the buildings. Furthermore, these trucks operate on predictable and stable circuits, making the same trip back and forth over and over again, a practice Walmart refers to as "Door per Store." Like a network of nimble freight elevators, the trucks play a crucial role in Walmart's spatial enterprise and are as much a part of its "architecture" as the supercenters.

The layout of DC 6094 is highly specific and tailored to Walmart's precise materials handling needs. Trucks bearing containers unload their contents onto conveyors that sort the merchandise onto short-term, high-density storage shelves to await "picking"—the selection of items for any given order and location. This process, enabled by the bar code's capacity to be read automatically, is regulated by the specific requirements of a given store and requires the assembly of a range of merchandise into one order. Depending on the requirements, these orders can comprise cases of merchandise or mixtures of single units. After an order has been assembled, it reengages with the system's automatic sorting equipment—belts, rollers, actuators, and scanners—and is routed to the appropriate docking bay and awaiting trailer that correspond to the correct Walmart store. This is also where Walmart's "cross-docking" operations take place. Soderquist recalls the development of this process:

> We tested the concept by building a long, narrow, extended arm on one of our new distribution centers and putting multiple doors on either side of the extension. A driver backed his truck into one of the doors on one side. As the merchandise was unloaded from that truck, some of it was moved to another truck on the opposite side bound for another distribution center. The merchandise was moved directly between trucks without any additional handling. . . . Cross-docking became the pattern for all new distribution centers.[44]

The malleability of the company's built products stands out in this description. While the process of optimization described above is seen more as a problem-solving venture, it nonetheless has architectural and territorial consequences. It also reinforces how the company sees its architecture: not as built enclosures but as interconnected systems of movement that can be managed and calibrated in pursuit of continuous movement:

> Throughout the day, all distribution center managers monitor the production process on their computer screens to see how the work is flowing and where any bottlenecks may be developing. They can move associates from one area of the distribution center to another at a moment's notice in order to keep the merchandise flowing. This is incredibly important, as the staggering volume of merchandise that each center receives and ships each day makes maintaining the highest level of efficiency a crucial priority. This type of process flow analysis is quite common in manufacturing, but it has been revolutionary for distribution centers.[45]

The conflation of the workers with the merchandise they are handling is apparent here. In Soderquist's account, managers can "move" people to areas that need more attention in the same way that they move merchandise from one truck to another. His acknowledgment of Walmart's appropriation of management techniques from manufacturing is also telling for its understanding of Walmart's role within regimes of production and circulation. However, these buildings are not just providing the armature for the automation of information and material management, they are automatic entities themselves, neither producing nor containing but, as described by Soderquist, *circulating*. According to Walmart's former vice president of logistics, Rollin Ford, "This is a fluid process, it's just constant, it never stops."[46] If this constantly circulating merchandise is conceptualized as data as much as physical material, Walmart's buildings are likewise not isolated objects but local manifestations of a dispersed communications network. The space they enclose is part of a continuous set of interiors connected, as it were, by the dynamic network of distribution.

In the distribution centers of Walmart and its materials handling subcontractor Dematic, this tendency to dissolve the envelope is rendered more plainly. In a series of images published in the company's promotional material, Dematic presents diagrams of various projects. While a physical envelope ostensibly surrounds each of these materials handling systems, it is consistently ignored or removed in the renderings. Although there is a pragmatic explanation for these visualizations—one has to remove the roof and walls to see the interior—they are also indicative of a larger attitude toward the buildings themselves. For example, in one illustration, the building's conventional edge is removed while the trailers are left in place. This is significant because, although the immediate enclosure is removed, the vessels that connect one interior with the next are included, making the physical limit of the building difficult to discern. Thus, Ford's statement that the Walmart distribution system "never stops" casts the operations of the company in a different light. Beyond the fact that the contents of the system never stop moving, more significantly, the system *itself* is constantly transforming at different scales of time. Following just a single object along its path, one misses the larger picture of millions of objects moving simultaneously within a dynamic and expanding organization. The single bar code is monitored at an instantaneous time scale, the containers carried by the trucking fleet change their position in a daily period, and new destinations in the form of new supercenters are added to the system weekly (requiring more trucks and in turn more distribution centers, which then allow for more stores to be built). Distribution begets distribution as the interconnected interiors continue to propagate.

If the supercenter is a building with content but no fixed form and the data center is a form with no content, the distribution center is where form and content merge. In the case of materials handling installations like those of Walmart, the belts and racks and other various conveyance mechanisms produce specific spatial and mechanical configurations that are connected directly to the trailers that transmit the items through the installations. While it so happens that there is a thin and conventional building enclosure that defines a condition of difference, its interiority is made redundant by the trailers shuttling between supercenter and distribution center. Indeed, as these buildings are completely sealed from external stimulus, the interior world of the trailer is continuous as far as the distribution center operators are concerned. Part of the wall rolls up to reveal an empty interior space. That space is filled with boxes of merchandise, and the wall rolls back down. It remains like that temporarily and then opens again to reveal a new and empty interior. In this sense, each trailer constitutes a room of the distribution center that is constantly on the move. These interiors, or semi-interior moments within a larger environment, are not nomadic but highly ritualized, making the same circuit day after day as they shuttle goods between centers.

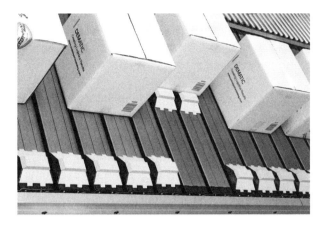

TOP LEFT: Flex-Sort Sliding Shoe Sorter, Dematic. Small automated "shoes" guide parcels to the appropriate conveyor, often to an awaiting trailer. Courtesy of Dematic, Inc.

TOP RIGHT: Conveyors merging in a Dematic distribution center. Courtesy of Dematic, Inc.

BOTTOM: Interior of a Walmart distribution center, 1989. Source: *Wal-Mart 1989 Annual Report*, 11.

Logistical Architecture Is Fugitive

Logistics is a temporal and interiorizing industry that shapes the things it encounters. In the case of Walmart's collection of buildings, gone are ideas of architecture as something stable and expressive of collective values. Instead, Walmart's architecture, here standing in for a more pervasive architecture of logistics, is contingent and fugitive. Its buildings form a hybrid network of low-definition configurations that are completed through their modification and instantiation, allowing a nimble response to unpredictable conditions. Because Walmart's architecture is imagined more as an operating expense than as a capital investment, the buildings are deployed as a means to an end.[47] The company's operations privilege reduction, removal, and abstraction. Technologies increasingly demand fast and remote decision making and condition the company's dynamic network of built elements. It is difficult to distinguish one of these installations from another. That is, while their internal properties, behaviors, and organizations might all be different, together they form an intertwined and constantly transforming set of shared interiors. In light of the logics shared by military and managerial logistics, one can best visualize Walmart's network of buildings by imagining it from a distance with its growth accelerated. It is at this point that one might witness the emergence of a new building type: a kind of ever-expanding form of logistically driven architecture that privileges performance and goes when and where it needs to. If one were to zoom in on the accelerated movements and the rapidly reconfiguring merchandise patterns of the automated distribution center's floor, one would find that these patterns and movements are legible only to the machines designed to read them. Larger shifts in territorial perception as a result of logistical vision enable the use of these elements. As places—the objects of this vision—become rendered as statistics, the spaces they inhabit are increasingly abstracted.

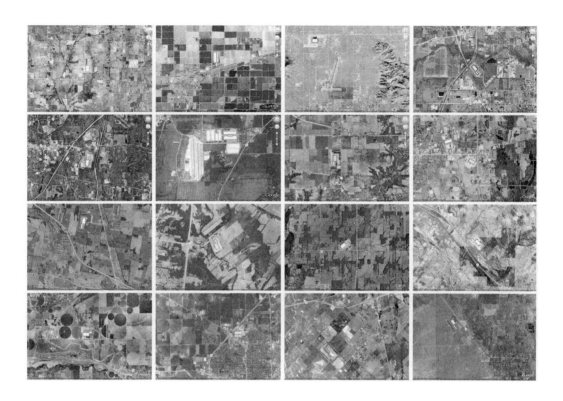

Selection of aerial photographs of typical Walmart distribution centers. Top row, left to right: DC 6095, Bentonville, Arkansas; DC 6299, Buckeye, Arizona; DC 7033, Apple Valley, California; DC 7083, Fort Pierce, Florida. Second row: DC 6054, La Grange, Georgia; DC operated jointly with Schneider Logistics, Elmwood, Illinois; DC 6092, Spring Valley, Illinois; DC 6017, Seymour, Indiana. Third row: DC 6066, Hopkinsville, Kentucky; DC 6048, Opelousas, Louisiana; DC 6043, Coldwater, Michigan; DC 6038, Marcy, New York. Fourth row: DC 6037, Hermiston, Oregon; DC 6012, Plainview, Texas; DC 7036, Sealy, Texas; DC 7026, Grantsville, Utah. Source: Google Earth.

3 LOCATIONS

From Intuition to Calculation

IN 1966, SAM WALTON, then a small-town discount merchant, traveled north from Bentonville, Arkansas, to the offices of IBM in Poughkeepsie, New York, to enroll in a retail training seminar; his aim was to learn how new technologies might help with his expansion plans for his company. In 1994, almost thirty years later, Howard Dean, then governor of Vermont, journeyed south to Bentonville, now the headquarters of the world's largest retailer, to negotiate with Walton's company about its controversial plans to open stores in his state, the last in the United States without a Walmart. During that interval, and thanks to a series of investments in information technology, infrastructure, and logistics, Walmart's retail empire spread steadily outward from Bentonville to cover the entire country (Plate 9). This process of expansion was driven by the company's own growth imperatives but also by ideological commitments to capitalism and the promotion of free trade.[1]

Walmart's site selection process began on the ground (by car), moved to the air (by personal aircraft), was launched into outer space (by satellites), and finally circulated through digital networks (by software). As a result, the sites in question are rendered in increasingly quantifiable and measurable terms. This shift from seeing space multidimensionally to seeing it one-dimensionally and remotely allows Walmart to manage its landholdings by imagining them as another part of the company's logistical network. However, in spite of the desire to manage sites as data, the contingencies of the local often require some degree of tactical maneuvering. Like the process of instantiating its prototypes, Walmart's approach to location requires an abstract system to be particularized, often through its network of buildings that act as couplings between these two conditions. While the global strategy remains general and the narrative smooth, the local instances illuminate some of the messiness and complexity of the system. The process of choosing where to site these buildings is increasingly mechanized and based on performance criteria and data analysis of a range of potential sites. By using personal aviation in early site selection, Walmart trained its executives to see territory in both abstract and comprehensive ways. So trained, these territorial managers were especially willing to experiment with technological systems that would reinforce those ways of seeing the world while also allowing the company to grow quickly. For Walmart, the communications satellite provided managers with the ability to supervise the entirety of their operation and also allowed them to visualize it in a variety of ways. Walmart's satellite network allowed it to develop a completely coordinated data exchange network, which, in turn, fed information to the company's real estate process through sophisticated demographics software. Such a transition from intuition to calculation creates new imaginations of space based on performance, mechanization, and fungibility: a logistics of territory.[2]

Walmart Is a Technological System

Sam Walton was conservative with investments in new technology but was always searching for ways to increase the company's efficiency. Hence his trip to Poughkeepsie, where he met Abe Marks, the first president of the National Mass Retailers' Institute (NMRI), a trade association for discount retail, and one of the speakers at the seminar.[3] Marks invited Walton to join the institute, and he quickly became an active participant; he served on the NMRI board for fifteen years. According to Walton, Marks "shared with me how he used computers to control his merchandise."[4] Marks recalls:

> What we helped him with in the early days was really logistics. It's like in the Army. You can move troops all over the world, but unless you

have the capacity to supply them with ammunition and food, there's no sense putting them out there. Sam understood that. . . . So to service these stores you've got to have timely information. . . .

. . . [Walton] became, really, the best utilizer of information to control absentee ownerships that there's ever been. Which gave him the ability to open as many stores as he opens. . . .

. . . Without the computer, Sam Walton could not have done what he's done. He could not have built a retailing empire the size of what he's built, the way he built it.[5]

Walmart has maintained close links to the association that was once the NMRI, even through a series of mergers and reorganizations. Now known as the Retail Industry Leaders Association (RILA), it "promotes consumer choice and economic freedom through public policy and industry operational excellence."[6] The 2010 RILA conference focused on logistics, and the program publication's cover featured an image of a field of spherical nodes redundantly stitched together with luminescent white lines, reminiscent of, if not in direct reference to, Paul Baran's diagram for the RAND Corporation some forty-five years earlier (see image on p. 59). Walmart's approach translates and spatializes this network thinking into a web of carefully located and coordinated installations. As the company grew, it demanded increased abstraction, if for no other reason than simply to cope with the increasing number of stores. Walton was enthusiastic about the possibilities of using private aircraft, and he and his executives took to the air to identify sites. As discussed further below, this change from being on the ground to being above it triggered a shift in the terms with which Walmart executives assessed locations. Because they were examining the landscape from above, they could more easily see larger patterns of infrastructural systems, traffic, population growth, and so on. As the number of stores continued to increase, the company further developed its extensive telecommunications system, which would also provide near-instantaneous communication throughout its network. Developments in satellite imagery eventually abetted this process to such a degree that Walmart executives no longer needed to survey land by plane—their "eyes in the sky," combined with advances in geographic information system (GIS) and real estate planning software, allowed them to make decisions in Bentonville. While site visits were still required, they were more of a formality to confirm the courses of action already developed by the real estate team and the prospecting software.

Walmart began using an IBM 360 system in 1972 to help coordinate its information management. At this point in its history, the company had only fifty-one stores, operating in Arkansas and the states immediately adjacent to it. In 1974, Walmart upgraded from a 360/20 to a 370/125. This process was not simply a matter of adding new software; it required changing the entire system and had significant material and cost implications, which some members of the Walmart leadership viewed with skepticism.[7] The retailer was proud of these investments, however, and began including images of its computer systems in its annual reports in 1975. The computer quickly acquired an important role not only in Walmart's daily operations but also in the company's self-image. Compared to IBM's marketing photos of products displayed in carefully organized showrooms, Walmart's annual reports offered a less pristine vision of corporate computing space. In a photo that appeared in the annual report of 1979, for example, the wood paneling and water-stained ceiling tiles in the room undermine the featured computers' modular character as envisioned by IBM designer Eliot Noyes. Nonetheless, IBM's slogan "THINK" is prominently displayed above one of the monitors. This photograph of the data processing center suggests that Walmart was deliberate about aligning its image with that of IBM, the modern and technologically innovative company providing Walmart's computers. In a photograph in the 1980 annual report, a modular floor, workstations, and storage devices are shown neatly ordered in a room devoid of evidence of any other activities. Walmart's imagery also suggests efforts to promote the technology's necessity and success to its shareholders. In other photographs, Walmart's data processing operators, phones to their ears and their eyes on monitors, complement the machinery. These images imply that data processing centers are like the automated control environments for which IBM's computer systems were instrumental (e.g., the U.S. Air Force's Semi-Automated Ground Environment, or SAGE, system). Walmart's technicians were initially responsible for ensuring the adequate supply and replenishment of inventory to its various stores. As this role has become increasingly automated, the data storage

In the late 1970s, Walmart began including images of its computer systems in its annual reports. This image, from 1979, shows the IBM 370 system that Walmart used to record daily store performance. Source: *Wal-Mart Stores, Inc. Annual Report 1979,* 11.

Walmart's data processing and communications center, Bentonville, Arkansas, 1979. According to the 1980 annual report, the center was "completed to assure around-the-clock communications throughout the Company." Source: *Wal-Mart Stores, Inc. Annual Report 1980,* 10.

apparatus has become significantly larger. However, the digital interface remains the primary site of Walmart's inventory management and real estate development. In this sense, the role of information technology for Walmart aligns with Noyes's statement that "if you get to the very heart of the matter, what IBM really does is to help man extend his control over his environment."[8] This role is further illustrated by recent photos of the control center in which technicians no longer fixate on a single monitor but rather keep track of an entire array of screens, each one constantly refreshing its readout (Plate 11).

An especially telling graphic from Walmart's 1986 annual report links the company's heavy investment in technology with its ideological mission. The image, organized in four bands, renders several photographs of Walmart management in ink and watercolor. The lowest portion of the image depicts a Saturday managers' meeting in which Walton, perched on one of the tables, reviews the weekly numbers. Extending from this group of managers is the plane of a desk on which one of Walmart's technicians is stationed in front of a computer monitor and wearing a communications headset. Rising almost from the back of his head, a large dish points south to Walmart's geostationary satellite. An American flag crowns the image and reinforces the words of Jack Shewmaker that appear in the lower right corner: "The development of efficient and cost-effective systems continues to move forward in support of our people development. The free flow of information and the continuous exchange of ideas with all our associates are cornerstones of Wal-Mart philosophy." Shewmaker's emphasis on the "free" flow of information and his rendition of Walmart management structure as open to anyone and characterized by continuous feedback echo the same free market principles that the retailer's executives are dedicated to defending. For Walmart, sustained communication and data tracking are not just good business: they are fundamentally linked to the company's ideological mission to propagate free market philosophies.

A photograph from the 1980 annual report shows Shewmaker pointing to a store location at the edge of the company's empire, reinforcing the zeal with which the company set out to expand its landholdings and increase its number of stores. In the eyes of Walmart's

Walmart data processing and communications center with attendants, Bentonville, Arkansas. Source: *Wal-Mart Annual Report 1981,* 10.

Walmart communications center operator and terminal, Bentonville, Arkansas, 1988. The original caption in the 1989 annual report reads, "Wal-Mart's overriding concern is the maintenance of its competitive edge." Source: *Wal-Mart 1989 Annual Report,* 9.

management, each new store meant a stronger defense against their fears of regulation. The caption to the Shewmaker image reads: "Wal-Mart Stores, Inc. has achieved an outstanding record of growth and profitability during the decade of the '70's. President and Chief Operating Officer Jack Shewmaker points out with pride the increased boundaries of 'Wal-Mart Country' from January 31, 1970, through January 31, 1980." In this context, "Wal-Mart Country" is a country of free enterprise but also a country of small government, deregulation, and Christian values.[9] The growth highlighted by Shewmaker was just beginning and—through his advocacy of aggressive investment in technology—would increase rapidly.

Store Locations Reinscribe Infrastructure

Based on its strategic plan, after Walmart identifies the general area for a new store location, the company's real estate team narrows the search to specific lots based on a combination of consumer demographic data, growth projections, and so on. After identifying a site that meets the company's criteria, the real estate team attempts to acquire the property, or at least the rights to build on it. In some cases, Walmart acts as the developer of the lot—that is, it buys the land and oversees construction of the building. Once rights are secured, Walmart begins the process of gaining municipal approval for the project. This process to determine whether the project is completed or abandoned has been well documented, often by scholars interested in understanding the dynamics of deliberative democracy or how small social groups can effectively challenge an organization as large as Walmart.[10] After the completion of a project, Walmart will sometimes sell the site to a property management company and then lease the site back. Essentially investing in Walmart, the property management company is then responsible for the maintenance of the store. Walmart historians Sandra Vance and Roy Scott point out that the company began using this "sale and lease-back arrangement" because it "afforded certain advantages: it was faster and more economical than using a developer; it permitted the company greater flexibility in choosing locations; it allowed Wal-Mart to develop a closer relationship with local banks;

Composite illustration including Walmart's home office, satellite receiving dish, operator and terminal, supplier negotiations, and Sam Walton and associates during a meeting. The caption, a quotation from Jack Shewmaker, reads: "The development of efficient and cost-effective systems continues to move forward in support of our people development. The free flow of information and the continuous exchange of ideas with all our associates are cornerstones of the Wal-Mart philosophy." Source: *1986 Annual Report from the People of Wal-Mart*, 8.

Photograph from Walmart's 1980 annual report of then president and chief operating officer Jack Shewmaker as he "points out with pride the increased boundaries of 'Wal-Mart Country' from January 31, 1970, through January 31, 1980." Source: *Wal-Mart Stores, Inc. Annual Report 1980*, 7.

and it enabled the firm to avoid percentage-of-sales clauses in leases."[11] Even though Walmart must evaluate each site individually, it always has several hundred sites in play at various stages of acquisition and development.

Walmart's basic approach to site selection in its early days was simple enough. It built stores out to the limits of the company's distribution range and then filled the area back in toward Bentonville with additional outlets. According to Don Soderquist's account:

> The real estate department maintained a rolling five-year development plan based on target numbers and locations that it established in concert with senior leadership each year. Regional real estate managers were responsible for developing future potential sites in their market areas based on demographics and cost-effectiveness. The overall plan was to grow out from a current store base and then fill in any major gaps between stores.[12]

When the company anticipated that too much stress would be put on a part of the distribution network, it would initiate the construction of an additional DC. This new building would then become the center of a new ring of development until *it* was overloaded, and then a new one was built, and so on.

The supercenters' locations are determined by a number of factors, but they all have direct relationships to local distribution centers. The growth patterns of the company are illustrated in Plate 9, which shows the Walmart stores and DCs in the United States as of 2013. Concentric growth is important: new stores are always built adjacent to existing ones, and the new locations are largely determined by the proximity of distribution centers.[13] Walton describes this process: "We figured we had to build our stores so that our distribution centers, or warehouses, could take care of them, but also so those stores could be controlled . . . each store had to be within a day's drive of a distribution center."[14] From the outset, this mode of conceptualizing Walmart's territory as concentric, calibrated, and, above all, controlled dominated the company's expansion. Rather than identifying receptive markets, regardless of their positions relative to corporate headquarters—as most of Walmart's competitors were doing—Walmart grew steadily outward from Bentonville in an effort to avoid exposing itself without first developing adequate logistical support mechanisms.[15] By mapping store locations relative to interstate highway infrastructure, one can see that Walmart effectively reinscribes the nation's transit network. For example, the store locations in North Dakota follow the route of Interstate 94 and are located at consistent intervals, each roughly half a day's drive from the next. The distribution centers' locations then become key to securing these delivery channels. David Glass, Sam Walton's successor as CEO, acknowledges that this strategy was seen as counterintuitive by many of Walmart's competitors: "For years and years we just simply expanded those circles out by strategically locating DCs. There was a tremendous flight from the inner cities to suburbs, and so our strategy was to go to Dallas or wherever and build stores in the suburbs; not because we wanted to be in small towns closest to Dallas but because that's where the population growth was."[16] Glass goes on to describe the process by which he and Walton would decide where to locate the company's first stores:

> We drew a circle two hundred miles around Bentonville, and we said we can put stores in that circle. We recognized that if you wanted to grow the business rapidly, you would need another distribution center, and so we decided to put up a second one. There was conjecture on the part of Wall Street analysts on whether we could operate these centers away from Bentonville. We built one in Searcy, Arkansas, in 1978. We drew a circle around it and made it work.[17]

Location and delivery—logistics, in other words—have been key components of Walmart's expansion strategy from the beginning.

The company was also aggressive in securing land. According to Walton, once they identified a site they liked from the air, they would immediately land nearby, attempt to find the owner, and make an offer on the spot. They would also do their best to remain anonymous. Sam Walton was a familiar face in the region, but some of his team members could maintain low profiles in their quest for real estate. Walton's son Jim was especially effective at this. According to journalist Bob Ortega:

> Beneath that Haight-Ashbury exterior beat the heart of a businessman. Jim Walton used his looks to his advantage, flying out to find store sites, landing, and hauling his bicycle out of the back of his plane to pedal

around a town without attracting the attention of local businesses. He would question property owners without mentioning his corporate connection.[18]

In this instance, the airplane allowed for nimble access to sites but the technology itself was used opportunistically and hybridized with other more "low-tech" options such as the bicycle.

Airplanes Override Terrestrial Infrastructure

In the beginning, Sam Walton intuitively made location decisions based on his experience as a retailer. He and his team scouted for prominent sites that were not too close to competitors or to other Walmart stores but close enough to Walmart's distribution facilities and to new growth. Walton preferred to be as involved as possible with any issues surrounding new store locations. In the early years of Walmart's operation, these locations were concentrated around northwest Arkansas, and Walton could manage them by driving from location to location. However, as the company continued to open new stores it became increasingly difficult for Walton to visit all his sites with a frequency that satisfied him. In his memoir, Walton refers often to his obsession with aerial reconnaissance and argues that it is one aspect that has set Walmart apart from its competitors. While Walton is less explicit about the genesis of his interest in flight, it could be related to slightly frustrated military aspirations:

> I wish I could recount a valiant military career—like my brother Bud, who was a Navy bomber pilot on a carrier in the Pacific—but my service stint was really a fairly ordinary time as a lieutenant and then as a captain doing things like supervising security at aircraft plants and POW camps in California and around the country.[19]

Without placing undue emphasis on Walton's biography, military associations with flight and surveillance reoccur in the discourse of Walmart's operations, retail growth strategies, and site selection. According to Walton, "Once I took to the air, I caught store fever."[20] His fervent approach to expansion enabled by air transport also granted him certain ways of understanding the terrain visible only from the pilot's seat. Walton describes the thrill of flying:

I loved doing it myself. I'd get down low, turn my plane up on its side, and fly right over a town. Once we had a spot picked out, we'd land, go find out who owned the property, and try to negotiate the deal right then. That's another good reason I don't like jets. You can't get down low enough to really tell what's going on, the way I could in my little planes. Bud and I picked almost all our sites that way until we grew to about 120 or 130 stores. . . . I guarantee you not many principals of retailing companies were flying around sideways studying development patterns, but it worked really well for us.[21]

As he points out, he flew only small propeller planes, like his early Air Coupe, Piper Tri-Pacer, and Beechcraft Baron, and his last one, a Cessna Chancellor 414A. These aircraft were agile in terms of maneuverability, and their size allowed access to the nation's numerous small municipal airports. Without the constraints of roads, Walton could fly directly from store to store. He could also scout for real estate from a privileged vantage point. John Huey, coauthor of Walton's autobiography, observed that Walton used his plane "pretty much like a station wagon. He would just go out, get in it, turn the key and leave. Never any checklist. One time we took off and the door wasn't closed yet. He would swoop down low and say, 'Okay, you look for the airport,' and the FAA would come on and tell him he wasn't allowed to be that low and he'd just turn off the radio."[22] This description suggests the casualness—and perhaps recklessness—with which Walton operated his aircraft. However, his willingness to challenge the limits of certain infrastructural protocols allowed his company to grow in an unprecedented way. By taking off without proper checks, flying too low, and landing without permission Walton was taking risks, calculated as they may have been. At the same time, his attitude suggests an effort to normalize the practice of air travel while also operating creatively within the constraints of an infrastructural network.

Airspace is a multidimensional medium *through* which one can navigate rather than a set of linear elements *along* which one travels. By looking at territory from the air, Walton was able to acquire a more comprehensive sense of the surroundings than if he were traveling by car. As Walton describes it:

There's no question whatsoever that we could not have done what we did back then if I hadn't had my airplanes. I bought that first plane for business, to travel between the stores and keep in touch with what was going on. But once we started really rolling out the stores, the airplane turned into a great tool for scouting real estate. . . . From up in the air we could check out traffic flows, see which way cities and towns were growing, and evaluate the location of the competition—if there was any. Then we would develop our real estate strategy for that market.[23]

While this was not a scientific process yet, Walmart would continue to refine its approach to site selection—especially in terms of its comprehensive view of its holdings and the abstraction that occurs in the process of surveying sites at a distance. The air, in this case, is a kind of thick medium through which, freed from terrestrial infrastructure, Walton could maneuver in an attempt to command a greater territorial vision.

Satellites Collapse Distance

As store numbers increased, Walmart needed a more comprehensive vision and a more informed decision-making process for selecting new store locations. To accomplish this, the company would travel more than 22,000 miles farther from the earth's surface, to a stationary point above the equator. Through the early use of a geostationary communications satellite, Walmart's command over its data expanded significantly. In 1984, the company committed $24 million to develop a satellite network of its own. This was more than a quarter of the company's entire operating budget. In its 1988 annual report, Walmart boasted the "completion of the largest private satellite communication system in the United States which links all operating units of the Company and the general office with two-way voice, two-way data and one-way video communication. The inauguration of this system featured a live broadcast from Sam Walton to all Wal-Mart associates."[24]

The satellite network was an economical response to the need for a comprehensive vision because it granted Walton access to his stores and his employees through a one-way video channel. The new satellite network also enabled easier and cheaper communication between different Walmart stores and allowed faster data transmission. This was important because the primary concern for Walmart continued to be its pursuit of optimization. Thus the company's executives devoted significant amounts of time to scrutinizing the performance data from each location. According to Soderquist, "We recorded and analyzed same-store sales increases every single week at Wal-Mart. Those were the first numbers we looked at every Saturday morning. At the first sign of weakness, we jumped to find out what might be the problem."[25] Walton himself drove this obsession and would arrive at his office on Saturday mornings as early as 3:30 a.m. to review the week's performance data before each meeting.[26] The data system provided nearly instantaneous access not only to Walmart's sales information but also to employees via a closed-circuit television network. Even though he could not be physically present in each store, Walton extended his command over his territory significantly through communications technology. Using the company's huge data network, Walton could, to some extent, transcend his physical limitations in order to communicate with his burgeoning force of employees.

Walmart's satellite network allowed its company headquarters to receive constant feedback from the various stores. Because Walmart preserved the centrality of its organization, company leaders became increasingly dependent on the network to maintain an awareness of operations.[27] A 1988 article in *Discount Store News,* a retail trade publication, noted that Walmart's network "provides real-time, round-the-clock transmission, with voice and computer data flowing between Bentonville and all locations, while video signals are broadcast only from headquarters to the stores and other facilities."[28] Walmart stores are referred to by number and not necessarily by geographic location. For example, Supercenters 5494 and 5495, which were opened sequentially, are in Idaho Falls, Idaho, and Glenolden, Pennsylvania, respectively, more than two thousand miles apart. The fact that the stores are designated in this way—as opposed to, say, by state—illuminates the company's collection of land and buildings as a numerical, quantifiable effort that allows for easy comparison, assessment, forecasting, and adjustment. Thus Walmart's stores serve as both data-gathering stations for recording shopping habits and transmission stations for reporting these findings back to Bentonville.[29]

At first, the satellite network was a risky proposition. Shewmaker describes the foundation of the system:

> I had this dream of an interactive communications system on which you could communicate back and forth between all the stores and the distribution centers and the general office. Glenn [Habern] came up with the idea of using the satellite, and I said, 'Let's pursue it without asking anybody.' . . .
>
> The technology didn't really exist to do this for retail in the early eighties. But we got together with the Macom & Hughes Corporation, and worked out a contract, and eventually we committed $24 million to build it. We launched it in 1983, and I mean, Sam liked to killed me the first two years. It was not an immediate success. But we got it working, and now, of course, everybody has one.[30]

As with the bar code, Walmart's eager, if risky, experiments with new forms of communication technology coincided with other technological developments (the profusion of data trafficking coupled with automated inventory management, in this case) to the retailer's advantage. Walmart uses the Satellite Business Systems (SBS)-4 K_u band satellite to relay its information.[31] According to Intelsat reports, this satellite was put into orbit on August 30, 1984, and was stationed at longitude 91°05' west (Bentonville is at 94°12' west). The terminology that has been used to describe the initiation of the system, or its activation, has been somewhat imprecise. When *Discount Store News* reported that Walmart had "launched" the world's largest private satellite communication system, the retailer was using just one satellite but had developed an extensive network, including one large hub at Bentonville and a small "portable earth station" at each store and distribution center. The SBS-4 acts as a relay for information traveling along the K_u band frequency range. Hughes Network Systems, the company that made the SBS-4, was instrumental in early satellite development and is responsible for the design and manufacture of some of the earliest commercial and military satellites. The SBS-4 consists of two concentric rotating drums wrapped in solar panels, the smaller of which can nest in the larger to save space during launch and transport. The coverage area of the satellite's "beam" includes most of the mainland United States and Hawaii. The image featured here suggests the satellite is operating in isolation, but of course the entire equatorial circumference is crowded

A drawing of the Boeing SBS-4 satellite used
by Walmart and its coverage area. Courtesy
of Boeing.

with neighboring satellites encircling the earth in geosynchronous orbit, sending images of the planet's surface back to us.[32]

Although at first reluctant to invest in a satellite system, Walton quickly came to appreciate its contribution. For the CEO, "the satellite turned out to be absolutely necessary because, once we had those [UPC] scanners in the stores, we had *all this data* pouring into Bentonville over phone lines. Those lines have a limited capacity, so as we added more and more stores, we had a real logjam of stuff coming in from the field. As you know, I like my numbers as quickly as I can get them. The quicker we get that information, the quicker we can act on it."[33] But Walton was not interested in how the system worked— he cared only about how it performed. His primary objective with the improvement of Walmart's computer systems was to gain the increased intelligence that came with them:

> I can pick anything . . . and tell you exactly how many of them we've bought over the last year and a quarter, and exactly how many of them we've sold. Not only overall, but in any or every region, every district, every store. It makes it tough for a vendor to know more about how his product is doing in our stores than we do. I guess we've always known that information gives you a certain power, but the degree to which we can retrieve it in our computer really does give us the power of competitive advantage.[34]

In his early days, he would spend his lunch hours walking through the aisles of Kresge and Woolworth's stores to gather information. Now his company uses one of the largest satellite networks in the world to gather intelligence:

> I can walk in that satellite room, where our technicians sit in front of their computer screens talking on the phone to any stores that might be having a problem with the system, and just looking over their shoulder for a minute or two will tell me a lot about how a particular day is going. . . . If we have something really important or urgent to communicate to the stores and distribution centers—something important enough to warrant a personal visit—I, or any other Wal-Mart executive, can walk back to our TV studio and get on that satellite transmission and get it right out there. And, as I told you earlier, I can go in every Saturday morning around three, look over those printouts, and know precisely what kind of week we've had.[35]

In this account, Walton demonstrates the potential, at least in his eyes, of both the omniscience and the omnipresence promised by his communications systems. His video network allowed him to be everywhere and his data screens allowed him to see everything at once, conflating his view with that of the satellite.

The particular example of communications satellites raises its own set of territory issues. As with any new communications system, regulation proved to be especially challenging. Confrontations with regulation, or lack thereof, served to highlight the capacity of satellite communications to override existing territorial boundaries. For example, Canada's first satellite, the Anik, was launched in 1972. According to satellite historian James Martin, "It was soon realized that the ANIK satellites would provide cheaper long–distance telephone or television circuits than those of the established common carriers. Antennas were set up in the United States to use the ANIK satellites, and for the first two years in orbit these satellites earned a return on capital investment that was virtually unprecedented in the telecommunications industry."[36] In other words, companies could circumvent national regulations through their satellite communications. By being inventive in developing their infrastructural services and by pursuing somewhat counterintuitive approaches, American telecom companies could save on operating costs while Canadian companies could increase their profits. According to David Rees, "Prior to the days of satellites, the task of government control was comparatively easy as either cable beach heads or larger antenna farms were needed to provide the services. . . . The arrival of satellites has introduced the ability of one country to influence greatly many aspects of other countries."[37] This erosion of political sovereignty as the result of the technological vision of logistics foregrounds some of the visual habits cultivated by a logistical imagination, which renders territory as a coordinate system and as a managerial field.

The first live-via-satellite television broadcast in the United States occurred on June 28, 1965. During that transmission, President Lyndon B. Johnson said, "This moment marks a milestone in the history of communications between peoples and nations. For the first time a manmade satellite of earth is being put into commercial service as a means of communication between continents."[38] Twenty-three years later, Walton and Glass inaugurated their new network with a live feed from Bentonville; in his remarks on that occasion, Walton referred to the company as "the nation's foremost pioneer in establishing a network of this type."[39] Platitudes about the corporation's achievements notwithstanding, this event marked a shift in Walton's understanding and engagement of territory. By using small private aircraft, Walton would hop from one store to the next and search for new sites in the process. His "eyes in the sky" were indeed still his. With the development of the satellite network, the ways in which Walton would "see" his territory changed significantly. The different stores were no longer directly associated through their location and physicality. Walton could simply choose a store number and broadcast to that store instantly on the company's monitors. The channel was only one-way, however; employees could see and hear Walton, but he could not see them. What he could see were the numbers: the consumer data that poured in through the retailer's communications channels. A photograph from Walmart's 1989 annual report captures this dynamic. Most of the image is devoted to Walton, who is perched on a stool and addressing a television camera. In the lower right, a small inset image shows his employees watching the broadcast at some remote site.[40] The satellite network allowed Walton's employees to see him when he deemed it necessary, while Walton was able to focus only on the numerical performance of their stores. This produced a kind of compound abstraction. With one shift in operating procedure, the employees and their stores disappeared from view and were replaced by sets of data concerned with narrow performance criteria. This dynamic, in turn, fed into a shift in the way new locations were chosen—abstractly and remotely. Whereas Walton's presence in his plane had been discreet, the satellite network absorbed and distributed his "presence" as he was able to inhabit the world of his own creation through its information channels. As a result of the satellite network, Walton could take to the air—or, more precisely, the airwaves—without his plane.

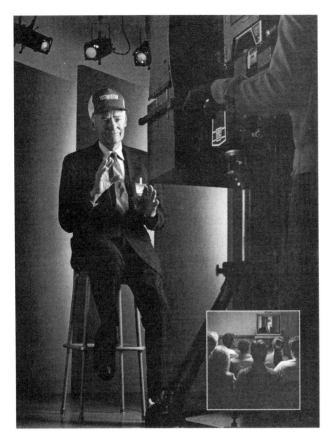

Image from 1989 annual report of Sam Walton broadcasting a message over the company's communications network, with inset image of an audience. Source: *Wal-Mart 1989 Annual Report*, 6.

At 7:30 a.m. on January 11, 1988, Sam Walton and David Glass inaugurated "Walmart TV" by broadcasting a message to all the company's associates. Photograph by the author of display in Walmart Visitor Center, 2007.

Software Turns Everything into Points

Surveying sites from his small aircraft, Walton gained a visual over-view of a given territory, enabling him to guess how an area might develop based on traffic, adjacent programs, density, and so on. As Walmart continued to grow, the retailer needed faster and more accurate ways of determining the best locations for new stores with reliable return-on-investment projections. The discount retail market had become more competitive, and there was pressure from shareholders to guarantee successful site selection. To accommodate this growing need for more accurate site and demographics data, Walmart's real estate division began to rely increasingly on software applications. This process, although technologically more sophisticated, remains consistent with Walmart's tendency to abstract territory by reducing it to quantifiable data. From the cockpit's oblique view to the flat satellite photo and now—with location software's capacity to render territory as data—to the single statistical point, this process of abstraction reframes territory as data. The company understands sites as quantities to be assessed in terms of performance: adopted if there is a match and abandoned in search of more compatible conditions if necessary.

Most location software relies on a combination of consumer databases in assessing a possible location's exposure to predetermined demographic profiles, or market segments. The software can survey the proposed area and determine whether it is a suitable match, based mostly on the likely return on investment. When there are several sites in one area considered for a new store, real estate planners can input information on all of them into a given software application and generate a series of reports that rank the sites according to their likely success. One member of Walmart's real estate division describes the process:

> We'd look at our market share, we'd look at our potential competition, at available retail sales—you could do it thematically—spreadsheet or database, and then you could come back and say here's a real opportunity to serve this market where we're not serving them today and then we would go out. We would probably start at a more regional level and work our way down to more of a block group and say where exactly do

we want to go. . . . Now the difference from the Sam Walton book is he would go out and fly his plane over the tops of stores to look at population. *Essentially we are doing the same thing,* we're just using data sets and putting that on maps, and we would give all that information to our real estate managers to go execute.[41]

Rather than physically moving through space and visually inspecting potential sites, Walmart's real estate executives now operate remotely from their (windowless) Bentonville offices. Site information is delivered to them through satellite imagery, demographic data, and mapping analysis software. Thus, without a potential site ever being visited, most of the process is already finished.

The challenge of locating potential sites for new stores from a centralized and remote corporate headquarters has prompted Walmart's real estate division to supplement its efforts with a range of computer software tools, all part of a process of measuring, recording, and indexing landholdings based on different factors.[42] These applications aggregate combinations of data and allow users to assess sites in terms of a variety of factors, including settlement patterns, growth predictions, traffic levels, user groups, and income levels. The data come from a variety of sources, some public and some proprietary. These sources include surveys of residents conducted by phone or mail or through sustained monitoring; the information gathered is fed into a territorial survey that merges behavioral and location data.

The public sector provides two main data sources: the decennial U.S. census and postal code information. In addition, some private companies develop their own demographic data or combine these data with those of the public-sector sources. Walmart often relies on information from one of these major providers, the Nielsen Corporation.[43] Nielsen is perhaps best known for its monitoring of television consumption trends through increasingly sophisticated technologies. However, it has diversified considerably and now offers a range of applications regarding site selection for retail businesses. The company, founded in 1923 by Arthur Nielsen and incorporated in 1929, has roots in the era of Taylorist industrial production in the United States and initially specialized in monitoring the performance and quality of manufacturing hardware. During the Great Depression, demand for the company's services diminished significantly, prompting Nielsen to look for other opportunities that would benefit from the precise accounting methods he had developed. As retailers struggled to stay in business, they were drawn to a service that promised to increase sales while reducing waste. Nielsen offered businesses comprehensive services, surveying customers but also synthesizing customer data in search of patterns and trends. However, in order to present these findings in a comprehensible way, Nielsen needed to invent new analytical categories. One of these was the concept of "market share," which Nielsen developed in 1935.[44] Market share can be understood as the number of customers in a given area shopping at a specific store, and determining market share became an early example of measuring the intersection between territory and consumer behavior.

Even though Nielsen would later be known for consumer behavior research in media, the company got its start in retail. With the growth of radio and the emergence of television, the advertising sector became both more lucrative and more competitive. If advertisers had a better idea of who was watching when, the thinking went, they could promote certain products at times when they would be most likely to reach potential customers. Nielsen maintained an interest in technology and, like Walmart, often seized new technological opportunities. In 1952, the company acquired a very early IBM computer, and by 1979, only two years after the introduction of the UPC, Nielsen had developed techniques for capturing and analyzing data from bar code scans. Given its interest in retail and in technology, the company would continue to develop products aimed at improving retail performance. Nielsen also began to turn to real estate—consumer behavior at a collective level—advising companies on where to locate new outlets.

Nielsen's process involves surveying consumers and transforming them into data points. Like the development of regional science, which sought to render territory as a statistical field, Nielsen transformed the ways the consuming public was understood. In this sense, resolution helped determine the quality of information and the consequent accuracy of the predictive models. More information was believed to yield better decisions. The planning culture at the time reinforced this mentality and invested significant energy and belief into such models.[45] In the case of television, these numbers became a kind of currency that networks would trade in, especially with their advertisers. Nielsen had to have monopolistic control over its numbers, because otherwise television networks and ad buyers would not be able to draw proper conclusions about relative popularity and thus worth. But this value was abstract: the income was speculative and linked to assumptions about buying habits and their correlation to advertising exposure. Similarly, these rankings relied on assumptions that such behavior could be predicted with some form of accuracy, assumptions that continue to hold a great deal of currency at other levels of prediction and measurement, including Walmart's real estate operations.[46]

While Nielsen has streamlined its offerings in recent years, until recently its website offered a range of tools designed to aid in the process of developing an appropriate distribution strategy. Even though these consulting services are provided at a more general level, Nielsen also offered "market and site analysis" for the established company looking to optimize its distribution strategy:

> With our market analysis and site analysis tools you will uncover potential real estate opportunities, eliminate overlaps in existing markets, and avoid inefficiencies in real estate planning and operations. In addition to expansion, you need to evaluate the impact of, and make intelligent and informed choices about, remodels, relocations and closures. In addition, you will be able to find your best customers and prospects and see where your competitors are located in relation to you and your customers. Nielsen's market and site analysis solutions offer flexible area definition and interactive mapping combined with our reliable data— in applications for businesses of all sizes.[47]

Nielsen promised customers that its market and site analysis would "uncover" hidden markets and unnoticed inefficiencies (politely referred in the quote above as "overlaps in existing markets" but often referred to as cannibalization).

The process of selecting locations for new stores naturally requires the identification of potential sites. In Walmart's case, according to a real estate division employee, the company articulates growth goals in its long-term plan along with market areas in which it hopes to build. Within those potential areas, real estate team members develop selections of possible sites, which they then process and assess using the tools described here. Demographics reports and area maps are often among the actual artifacts that the company uses to choose sites. Reports from Nielsen or other providers, such as Esri or the more retail-focused Sites USA, break down a prospective area's residents into different categories based on factors like age, income, and marital status. For clarity's sake, the providers place these consumers into certain market "segments" that generalize the likely behavior and consumer demands of given groups. Esri has developed sixty-seven different demographics clusters, which it uses to generate profiles for the types of people inhabiting an area.[48] Retailers like Walmart have certain consumer target ranges in mind and look for sites with the highest concentrations of members of those groups. Other factors include driving time, competing locations, and overlap with other outlets of the same business.

Cartographic images created by these companies illuminate the ways in which territory is abstracted in pursuit of market performance. For example, a market optimization study from Sites USA, using the company's tool REgis, shows a range of potential sites and ranks them according to their proximity to desirable households. Maps like these might include postal code divisions, local and national highways, shopping areas, and demographic segments (e.g., Esri uses labels like "Boomburbs," "Metro Renters," and "Up and Coming Families" to describe groups of people), as well as the potential trade areas surrounding each site. A map from Esri shows a range of possible sites in the Greater Los Angeles area in relation to other existing locations and transport infrastructure.

According to one GIS expert on the Esri staff, "Common business challenges, such as site selection and trade area analysis, can be solved with the push of a button using GIS."[49] Moreover, "done correctly, GIS exposes hidden relationships and helps everyone explore and investigate market conditions and performance."[50] Site selection software is promoted as a quasi-magical revelatory process in which "hidden relationships" are exposed with a simple mouse click. This notion is seductive, especially when organizations are confronted with increased competition and pressure to continue growing.[51] Equally enticing is

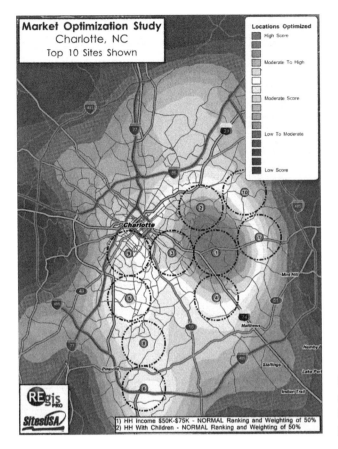

Sample visualization indicating potential store locations and the demographic groups in range. Source: 2010 Sites USA REGIS promotional brochure.

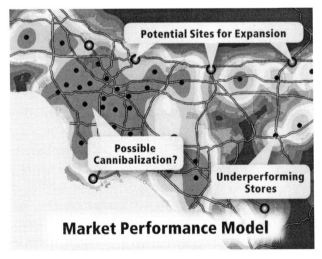

Sample map of an assessment model to evaluate performance of current store sites and potential sites of expansion. Source: 2010 Esri Business Analyst promotional brochure; reprinted by permission. Copyright 2010 Esri. All rights reserved.

the promise of the ability to command territory from the comfort of one's desk chair, which in Walmart's case is somewhere inside the Sam M. Walton Development Complex. Desktop computers linked to the company's large data network and satellite system provide access to the world beyond and allow development at a distance with limited encounters with the collateral consequences of such automated location processes.

A crucial step in the site selection protocol is the delineation of the so-called trade area, the territory that contains the location's potential consumers. Trade areas are calculated primarily in terms of the time it takes to travel to the location or in terms of distance (e.g., a radius of one mile, three miles, or five miles). In an idealized model, the trade area is always a circle around the site. Before the development of location software, store planners used analog tools to delineate trade areas based on the specifics of the individual locations. The potential values of proposed locations were also calculated by hand. The "location table" was one method that planners used in attempting to rationalize the process of site selection through quantitative terms. In this approach, a map of a given area is attached to the top surface of a table, and holes are placed through the table in locations on the map corresponding to different geographic factors that are likely to affect the potential new site. A piece of twine is then threaded through each hole, and the top ends of all the pieces of twine are knotted together above the table's surface. Attached to the lower ends, beneath the table, are varying weights based on different values. In this way, one can test different relationships, as each new configuration, through different distributions of weight, pulls the knot above the table to a different point of equilibrium. Each resting point then corresponds to the optimum location for the given assignment of relative values of the different elements (population centers, access to infrastructure, and so on). In what is basically an analog precursor to the real estate software described above, the location table follows the larger impulse to mechanize the process of location.

Real estate location and mapping software further expands the possibilities of the selection process by eliminating the need to identify a particular site in the first place. Using "prospecting" software,

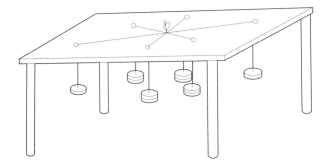

Location tables were analog tools for modeling optimal sites. Drawing by the author based on diagram in Peter R. Attwood, *Logistics of a Distribution System* (Aldershot, England: Gower, 1992).

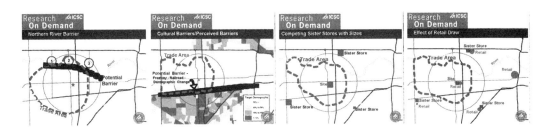

Tutorial from the International Council of Shopping Centers indicates the steps to establish a trade area. Screen shots of "Creating Retail Trade Areas," David Daleiden of Weingarten Realty Investors/ICSC, part of ICSC "Research on Demand" series.

companies can choose target markets (e.g., households with two children and earning $50,000–$70,000 annually) and generate maps of locations in given territories ranked according to the criteria. Rather than finding available sites first and then assessing those sites' appropriateness, these applications find territories to reflect the presence of certain types of consumers and the priorities of the retail market. As the name suggests, prospecting software presents the city as a resource to be mined and promises to reveal the best places to start digging.

Walmart chooses sites according to performance criteria and forecasts about future consumer behavior. Performance in this case is measured mostly in terms of profitability, but also considered are customer traffic and month-to-month same-store improvement. However, as it maintains a constant overview of its operations, Walmart always assesses the performance of an individual store relative to those in the larger network. New store locations are thus part of a dynamic system intent on encumbering territory and saturating a given market with the least amount of investment possible—an effort to do the most with the least. The single location is less important than the aggregated system of sites. In focusing on questions of performance, Walmart demonstrates its concern with a set of criteria based on tax rates, gasoline prices, real estate catchment areas, and so on. In other words, it focuses on a logistical-economic field of requirements and sometimes ignores certain political distinctions or engages them only when necessary. For instance, state boundaries and municipal divisions are considered significant only when they might disrupt the company's standard procedures or impact costs. This has implications for architecture. As Walmart deploys buildings as part of its specific territorial agenda, the structures themselves become implicated in this process of territorial control. With its focus on certain aspects over others, Walmart can supersede political boundaries by carefully crafting its own parameters of market coverage. Walmart acts at a coordinated regional level, which makes it difficult for individual states and cities to reckon with the company. However, while the stories about automated location assessment and digitally optimized store rollouts suggest tidy and untroubled expansion, the encounters of Walmart's general system with the specifics of actual places reveal a far messier process.

Buildings are deployed to mediate between the calculative and measured aspects of territory and the physical properties of site and land. The remainder of this chapter looks at two examples of Walmart's semiautomated location process as it has run up against conditions that have frustrated the company's imagined smooth operations.

Walmart Makes Its Own Borders

Vermont was the last state in the United States to have a Walmart store built within its borders. Driven by the conviction that the Bentonville-based retailer's presence in the state would increase traffic, threaten local businesses, and produce sprawl conditions, local opponents waged a tenacious policy and media campaign that kept the company at bay for several years. News media seized on this struggle between the small state and the large corporation, using bellicose headlines like "Battle of Vermont: Wal-Mart Plots Its Assault on Last Unconquered State," "Wal-Mart Lost Battles, Won the War: Vermont Store Opens," and "Waging War on Wal-Mart."[52] Beyond journalistic histrionics, both sides of the conflict employed unconventional tactics in pursuit of their aims, and each adopted an aggressive and oppositional stance toward the other. In spite of resilient opposition, Walmart continued its high-profile policy-based efforts to establish a store in Vermont. Simultaneously, the company proceeded systematically to build a physical line of stores just outside the state's border. This "blockade" of retail outlets proved more potent than policy negotiations because Walmart effectively saturated the market without ever entering it.

Walmart got its start serving a dispersed clientele in rural areas and tended to find locations on the edges of, or outside, cities. This land was often cheaper and less regulated than land closer to city centers, but it also reflected the distributed and rural nature of Walmart's target consumers. And although regulation was less of an issue in the retailer's early days, as it grew, the company benefited from sites outside cities because in those areas it could acquire land and buildings more quickly and easily. Walton writes, "We never planned on actually going into the cities. What we did instead was build our stores in a ring around a city."[53] Walmart's consistent pursuit of these strategies is confirmed by a study that found that 49 percent of Walmart locations are within five hundred meters of a city boundary, and only 18 percent of stores are within one hundred meters of a city boundary.[54] While Walmart has no official policy, the precision of its location strategies suggests a deliberate effort to remain outside municipal boundaries and in areas of "weak citizenship," where its entry is less likely to be contested.[55] This approach is combined with a sophisticated set of location tools that help the retailer identify its target markets and assess potential locations in terms of audience, proximity to logistics networks, likelihood of resistance, and, of course, cost.

In Vermont, faced with Walmart's imminent arrival, concerned citizens and various government agencies mobilized their resources to prevent the company's entry into the state. They adopted most of the usual approaches, including petitions, demonstrations, and strict enforcement of design guidelines. The Vermont opposition also pursued more inventive measures. For example, in an effort to raise awareness of the situation, the National Trust for Historic Preservation included the entire state in its annual list of "Eleven Most Endangered Places" in both 1993 and 2004.[56] Although it has no immediate policy impact, inclusion on the list holds significant sway over public opinion.

While Walmart cooperated with the demands of various Vermont municipalities, the retailer proceeded to surround the state with outlets in an attempt to lure the members of its inaccessible target market across the border into New York, Massachusetts, or sales tax–free New Hampshire. One reporter even suggested that Walmart was building a "Maginot Line of four open or soon-to-open stores along the state's border."[57] If Walmart could not enter Vermont, it would distribute its locations as close to the border as possible to ensure saturated coverage. There are now seven Walmart locations within five miles of the Vermont border (two are less than two thousand feet away) and another six in a slightly larger ring around the state.[58] Taking a standard twenty-mile radius as an index of coverage, the Vermont border is effectively sealed by Walmart stores (Plate 10). If the opposition's campaign against Walmart was predicated on defending local qualities and difference, then Walmart's spatial tactics were a

PLATE 1

This illustration from *Army Logistician* represents
enclosure and inventory in the same manner. Source:
Charles B. Einstein, "Modeling the Wholesale Logistics
Base," *Army Logistician* 15, no. 6 (November/December
1983): 17.

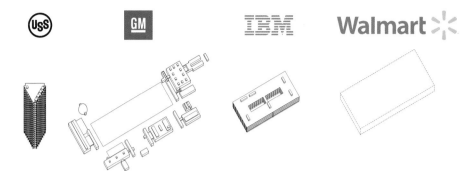

PLATE 2

Corporate logos and headquarters of U.S. Steel, General
Motors, IBM, and Walmart. Illustration by the author.

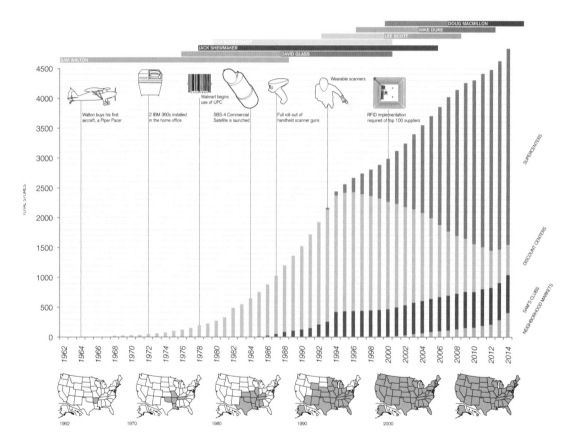

PLATE 3

Walmart store quantities and types since the company's
founding in 1962, with annotations concerning location,
technology, and leadership. Illustration by the author.

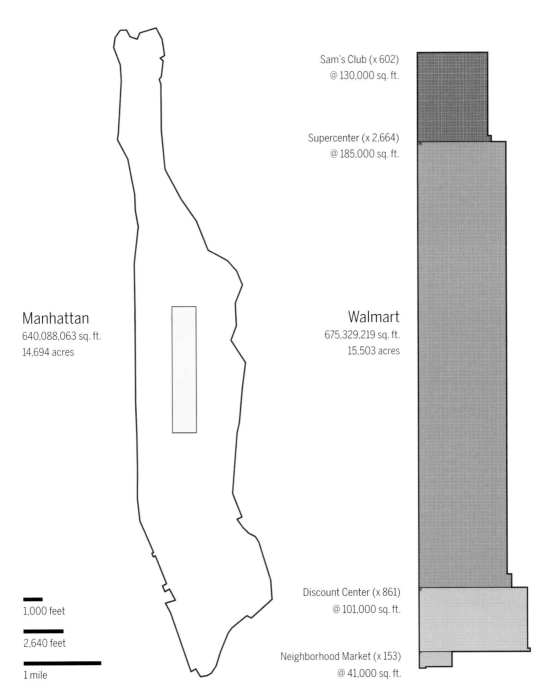

Sam's Club (x 602)
@ 130,000 sq. ft.

Supercenter (x 2,664)
@ 185,000 sq. ft.

Manhattan
640,088,063 sq. ft.
14,694 acres

Walmart
675,329,219 sq. ft.
15,503 acres

1,000 feet

2,640 feet

1 mile

Discount Center (x 861)
@ 101,000 sq. ft.

Neighborhood Market (x 153)
@ 41,000 sq. ft.

PLATE 4
A comparison between the area of Manhattan and the
area of all U.S. Walmart locations (excluding parking).
Illustration by the author.

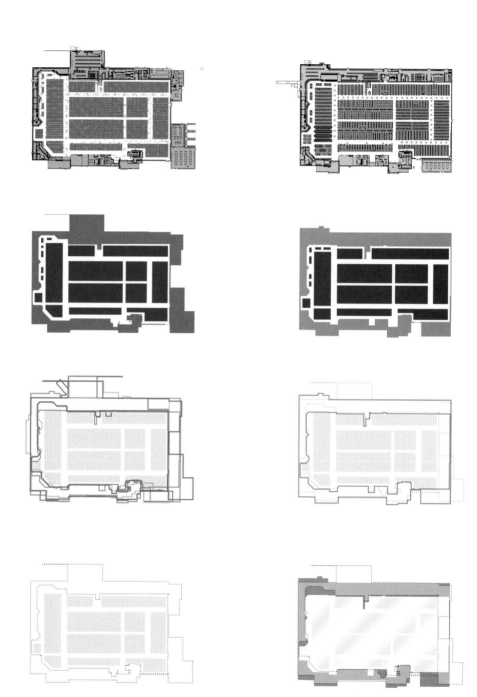

PLATE 5

Comparative diagram of Walmart's Prototype 150 with three instances. FROM LEFT TO RIGHT: Prototype 150; Walmart 2185, Selinsgrove, Pennsylvania; Walmart 1820, Kittanning, Pennsylvania; Walmart 2953, Swansea, Massachusetts. Illustration by the author.

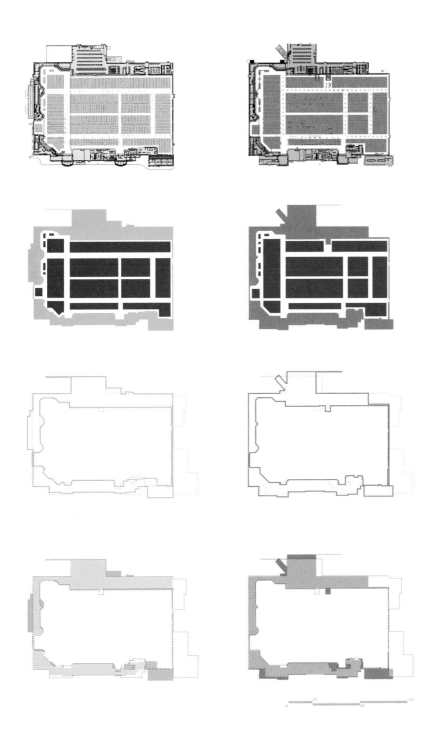

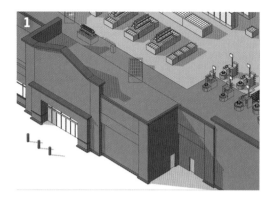

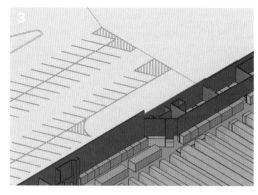

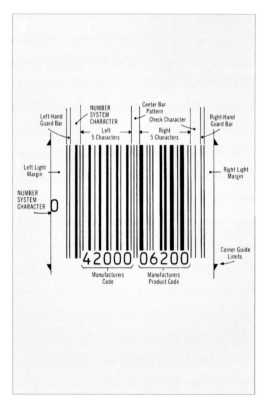

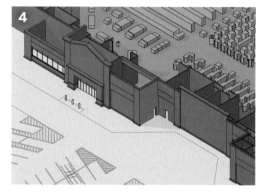

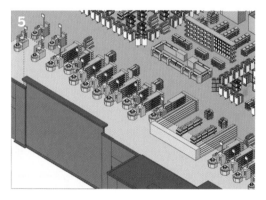

In the barcode diagram:

NUMBER SYSTEM CHARACTER

Left-Hand Guard Bar

Center Bar Pattern

Check Character

Right-Hand Guard Bar

Left 5 Characters

Right 5 Characters

Left Light Margin

Right Light Margin

NUMBER SYSTEM CHARACTER 0

Corner Guide Limits

42000 06200

Manufacturers Code

Manufacturers Product Code

PLATE 6
Supercenter: Content but No Form

Composite drawing of Walmart supercenter prototype. Illustration by the author based on Walmart construction documents and site visits.

1. The space between the entrance and the cash registers is part of the malleable "crust" that Walmart uses to adapt its collection of prototypes to specific contexts.

2. The bar code and its attendant information-processing apparatus are essential to Walmart's operation.

3. The interior facade of the building's mantle is a site of interface and comprises primarily display cases and refrigerated merchandise, accessible from the front and loaded from inside.

4. The exterior design of Walmart is often the target of criticism from local communities. Prototypes allow for flexible modification during the design phase.

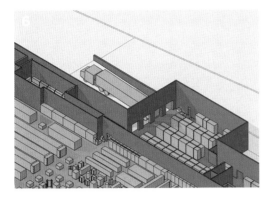

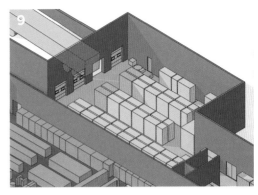

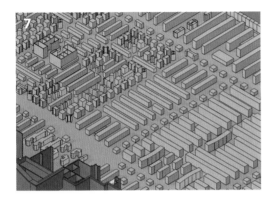

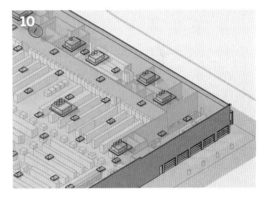

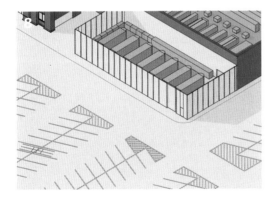

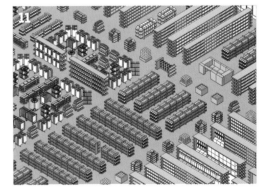

5. Walmart's point of sale consoles are the sites where data are collected and transmitted to the data center for analysis and to the local distribution center if new merchandise is required. Walmart holds patents on various cashier technologies (USPTO US6491218 B2).

6. Because the retailer can calibrate its replenishment process, on-site merchandise storage is reduced to a minimum and the supercenter acts more as a staging area for goods being unloaded from trailers.

7. The merchandise floor of each prototype is carefully scripted to ensure that inventory is moving steadily. The open aisles separating the zones are for promotional merchandise, historically displayed while still on shipping pallets. Walton called this zone "Action Alley."

8. The garden center occupies a semi-enclosed zone between parking lot and buildings.

9. Walmart's fleet of tractors and trailers forms the link between supercenter and distribution center as they shuttle between the two, often several times a day.

10. The roof is a crucial interface in Walmart's infrastructural system. As it has no symbolic obligation, its expression reflects the building's requirements below. It also supports communications technologies that allow each store to communicate with the company in general.

11. Requirements for optimized merchandise layout are the priorities for the design of Walmart supercenters.

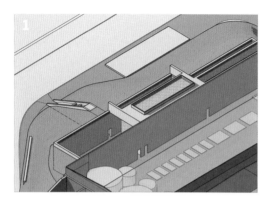

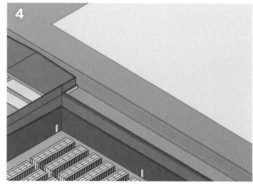

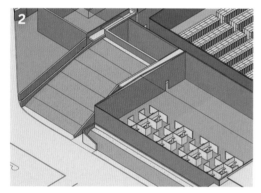

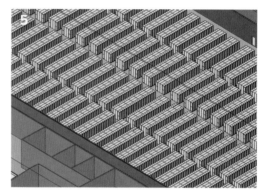

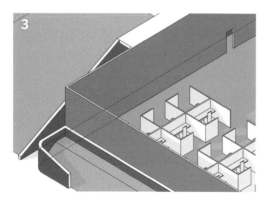

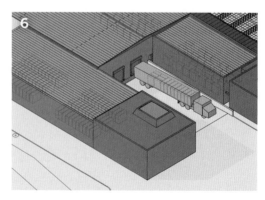

PLATE 7
Data Center: Form but No Content

Composite drawing of Walmart data center. Illustration by the author extrapolated from aerial photographs, site visits, and descriptions of data centers in Luiz Barroso and Urs Hölzle, *The Datacenter as a Computer: An Introduction to the Design of Warehouse-Scale Machines* (San Rafael, Calif.: Morgan & Claypool, 2009).

1. Large exhaust and intake vents are obscured by the earthen berm that surrounds the data center.

2. Data center employees enter from the rear of the building, not visible from the road.

3. The data center is more like a very large computer than a building designed for use and inhabitation. Consequently, much of the footprint is dedicated to data storage with limited office space.

4. The retaining wall for the earthen berm defines a large volume, into which additional buildings are nested.

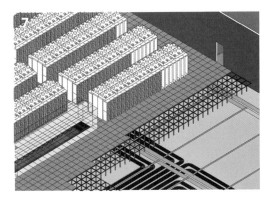

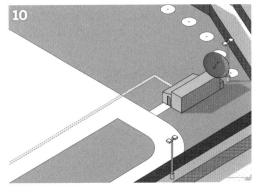

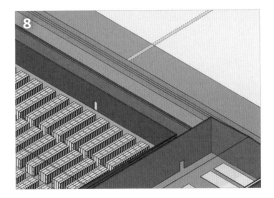

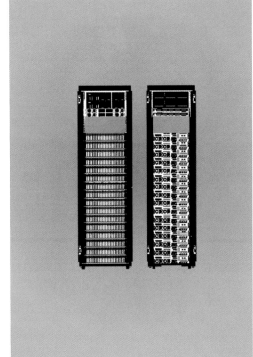

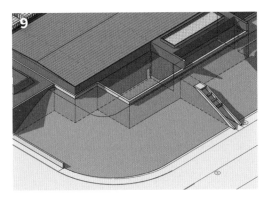

5. In a typical data center, the array of servers is constantly updated as new technologies become available.

6. The loading dock, as with Walmart's supercenters, is hidden from view.

7. A plenum floor system allows flexible configurations of racks, cables, and environmental conditioning.

8. The berm and retaining walls define a clear perimeter for the data center while the interior contents are typically more flexible.

9. The building's low profile and small obscured openings suggest an architectural language related to bunkers or to infrastructure.

10. The large satellite dish connects Walmart's data center to its private communications network.

11. Server rack detail.

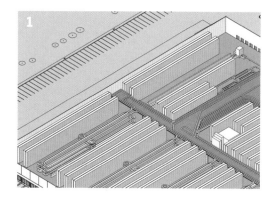

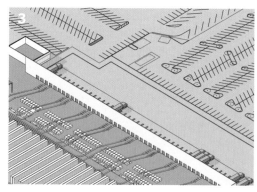

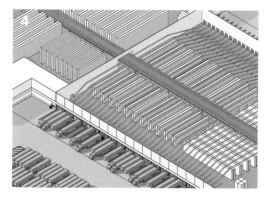

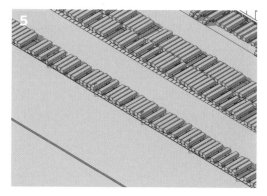

PLATE 8
Distribution Center: The Content Is the Form

Composite drawing of typical distribution center. Illustration by the author based on drawings and diagrams from Dematic.com, site visits, and Jolyon Drury and Peter Falconer, *Building and Planning for Industrial Storage and Distribution,* 2nd ed. (London: Architectural Press, 2003).

1. Workers assemble orders through automated and semiautomated picking modules.

2. Distribution center workers, augmented by a range of technologies, navigate the DC floor.

3. In a process called cross-docking, suppliers can unload their merchandise to be directly loaded on another truck ready to depart for a Walmart location.

4. Automated conveyor systems transport the assembled orders from the receiving area to the loading area.

5. Walmart has its own fleet of trucks and trailers, which allows it more control over the distribution process and more opportunity to reduce costs.

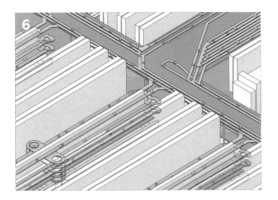

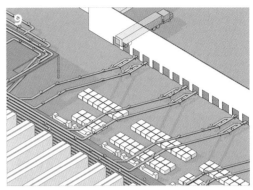

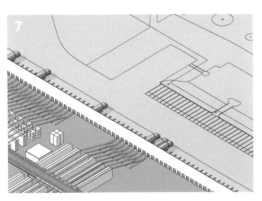

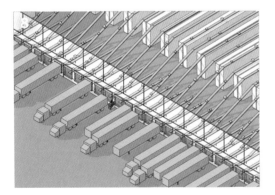

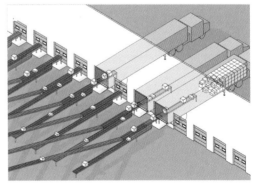

6. Distribution centers are emptied and filled every twenty-four hours. Because this process is piecemeal and continuous, the interior appears to always be the same.

7. Walmart assigns each loading bay to a single store location.

8. Automated rollers transmit merchandise to DC workers who load it and stack it in the trailers.

9. Objects are treated as information, and their bar codes automatically direct them to the correct waiting trailer.

10. Scanners read the bar code information on each parcel as it passes through a series of gates. When the right chute appears, small rubber shoes redirect it.

11. The bay doors connect the interior of the DC to the interiors of the trailers to the interiors of the supercenters.

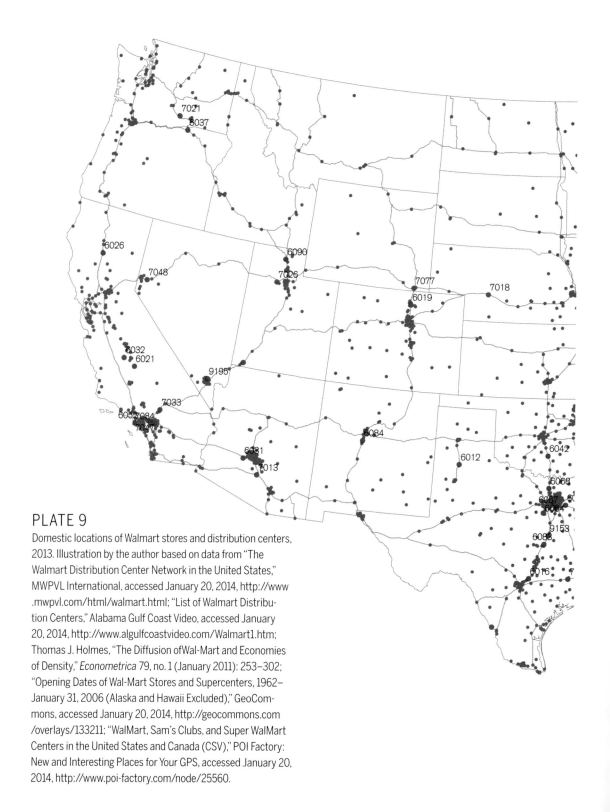

PLATE 9

Domestic locations of Walmart stores and distribution centers, 2013. Illustration by the author based on data from "The Walmart Distribution Center Network in the United States," MWPVL International, accessed January 20, 2014, http://www .mwpvl.com/html/walmart.html; "List of Walmart Distribu-tion Centers," Alabama Gulf Coast Video, accessed January 20, 2014, http://www.algulfcoastvideo.com/Walmart1.htm; Thomas J. Holmes, "The Diffusion of Wal-Mart and Economies of Density," *Econometrica* 79, no. 1 (January 2011): 253–302; "Opening Dates of Wal-Mart Stores and Supercenters, 1962–January 31, 2006 (Alaska and Hawaii Excluded)," GeoCom-mons, accessed January 20, 2014, http://geocommons.com /overlays/133211; "WalMart, Sam's Clubs, and Super WalMart Centers in the United States and Canada (CSV)," POI Factory: New and Interesting Places for Your GPS, accessed January 20, 2014, http://www.poi-factory.com/node/25560.

1. The state of Vermont.

2. Walmart locations within twenty miles of the Vermont border.

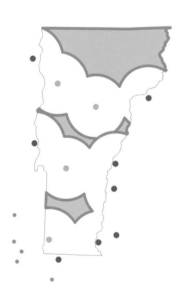

5. Vermont Walmart store locations and catchment radii.

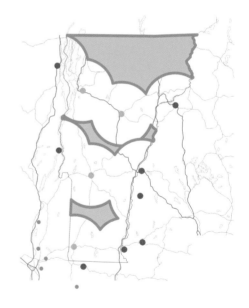

6. Walmart locations in Vermont and its vicinity, including highway systems and waterways.

PLATE 10

Walmart locations in and around Vermont, 2011.
Illustration by the author based on information from
Walmartstores.com and Google Maps.

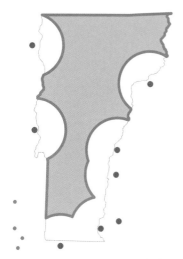

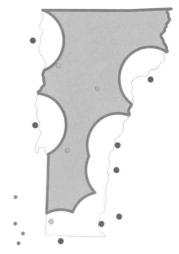

3. Walmart locations at the Vermont border with indication of twenty-mile catchment radii.

4. Locations of Walmart stores in Vermont.

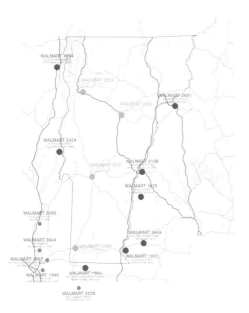

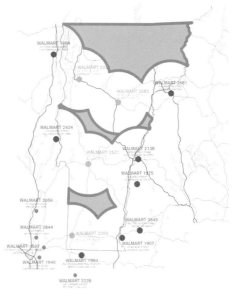

7. Walmart locations in Vermont and its vicinity, with store numbers, as assigned in the sequence of construction.

8. Walmart's territorial saturation in and around Vermont.

Our Data Center Tracks
Over 680 Million SKU's Weekly.*

Vested Interest:
Delivering More
Kellogg's® Pop-Tart®
Toaster Pastries
To Pensacola.

*© 2005 Kellogg NA Co.

Thanks to over 75,000 associates in Logistics and in our Information Systems Division, Wal-Mart has "the firepower" behind our retailing strategy that strives to have what the customer wants, when the customer wants it. With the Data Warehouse storage capacity of over 570 terabytes – larger than all of the fixed pages on the Internet** – we have a remarkable level of real-time visibility into our merchandise planning. So much so that when Hurricane Ivan was heading toward the Florida panhandle, we knew that there would be a rise in demand for Kellogg's® Strawberry Pop-Tart® toaster pastries. Thanks to our associates in the distribution centers and our drivers on the road, merchandise arrived quickly.

*Item/store combinations tracked worldwide
**"How Much Information" – 2003

PLATE 11

The background of this photograph offers a rare glimpse into Walmart's data and communication center. In the foreground is an example of the consumer items that propel the retailer's massive logistical system. Source: *Wal-Mart 2005 Annual Report*, 9.

From left to right, Mayor Jeff Wennberg of Rutland, Vermont, and Walmart associates Chet Landon, Gail Scribner, and Brenda Heath pose for the 1997 annual report and "proudly show off a revitalized downtown." Source: *Wal-Mart 1997 Annual Report*, 9.

Walmart stores in and around Vermont. TOP ROW, LEFT TO RIGHT: Albany, New York; Schenectady, New York; Saratoga Springs, New York; Ticonderoga, New York; Plattsburgh, New York. MIDDLE ROW, LEFT TO RIGHT: Williston, Vermont; Berlin, Vermont; Littleton, New Hampshire; Rutland, Vermont; Lebanon, New Hampshire. BOTTOM ROW, LEFT TO RIGHT: Claremont, New Hampshire; Keene, New Hampshire; Hinsdale, New Hampshire; Bennington, Vermont; North Adams, Massachusetts. Photographs by the author.

significant threat. By encircling the state with precisely targeted retail locations, Walmart effectively acquired the market territory it was pursuing without ever entering Vermont. The state border that served as a political boundary was trumped by the "catchment areas" of the store locations, and their strategic constellation effectively inscribed a new kind of elastic border within and around Vermont. Faced with the increasing out-migration of its retail tax base, in 1997 Vermont finally approved Walmart's entry into the state.[59]

Walmart subsequently built four stores in Vermont, in Williston, Berlin, Rutland, and Bennington. All are variations on typical Walmart formats, in part owing to the pressure then-governor Howard Dean applied on behalf of his constituents. After flying to Bentonville to meet with Walmart CEO David Glass, Dean said, "We had a good meeting. I don't think they'd had many governors come to meet with them. I wanted them to understand that we're not against Walmart but that we're just against suburban sprawl . . . [and] they agreed to consider downtown locations in the future."[60] All four of the Vermont stores are located in towns at crossings of significant state roads or interstates, which avail them as much consumer traffic as possible. In Rutland, Walmart seems to have taken Dean's request seriously. As part of a city revitalization project, the store opened at one end of a shopping center in the center of the town. The company's 1997 annual report promoted the Rutland location as evidence of Walmart's interest in maintaining healthy and vital small towns. The company's record might suggest that its interests are elsewhere, but this particular arrangement is an exception to its standard model of growth.

In most cases, the particularities of the actual architecture are secondary to their collective presence. To produce its buildings, as discussed in chapter 2, Walmart relies on a collection of store models called "prototypes" that combine specificity of plan and looseness of form. These prototypes reflect the tight scripting of the retailer's logistics operations while allowing for modifications required by local conditions. Some of the buildings in and around Vermont are based on the same prototype, but minor variations in their instantiation produce the appearance of difference. While Walmart maintains a coordinated and global view of its network, it does not broadcast it through

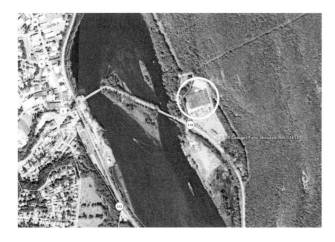

The Walmart in Hinsdale, New Hampshire, is immediately adjacent to the Vermont border. Source: Google Earth, with annotation by the author.

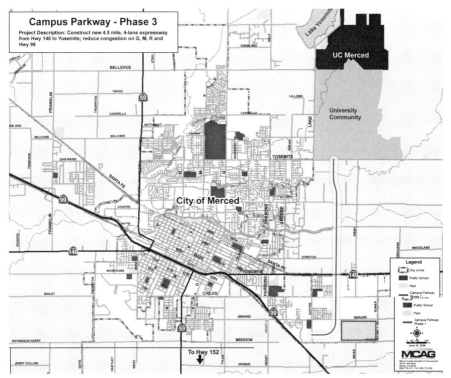

Campus Parkway - Phase 3
Project Description: Construct new 4.5 mile, 4-lane expressway from Hwy 140 to Yosemite; reduce congestion on G, M, R and Hwy 99

City of Merced plan, including new parkway to connect Highway 99 with the University of California, Merced, campus. The proposed Walmart distribution center site is indicated in the lower right. Public document courtesy of the City of Merced, California.

its architecture. In Hinsdale, New Hampshire, for example, a Walmart supercenter (not permitted in Vermont) is located almost immediately over the Vermont border—any closer and it would fall in the Connecticut River that separates the two states. The store is situated to play down its proximity to the border: dense riparian forest obscures views of the river/border, and the building is oriented so that shoppers see only the surrounding tall hills. The single retail unit, when understood collectively, becomes a territorial instrument capable of securing space within an established logic of market control. Architecture is no longer just a system of isolated buildings but instead is an interlinked network, the parts of which are united in a common purpose. Rather than developing the symbolic content of its buildings, Walmart emphasizes their symbolic presence.

Walmart Locations Anticipate Infrastructure

If Walmart's entry into Vermont demonstrates the geopolitical possibilities of its buildings, its process of developing a distribution center in Merced, California, illuminates larger regional and infrastructural implications. If one examines a map showing Walmart's distribution centers and the U.S. Interstate Highway System, the continuity of Walmart's operation is apparent (Plate 9). The distribution centers and their hundred-mile radii act as relays from one coverage area to the next.[61] A closer look at this system reveals a significant gap in California's Central Valley. This is the core agricultural region of the state and a site of significant population growth. To mend this gap in its distribution coverage—and in anticipation of future growth—Walmart gained approval for the construction of a new distribution center in Merced, a town of 90,000 and host to the newest campus in the University of California system.

As with its efforts to enter Vermont, Walmart encountered substantial resistance by local residents when it sought approval to build a new distribution center in Merced. The most vocal residents lived in the area immediately west of the proposed building site, which was almost literally in their backyards. Their arguments were similar to those made by the local opposition in other Walmart battlegrounds: they

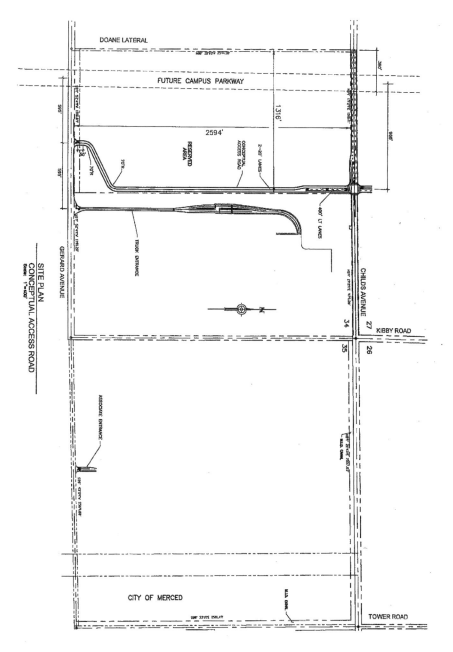

Site plan for proposed Walmart distribution center, Merced, California, indicating infrastructural connections, including associate (employee) entrance, truck entrance, and "conceptual access road." Public document courtesy of the City of Merced, California.

were concerned about potential traffic increases, noise, pollution, and safety. Walmart countered with data regarding job creation, environmental remediation, and landscape improvements that would mitigate the new building's impact. The particular regional character of both the proposed distribution center and its proponents' arguments was significant. In September 2009, the Merced City Council approved Walmart's proposal, but it was quickly met with a lawsuit by the citizens' group Merced Alliance for Responsible Growth (MARG), which alleged that the city's approval process for Walmart's proposal violated the California Environmental Quality Act.[62] After a number of challenges and appeals, MARG's appeal to the California Supreme Court was declined. This allowed the project to go forward, but Walmart decided to delay construction of Regional Distribution Center 7073 until after 2015.[63] In 2010, John Ramirez, a lawyer working on behalf of the city, argued, "This project is critically important for the city of Merced. . . . The economic recession has devastated the city, and the city has specifically targeted this piece of property for job creation and industrial use."[64]

In spite of Walmart's tendency to reduce sites to abstract performance criteria, the process of committing to particular sites remains difficult. The company prefers to commit as quickly as possible, but as site selection remains focused on each location's potential performance within the company's larger operations, Walmart must continue to assess the cost associated with a protracted dispute over a proposed site. If, at a certain point, local opposition become too costly for the retailer, it can simply back off and try to establish a location elsewhere. A judge in the Merced case acknowledged this: "This matter has been pending since '06. It's been four years. . . . Wal-Mart may pack it up and go down to Madera. They *want* Wal-Mart down there."[65] In the end, this outcome is exactly what Walmart's opponents are hoping for. By hamstringing the company with bureaucratic inconveniences, MARG and other opponents hope to make it too costly for Walmart to stay in town. Walmart had to weigh the expense of fighting the opposition in Merced against the company's desire to establish a regional distribution center there, as the absence of a DC in that part of the country was hampering Walmart's growth and indirectly costing the company money through an overall drag on operational efficiency.

Since Walmart maintains a regional view of its operations, one location is often interchangeable with another. Even though its plans to build new stores are often thwarted, other options fulfill the same performance criteria.[66] One document is particularly revealing about how Walmart operates at the territorial level. In a presentation to the Merced City Council on September 21, 2009, the distribution center project team included a map of Walmart distribution centers in the western United States. While the standard state and municipal borderlines are shown on the map, they are overwritten by heavy contours that delineate the boundaries of Walmart's respective distribution zones. Areas in Northern California and parts of Oregon and Nevada are too large to be serviced by a single distribution center (DC 6026 in this case). In order to determine the locations of new DCs, Walmart indexes demographic data and real estate availability with its own growth plans and existing facilities. The small number of DCs in the western states corresponds to fewer Walmart stores and uneven population distribution. Thus DC 6037 serves a relatively small number of Walmart stores in the Pacific Northwest compared to the larger number in Central California served by DC 6021. Federal divisions are less relevant to Walmart than the performance of its system. Walmart has a decidedly regional approach to planning that overrides the historic state boundaries in favor of a dynamic system of territorial shapes. These boundaries are elastic and can be modulated quickly with the introduction of new stores. It follows, then, that the construction of the DC in Merced will establish its own new regional jurisdiction and a new shape on Walmart's distribution map. This map's fixed image, however, obscures its actual fluidity. If DC 7073 is completed as planned, another zone will need to be added to the map—and this likely will not be the last regional distribution facility for Walmart or the last revision of the map.

Given Walmart's location habits, it is no surprise that Merced neatly straddles the distribution zones covered by DC 6026 and DC 6021. The actual location of the proposed distribution center is in an agro-industrial area on the southeastern edge of town. The 230-acre site will contain the distribution facility (1.2 million square feet) as well as parking and maintenance areas. The DC will be in constant operation, employing roughly 1,200 people. The site is close to the

Mission Avenue interchange of State Highway 99 and the smaller State Route 140 and is immediately adjacent to a new expressway spur referred to as the Campus Parkway, which will connect Highway 99 with the recently opened campus for the University of California, Merced.[67] This proximity reinforces how carefully Walmart selects its sites. The site drawing's speculative language is also illuminating. For example, the project site plan labels the right-of-way "Future Campus Parkway," and another site drawing refers to a "Conceptual Access Road." This future tense suggests Walmart's comfort in trading in speculation as it works to remake the city at the infrastructural level.[68]

Logistical Territory Is Fungible

Walmart's approach to its retail locations involves a collective and nimble view of operations. Similarly, "sites" for Walmart are equally interchangeable and amount to another set of numbers, another node in the abstract data field over which the company's real estate analysts pore and through which its data-cum-merchandise are directed. In taking this approach, the company produces a kind of space that conforms to its requirements. By projecting a version of the world based on performance criteria onto a given area, Walmart privileges certain characteristics over others but also helps to bring them about. In this regard, the notions of reproducibility, indifference, and equivalence can be extended through the adoption of a term familiar to economics: fungibility. More than simply describing an interchangeable set of things, fungibility implies a certain relationship to the particular instance and generic conditions. A classic definition states:

> Where a thing which is the subject of an obligation . . . must be delivered *in specie*, the thing is not fungible: i.e. that very individual thing, and not another thing of the same or another class, in lieu of it, must be delivered. Where the subject of the obligation is *a* thing of a given class, the thing is said to be fungible: i.e. the delivery of any object which answers to the generic description will satisfy the terms of the obligation.[69]

While the concept of fungibility is most commonly applied to commodities, it can be applied to territory in the case of Walmart's real estate practices. The company understands sites in terms of performance

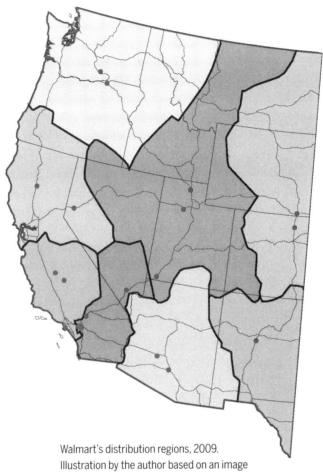

Walmart's distribution regions, 2009.
Illustration by the author based on an image
in a digital presentation by the Walmart distribution center project team to the City
of Merced, California, September 21, 2009.

characteristics, for each location functions as "a thing of a given class" and as an object that "answers to the generic description" in spite of its otherwise specific qualities. In other words, while both sets of conditions are embodied in any given site, Walmart's expansion protocols foreground the fungible aspects of real estate.

In 2002, for instance, Walmart's plan to construct a supercenter in Inglewood, California, was consistently frustrated. With the strong support of labor unions, which opposed Walmart's hiring practices, the Inglewood City Council instituted an emergency ordinance that prevented construction of retail spaces of more than 155,000 square feet. Walmart quickly gathered enough signatures from area residents to force a public vote and threatened to sue the city. The city repealed the ordinance but continued to resist the company's advances. In 2004 the retailer successfully lobbied for a ballot measure that would allow construction to proceed without public hearings or environmental impact reports. The measure's resounding defeat—by a 20 percent margin—was a major victory for the diverse, pro-labor community. Yet Walmart appeared unfazed; as spokesperson Bob McAdam asserted: "If we win, that's all it means. If we lose, it will have no implications beyond that. We're still going to meet our goal of building the stores we predicted we'd build."[70] Walmart gave up on Inglewood, but McAdam's statement is a reminder that the numbers-driven, logistics-focused company understands territory in terms of performance and not of place; for Walmart, individual sites—singular and unique to locals— are more or less interchangeable. The retailer's hybrid approach to its constructed environments, its deployment of buildings as fungible components of distribution networks, dissolves certain well-worn distinctions and results in buildings and landscapes that operate in both architectural and infrastructural registers. Even if Walmart's real estate planners see the United States as a field of data, this outlook has spatial implications. The process of choosing sites has relatively little to do with notions of social considerations or public space; rather, like the rest of Walmart's operations, it is concerned with efficiency and optimization. While municipal governments, for the most part, have yet to manage significant regional coordination of resources, Walmart acts as a regional planner and governor of its own territory.

In the examples included here, Walmart planners exceed static political designations with additional and contingent notions of division and organization. This approach cultivates modes of corporate geographical perception that respond to performance criteria rather than political boundaries. While the citizens in Walmart catchment areas are united by demographic consistency or shopping habits, it is possible to consider how regional affiliations could be more effective than state associations in involving them in political processes. As these regional definitions are understood to have flexible, elastic borders, they also suggest the capacity for multiple affiliations and increased opportunities for active participation, even simply at the level of public presence. Moreover, Walmart's geographical architecture amounts to more than just the deployment of consistently branded buildings because its size and influence actually have the substantial capacity to transform cities directly.

Weaving together military technology with consumer marketing trends, Walmart has developed a highly rationalized process of selecting store locations that focuses on performance and market coverage. This trafficking in territory, this management and deployment of land area, is a reminder that logistics is not only about optimizing supply chains, but it also informs Walmart's entire mode of thinking. Just as people, goods, and information are moved through space, so are the places themselves. The decoupling of place from space is destabilizing but also potentially invigorating because it challenges assumptions about some of the values under which such designations have operated. For example, Marc Augé's identification of the "non-place," while a negating definition, is not negative from a qualitative point of view. Rather, Augé attempts to establish the features and logics of emerging conditions of what he calls "supermodernity."[71] In Elden's efforts to distinguish between place and space, he observes that "two different things in size and shape can occupy the same *place*, but clearly not the same *space*. And when something moves, it is its place that has changed, not its size or shape."[72] His claim that "space, not place, claims for exclusivity" can be extended and complicated as one imagines the replication of Walmart store locations. As the retailer continues to anticipate new locations, multiply its real estate holdings, and deliver new buildings, the process of real estate production becomes logistical in its own right. In his contribution to a publication for the Urban Land Institute titled *Just-in-Time Real Estate* Luis Belmonte treats real estate as handled not by brokers or agents but by providers he further identifies as supply chain "outsourcers" for global supply chain companies. He argues that when it comes to the design of buildings, "dollars are better spent on design that incorporates flexibility and enhances the flow of goods."[73] The title of the book suggests that real estate, more than providing support buildings for the world of on-demand production and consumption, is equally capable of being produced and deployed as needed, enrolled "just in time" into the logistical as it expands outward across urban territory.

4 BODIES

Coping with Data-Rich Environments

TROY: This is a Jennifer unit, m'kay? It's what tells us what to pick.

DAVE: So, she talks to me?

TROY: Yes, she does!

JENNIFER: 00 08 00

TROY: Did you hear her?

DAVE: I hear her, she talks fast!

TROY: Jennifer, slower.

JENNIFER: Slower.

TROY: Jennifer, slower.

JENNIFER: Slower.

TROY: Jennifer, slower.

DAVE: Oh . . . wow . . .

JENNIFER: This is slowest.

TROY: This is slowest.

THIS EXCHANGE, transcribed from the television series *Undercover Boss,* is part of an interaction between Troy, a distribution center employee of the retailer Oriental Trading Company, and Dave, the CEO of the company in disguise.[1] Dave is being trained to select inventory to fulfill online orders using the company's voice-directed picking system, Jennifer, designed by Lucas Systems. Jennifer is not a real person but a combination of software and hardware designed to translate digital input into comprehensible signals for the human ear and to translate voice input into a format useful for the computer. In spite of this, as is evident in the example, Jennifer's suggested humanity is quickly adopted by both speakers, who continue to refer to the system using feminine pronouns. This suggests a willingness to accept the premise of the interface but also to agree to cope with the overwhelming and incomprehensible amount of data that is part of the logistics environment.

This chapter takes a wider view of the distribution interior in order to survey the range of technologies deployed within the logistical environment and the ways these technologies condition workers in turn. The scope of the discussion is broadened here beyond Walmart's operations to explore the materials handling field more generally, especially as it applies to logistical systems' relationships with humans—how it interacts with and augments human workers and how it absorbs or excludes them. As logistics is required to manage data at both volumes and speeds that exceed any human capacity, companies must rely on digital and automated technology while still maintaining their human labor forces. The humans who operate within the space of the automated distribution center environment develop relationships at multiple scales: as individual bodies, they become, to varying degrees, absorbed by the installations, effectively becoming part of the architecture; as a collection of bodies, they demonstrate an inverse to the more commonly understood dynamic between humans and technology—that is, rather than the various technologies being mechanical augmentations of the bodies themselves, the collection of workers constitutes an organic extension of the computer systems that control the environment but lack the dexterity and cost-effectiveness to execute the commands. Finally, in cases where the distribution center floor has become almost completely automated, the human occupants, while marginalized, nonetheless bear witness to a dynamic environment that indexes our own desires. The focus of this chapter is what happens when humans find themselves inhabiting building-sized machines.

Rather than simply housing tools to employ and vehicles to operate, the fulfillment center environment demands a mode of inhabitation and engagement conditioned by logistics. If architecture, and the built environment more generally, mediates between the various scales of logistics and its tendencies toward abstraction while also becoming increasingly concretized, then how ought one make sense of the human inhabitants/components of such a system? Scholarship in labor, prosthetics, and technics provides some initial approaches. While I borrow from all three, these technologies are indicators of new categories and new spaces governed by the rule of logistics. Compared to, say, Frederick Winslow Taylor's scientifically managed shop floor, the metrics, organizational criteria, and operational goals of distribution centers, while similarly oriented toward efficiency, are monitored automatically and measured in terms not of units produced but of items "picked." The workers in these spaces are less concerned with "output" (the systematic transformation of raw material into a finished consumer product) than with "throughput" (the rate at which inventory is moved into and out of a distribution center), and the environments they inhabit possess an inscrutability that results from the machinery that keeps the systems running.[2] The effect of this is a vibrating interior condition in which merchandise is replenished as quickly as it disappears, producing a condition that is as full as it is empty but knowable only to the software that orchestrates the interactions and increasingly determines the paths of the workers as they navigate mile after mile of storage racks. If industrial developments of the early twentieth century brought with them their own "machine aesthetic" and an "architecture of the first machine age," and if logistics is linked to a third machine age, an age of globalization and neoliberal trade policies, then it follows that logistics might influence the ensuing architecture of its own period. However, as the "audience" for logistical production is largely the software that helps choreograph its circulation paths, the resulting effects, while signaling an emergent logistical aesthetic, cannot really be read in their original.

Logistics' distribution centers and fulfillment centers, although implicated in longer chains of resource extraction and transformation, are not explicitly concerned with production. Strictly in terms of the merchandise they process, distribution centers do not effect significant material change on the goods they circulate because the buildings serve only as switches and relays in much larger logistical networks. As a result, both the tasks of those working in them and the ways they might be understood are different from those associated with other forms of industrial enterprise. For example, Walmart distribution centers evoke the shop floors described and analyzed by

Frederick Winslow Taylor as he developed his system of scientific management. Through careful and repeated measurement of the time and action needed for each job, Taylor developed standards against which workers could be assessed.[3] With his method, one coherent system of oversight could enroll all the elements of production: the space, the tools, the tasks, and the workers. Indeed, as he saw little distinction between tool and worker, Taylor approached the problem of optimization by "applying similar methods to the machinists as he did to the boring lathe itself."[4] However, in comparison with the managers of early twentieth-century sites of mass production, the managers of distribution centers pursue different goals and, consequently, produce different kinds of attitudes toward their workers. One way to understand this distinction is through the broader philosophical shift in emphasis from the subject to the body, as it becomes entangled in organizational and managerial systems. In his foreword to Friedrich Kittler's *Discourse Networks 1800/1900*, David Wellbery writes: "One widespread reading of post-structuralism claims that it eliminates the concept of the subject. It would be more accurate to say that it replaces that concept with that of the body, a transformation which disperses (bodies are multiple), complexifies (bodies are layered systems), and historicizes (bodies are finite and contingent products) subjectivity rather than exchanging it for a simple absence."[5] In descriptions of the coordinated efforts of the distribution center corps, the predicament of the body remains central. This predicament is additionally complicated by various means of digital augmentation that serve to erode the body's borders further.

The distribution center, while subject to many of the same managerial principles as the factory, differs from the factory in the kind of labor it demands. While workers are no less scrutinized and disciplined in pursuit of efficiency, their tasks do not transform one material into another or assemble complex technological artifacts. Workers in a DC collect items to be shipped somewhere—to an awaiting supercenter in Walmart's case or directly to customers in the case of online sellers such as Amazon (which, like most e-retailers, refers to its distribution buildings as fulfillment centers). Humans act as relays between various systems of automated sorting and retrieval. The automation also

Analog "break-pack" picking at a Walmart distribution center. The DC worker checks the inventory against the order list in her left hand. Source: *Wal-Mart Annual Report 1985*, 9.

A "Put-to-Light" system by Dematic, a materials handling and logistics automation company. Workers are prompted by light cues as they assemble orders in plastic totes moving along conveyors. Courtesy of Dematic, Inc.

extends to the management of workers themselves. For example, in a profile of a new Amazon order fulfillment center in the United Kingdom, the *Financial Times* reports:

> Amazon's software calculates the most efficient walking route to collect all the items to fill a trolley, and then simply directs the worker from one shelf space to the next via instructions on the screen of the handheld satnav device. . . . "You're sort of like a robot, but in human form," said [one] Amazon manager. "It's human automation, if you like." Amazon recently bought a robot company, but says it still expects to keep plenty of humans around because they are so much better at coping with the vast array of differently shaped products the company sells.[6]

A technological threshold continues to make the dexterity of human workers more affordable than other options.[7] As John McPhee points out in his account of the UPS worldwide air hub in Louisville, Kentucky, "Automation alone will not do everything for 8 million packages a week."[8] However, he also identifies trends in distribution center technologies and requirements toward making workers' jobs simpler and easier: "Sortation used to require a more complex application of human thought, but in the development of the UPS air hub the intellectual role of the workers 'out in the sort' underwent a process of 'de-skilling'" to such a degree that the main task of many of the workers monitoring the stream of parcels is to simply make sure that they are "label-side up."[9] While similar, the assembling of orders in a distribution or fulfillment center requires workers to have a more sustained and active involvement with the technology that they handle, wear, or inhabit, always with bodily implications.[10]

Distribution Center Workers Occupy a Space between Objects and Information

Recording twenty million customer transactions a day, Walmart's private database is one of the largest in the world.[11] According to one estimate, the world's Internet users create 2,500 petabytes of data per day, with Walmart alone responsible for 2.4 percent of that volume.[12] The retailer maintains a vast store of information because efficient inventory management allows a large company with very thin margins to maintain profitability. While the goods in transit through these buildings must be physically moved and are inherently material, Walmart manages merchandise as if it is immaterial—as if it is only information.[13] Correspondingly, the distribution centers function like gigantic computers whose inhabitants straddle the concrete realm of things and the abstract realm of information. The specific information about the items for sale is important only insofar as the items can be strategically distributed to maximize that profit. In making decisions about where these products can best be used, Walmart analysts work with large databases to anticipate needs and market opportunities. This conflict between high-speed digital networks and relatively slow terrestrial networks creates the conditions under which Walmart distribution center employees must work.

The condition of these operators is suggested by one of the company's promotional images: that of an employee dressed as an oversized credit card. The costume includes black trousers and cartoonish yellow shoes and gloves (with only four digits), and beginning at the torso it takes the form of a large Walmart credit card. Part human cartoon and part plastic card, this hybrid embodies the predicament of the distribution center worker. In one sense, this walking credit card transforms the Walmart employee into a consistent and recognizable format that contains a wealth of information not immediately apparent to external viewers. Company credit cards help Walmart track and predict consumer behavior, not only what customers are buying but also at which branches they shop, how frequently they shop, how far they drive from their homes to reach a Walmart, and so on.[14] Each shopper with a credit card helps refine the company's purchasing and supplying behavior. Even if a shopper has no card, the purchases are still recorded and indexed with date and time information. These data can confirm merchandising decisions and can also identify surprising or latent patterns. For example, by indexing weather conditions and correlating them with customer purchasing habits, the company has discovered that shoppers in southern states buy large amounts of Pop-Tarts when hurricane warnings are issued.[15] As a result, the company places rush orders for large quantities of Pop-Tarts when a significant storm system is brewing (Plate 11).

The consequences of this tracking and forecasting method are manifest in the organization and behavior of Walmart's distribution network. The credit card mascot reflects the increasing resolution of the company's image and its inventory needs. It is also an honest, if blunt, depiction of how the company imagines many of its employees. Just as the card is a traceable producer of information, so is the worker in the distribution center. DC employees are checkpoints through which certain merchandise must pass and therefore are still vital to the overall functioning of the transmission network. However, they are data points as well: managed, hoarded, and deployed in the same way the company's consumer information is wielded. The various guises and augmentations of the distribution center worker help us to better understand how that worker fits in the larger organizational landscape of Walmart's logistics operations.

Logistical Environments Demand New Forms of Literacy

The form and position of a distributions center result from the direct translation of efficiency protocols into a three-dimensional space. The standardized materials handling equipment forms a kit of parts whose overall arrangements and constitution are customized to reflect the needs of a specific operation. This system is a combination of conveyors, rollers, shelves, struts, sensors, and actuators that process the company's merchandise. Trailers are pulled up to receiving docks and the merchandise they carry is unloaded into the DC, put onto conveyors that carry it to the picking module. Based on the inventory needs of different stores, as dictated by the Walmart home office, DC employees break down the new inventory into smaller cartons. These smaller units are then placed, either directly or in totes or boxes, on conveyors that take the merchandise to the receiving bay at the other end of the facility. This process is enabled by a host of technologies that help workers translate input that is otherwise developed for and by computers. The bar code is an early example—it performs such a translation but it also requires an attendant suite of scanning technologies to capture the code and translate it to legible output. As these technologies developed and were subjected to increasing demands for faster order processing, translation shifted from legible output to audible output, thus "freeing" the hands of the DC worker to operate more quickly.

The bar code symbol is a language written by machines for machines. The bar code is also the primary means of tracking merchandise from supplier to consumer within the logistical sequence. To keep shelves stocked with the right amount of inventory at the right time, Walmart connects checkout data with inventory levels, all via the bar code. In a process known as "replenishment," distribution center employees called "pickers" assemble orders based on lists generated by Walmart's inventory management software. Both workers and the computer system rely on the bar code as the means to navigate the distribution center and to communicate workers' positions and those of the particular inventory items they are selecting. So that they can translate the codes and, thus, access Walmart's large store of data, employees are equipped with wireless scanners. The scanners are primarily a means of communicating with Walmart's computer database and act as the "eyes" of the management offices in Bentonville. At first glance, such a portable scanner might be understood as a mechanical extension, or servomechanism, for an individual. However, because the function of the device is not directed to the worker but rather beyond the worker, the worker–scanner combination functions more as an extension of the central office in Arkansas and places the human in the servant role—mechanically autonomous but bound to the demands of the computer.

The bar code scanner remains a discrete tool separate from the body of the worker. Depictions of such scanners in various patent applications made by Symbol (and now its parent company, Motorola) reinforce the discrete nature of these tools. For example, in U.S. Patent 6,216,951, the scanner is shown at rest in its cradle. The operator can return the scanner, or "scan gun," as it is often called, to a position independent of the user. Rather than "holstering" it in a container on his or her body, the user places the scanner in a stationary charging receptacle connected to the warehouse computer system. This image reinforces the concept of the scanner as a technology beyond the human operator that can be selectively engaged and disengaged over the course of the working day. Walmart also uses larger scanning devices referred to in its 1997 annual report as "magic wands":

> That "magic wand" is actually a handheld computer, linked by a radio-frequency network to in-store terminals. It's a high-tech conduit to an internal information system that gives every associate a window on the world of Wal-Mart merchandise. . . .
>
> The computerized wands are amazing enough, "seeing through walls" to find what our customers want, when they want it.[16]

The architectural imagery in this description suggests the powers of visibility granted by the scanner as well as its ability to overcome the visual limits imposed by buildings.

The "wearable scanner" by Motorola further expands the human–tool relationship. This system "allows workers to move freely through inventory aisles and still be able to scan, access information and perform data entry," with the scanners part of them for the entirety of their shifts.[17] DC workers using wearable scanners still have control over all of their cognitive and motor abilities, and the interfaces strapped to their forearms and wrapped around their fingers give them access to one of the world's largest databases. More important, the interfaces also give the database access to the workers. They are feeling, lifting, and moving as usual but they are also "seeing" for the central servers. With their wearable scanners, DC employees can distinguish among the varieties of inventory otherwise obscured by the encrypted exteriors of shipping containers, pallets, and cardboard boxes.

U.S. Patent 5,898,161 describes an early version of Motorola's wearable scanner. A scanner is worn as a "ring" and connects to a console worn around the wrist that in turn connects to a battery pack at the waist. The operator points at the bar code to be scanned and depresses a button on the side of the ring on his or her index finger to register the information. A drawing in the patent renders a man from the waist up but distorts the body to illustrate the scanner system's various features, including arm computer, ring scanner, and battery pack. While the drawing's primary duty is not to depict the human body accurately, the strangeness of the distortion is worth dwelling on for a moment because it suggests the effects of this technology. For example, as the

An early handheld computer for inventory management. Walmart calls this the "magic wand." Source: *Wal-Mart 1997 Annual Report,* 12.

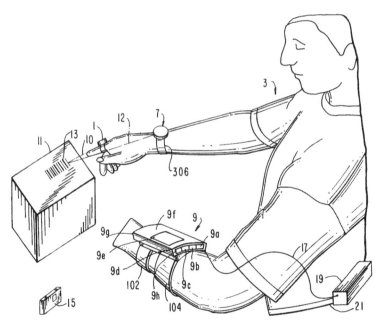

Patent diagram shows a distribution center employee using Symbol's (now part of Motorola) wearable computer to scan an item's bar code. Source: Symbol Technologies, "Wrist-mounted optical scanning and pointing system," U.S. Patent 5,898,161, 1999, 1.

depicted operator is at work scanning a bar code on a box, his eyes appear to be closed. In fact, some scanning technology, especially that related to voice-directed picking, claims to be "eyes-free." While the promise is that operators' eyes will be "free" so that they can perform other duties, such a phrase could be interpreted to mean that eyes become unnecessary through this specific kind of augmentation. In this case, the scanner on the operator's right index finger does the visual work. The patent drawing is striking for its decision not to show the man's left hand, which is perhaps omitted so that the rest of the box is visible. In any case, the apparent amputation of the left hand echoes the often-touted mobility attribute "hands-free."

A similar diagram, this one from U.S. Patent 5,514,861, describes the working space for such augmented and amputated operators. If the ability to maintain an overview of operator locations (by monitoring radio-frequency signals) is one of the benefits of wireless scanning technology, then the invisible ceiling grid in the patent diagram inscribes this advantage graphically. The locations of workers, the drawing suggests, can be tracked relative to a superimposed coordinate system. Like the inventory being handled and sorted in the distribution centers, the operators are marshaled and directed to "keep the merchandise flowing."[18] The patent illustration makes clear the integrated nature of the distribution center space. The workers, though apparently free to move about the space, are nonetheless incorporated into the larger information network and inventory control system. Furthermore, wearable scanners are necessary for the operators to navigate this information-rich/information-poor environment. The devices augment their vision as they become trained to understand otherwise illegible surfaces. Distribution center operators, with the help of their wearable scanners, can indeed "see through walls."

A picker in a distribution center typically carries a list of orders in one hand and a scanning gun in the other. To alleviate the awkwardness of this arrangement and to increase the number of orders each operator can process in a given time period, some companies in recent years have adopted "voice-directed" picking systems. In such a system, rather than carrying a list of items to pick, an operator wears a headset with earpiece and receiver through which he or she receives and confirms

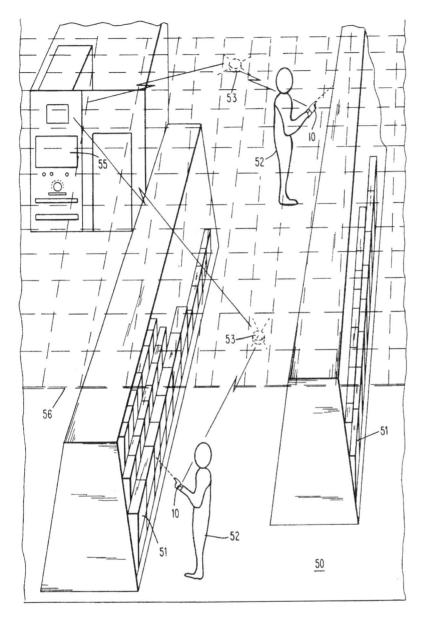

Symbol's patent drawing for an inventory control system capable of monitoring worker activities. Source: Symbol Technologies, "Computer and/or scanner system mounted on a glove," U.S. Patent 5,514,861, 1996, 4.

instructions. The headset is connected to a small computer holstered at the waist that is in turn connected to the larger DC network. After a setup process using voice recognition software, the operator communicates by voice with a computer program. A synthesized voice directs the worker to different locations in the distribution center, prompting him or her to pick certain quantities of particular items. The worker then vocally confirms the completion of each task. This approach is popular with managers, who cite improvements in both the numbers of orders processed and their handling accuracy. Voice-directed picking also allows operators to work both "hands-free" and "eyes-free," since they communicate primarily in an audible format.[19]

In promotional videos for Dematic, a materials handing company, voice-directed picking software is introduced and explained in a way that quickly humanizes its features. According to one video's narration: "The system is designed to tell you, step by step, exactly what needs to be picked for every order. You don't need a list, so your hands are free to pick the order. . . . Just like you recognize the voice of a good friend on the phone, the system learns your voice. It knows how you pronounce words."[20] However, in spite of these claims of familiarity, it is not another human delivering orders, but humanlike speech synthesized and delivered by a disembodied source. Voice-directed picking shifts authority away from DC supervisors and places it in the software system. This shift is rendered plainly in a promotional video in which the narrator refers to this inventory control software as "The Voice." For example: "The Voice will send you to a pick location. Once at the correct location, you can either say the check digit number, scan the location bar code, or scan the product ID. This verifies that you are at the correct picking location. The Voice will tell you how many units to pick."[21] With authority placed in the software, control is transferred from local floor managers to another unknown and remote site. In the case of Walmart, inventory data and models are stored and processed in the home office in Bentonville. This distance makes it increasingly difficult for operators to engage the system, because they have nobody to talk to.

Some companies are trying to humanize the synthesized verbal commands in voice-directed picking. The company Lucas Systems, Inc., in

A sequence of still images from a Dematic promotional video about voice-directed picking. Source: Dematic, Inc., "Voice-Directed Picking," promotional video.

partnership with Motorola, developed the Jennifer VoicePlus voice-directed picking system, whose dialogue opens this chapter. This system of software, voice synthesizers, receivers, and scanners is not only humanized but also gendered. According to one Lucas spokesperson, "We've named, or termed, our system 'Jennifer' to kind of give the technology a bit of a human look and feel and sound. And Jennifer is kind of like having a supervisor stand over your shoulder. So as you're a worker out on the floor, wearing your headset you have someone speaking into your ear telling you where to go and what to do."[22] Operators are trained to compete with their own previous performance records in order to constantly improve. The software system can also indicate how much work remains in a job or how fast the operator is picking. The operator can access this information by asking, "How am I doing?" One employee in the promotional video gushes, "You just have to listen to where Jennifer tells you to go, go get the product, and put it in the tote. And there's no way of making errors with Jennifer because you give her a number that tells her that you're at the right location."[23]

Location confirmation is one type of sustained feedback necessary in this kind of picking system. Jennifer's voice has a metallic shimmy as it breathlessly relays strings of numbers, verifications, questions, and commands. As speed remains an obsession, the voice speaks quickly, almost without pauses between words. Here is a sample exchange between an employee and Jennifer:

JENNIFER: Sixonethreefour.
EMPLOYEE: Nine four three.
JENNIFER: Pickoneinnerpackofsix.
EMPLOYEE: Grab one.
JENNIFER: Oneinnerpackgrabbed. Pickthreeeach.
EMPLOYEE: Grab three.
JENNIFER: Bravo, putfiveeach.
EMPLOYEE: Eight seven, put five.
JENNIFER: Alpha, puttwoeach.
EMPLOYEE: Five eight, put two.
JENNIFER: India, puttwoeach.
EMPLOYEE: Seven zero, put two.

JENNIFER: Sixonethreeone.

EMPLOYEE: Seven six four.

JENNIFER: Pickoneeach.

EMPLOYEE: Jennifer, what is item.

JENNIFER: Itemonezerozerofivesixeightninesix.

EMPLOYEE: Grab one.

JENNIFER: Bravo, putoneeach.

EMPLOYEE: Eight seven, put one.[24]

This seemingly nonsensical conversation is a precisely encrypted exchange but also a kind of training session as Jennifer directs the employee to operate more like a machine. Such feedback mechanisms are familiar tools of the disciplined institution, from Robert Owen's experiments in self-assessment to the scientific management of a Taylorist shop floor to the cybernetic entanglements articulated by Norbert Wiener.[25] However, feedback in this case is not a matter of reciprocal calibration but a unilateral and ceaseless stream of numbers posed as questions and correctives. If wearable scanners help workers see like computers, voice-directed picking helps them operate like computers.

Since the communication is audible rather than written and one program can be scaled up to a large number of employees, the economies of scale allow for a great degree of customization while lowering a company's need to invest in or train employees. Southeast Frozen Foods offers one example of the flexibility of a voice-directed picking system.[26] Some of the company's distribution center workers speak English and others speak Spanish, and the voice system, made by Vocollect, can be easily adapted to communicate in operators' native languages. Workers do not need to read the labels on the cartons, they only need to recognize the numbers and scan the bar codes. In this sense, the computer system demonstrates a greater capacity for communication with workers than many human managers. Another example comes from an article in *Logistics Management* that profiles a supplier's use of voice-directed picking. The supplier's vice president of logistics states: "The main reason we like voice is because it isn't hard-wired or confined to a specific location such as pick-to-light. . . . We also find voice to be faster than RF and not as cumbersome; but perhaps the best part was that it is hands-free and eyes-free."[27] Like logistical systems more generally, voice-directed picking is neither confined to a place nor governed by a visual regime, and this in turn allows for easier accumulation and liquidation of resources, human or otherwise.

Voice-directed picking's actual hardware includes standard communications equipment. Workers receive instructions and vocalize confirmations through headsets. But they are not speaking to a human at the other end of the communications channel. Rather, their confirmations are part of a feedback process in which their voice signals are translated to signals understandable to the voice recognition software, the responses are processed, and in turn they are translated back into signals comprehensible to humans. In this sense, operators are not "talking" to "The Voice" but are entering data into a set of algorithms that provide responses. Managers praise voice-directed picking systems for the ease with which operators can learn to use them. Workers can be trained in a matter of hours rather than the days or even weeks required for other systems. Thus there is little incentive for companies to invest in their employees. Since fewer resources are necessary to bring new employees to a satisfactory performance level, voice-directed systems significantly diminish the consequences of high turnover. Workers, like the software that commands them, can be replaced quickly, with only limited and temporary reductions in productivity. The new forms of literacy demanded of DC workers are impossible to achieve without the aid of some kind of augmenting technology to mediate between computers and humans.

Logistical Environments Demand New Forms of Mobility

Logistical environments pressure workers to adapt to new communications regimes and to adopt new forms of mobility. Distribution centers, in keeping with the traits of logistics, imagine and calculate space volumetrically. In the same way that a container ship's manifest locates merchandise in three coordinates, the contemporary automated or semiautomated logistical environment locates wares vertically as

Voice-directed picking systems allow distribution center employees to work with both hands free. This often results in increased pressure on workers to meet escalating performance standards. Source: Vocollect, Inc., "Voice-directed portable terminals for wireless communication systems," U.S. Patent 8,128,422, 2012, 2.

well as horizontally. This shift from surface to volume results, in part, from the pressure to maximize real estate investments by lowering the cost per unit area as well as by improving the efficiency of operations. Moreover, developments in picking and conveyance technology have required building design to evolve in response. The mechanisms used to move human pickers through space signal these workers' nearly complete absorption into the logistical apparatus.

A device known as a pallet truck or pallet jack enables an operator to move and place large quantities of goods that would otherwise be impossible for one person to lift or carry. During World War II, the military popularized the now ubiquitous shipping pallet to aid in the allocation and shipment of matériel and other provisions. The pallet became a crucial module in military logistics operations because planners and suppliers could depend on its standard format. As long as things to be shipped were placed on and secured to pallets, it could be trusted that they would fit into vehicles for transport in the most efficient way.[28] Often arriving at a distribution center on pallets, some merchandise must be broken down into smaller units and routed on the DC's conveyor system to the appropriate holding area, where they wait to be picked to fulfill an order. In other cases, pallets remain intact and are transported to the appropriate part of the distribution center from which the merchandise they hold can be picked directly.

In all cases, these large and heavy modules must be moved through the space of the facility, a need fulfilled largely by an array of pallet transports. The hydraulic pallet jack is the most basic configuration. The operator slides the forks of the jack between the pallet stringers and pulls down on the steering column to lift the pallet high enough off the ground to move it. A press photograph from pallet truck manufacturer Crown, showing operators using pallet trucks to load and unload pallets from trailers attached to loading docks, illuminates the interiorizing conditions of the distribution center. The rolling doors that seal the backs of the loading docks are visible, as is the inside of each trailer—basically understood as another space of the distribution center. In fact, as the rolling doors stay closed when there are no pallets to load or unload, it is not inconceivable that the trailers are on the other side of the doors at all times. The fact that the bodies in the image are

Interior view of one of Walmart's "High Velocity Distribution Centers," where a mechanized pallet truck operator loads goods into a trailer. Source: *Wal-Mart 2007 Annual Report*, 17.

Pallet trucks from Crown augment the movement of heavy inventory. In this case, distribution center workers load pallets into waiting trailers through loading bay doors. Source: Crown PC 4500 Series brochure.

obscured by the technology they inhabit is also significant. An earlier image from a 1949 materials handling manual in which a range of trucks are rendered in silhouette presents this even more plainly. In one case, that of a high-lift platform truck, the figure of the driver is literally fused with the body of the vehicle and capable of delivering several hundred pallets per hour.

Crown makes a range of products for transporting palletized merchandise, including what it calls stockpickers. These devices, a hybrid of pallet truck and loader crane, prefigure another family of semi-automated high-density materials handling equipment sometimes referred to as man-on-board automated storage and retrieval systems (ASRS). In using a stockpicker, an operator occupies a cab connected to a crane and rail system that moves between aisles both vertically and horizontally. In the case of man-on-board ASRS, the operator can manually direct the cab, but the picking order sequence more often dictates movement. The mechanism, outside the control of the operator, moves the cab to the appropriate inventory position and the operator picks the correct number of units before signaling to the system to move to the next point. The operator spends the day suspended between two high-density storage shelves, being shuttled back and forth and up and down as orders are fulfilled. Suggesting another kind of radical incorporation, the operator is mostly controlled by the central network in that not only are the operator's movements and actions determined by an external set of directives, but also the person is physically transported to each location by the mechanical force of the crane. Whereas the mobile stockpicker remains identifiable as a vehicle that an operator can enter, exit, and drive around, the picking crane is much more a piece of the building in that it both dictates the actions and controls the movements of the operator. An image from Dematic's systems overview brochure shows three aisles, each with a cab and operator. These three units move horizontally and vertically as their occupants take inventory units from very high shelves and place them in order trolleys. In some cases, the human inhabitants of such systems are almost impossible to discern.

An early version of a man-on-board picking crane, in which the operator becomes part of the building system. Source: Jolyon Drury and Peter Falconer, *Building and Planning for Industrial Storage and Distribution,* 2nd ed. (London: Architectural Press, 2003). Courtesy of The Robert Elwall Photographs Collection, British Architectural Library.

Diagram suggesting the augmentation of power truck operators by their vehicles. Source: Material Handling Institute, *Materials Handling: Techniques, Case Studies, Equipment,* Proceedings of the Third Annual Materials Handing Conference, Philadelphia, Pennsylvania, 1949 (New York: American Society of Mechanical Engineers, 1949).

Logistical Environments Demand
New Human–Machine Assemblages

Distribution centers are environments in which many necessary functions are automatically executed. Yet, because of their size and nature, these buildings still require human labor to operate. The difficulty in modeling the demands of the inventory system also makes optimization a special challenge. Likewise, the economy of human labor for carrying out simple tasks, like moving small boxes, continues to trump that of machines, which could do these jobs but only at considerable cost and possible obsolescence. By accepting that the goods Walmart handles can be understood as both information and material, the distribution center functions more as a processing device than as a storehouse or a place of inhabitation. Broadly considered, these automated buildings function much in the same ways that early theorists of computers described those arrangements: "a wide class of calculating, data-processing, and information-storage-and-retrieval machines."[29] In a typical distribution center, workers experience direct and sustained contact with machines and a ceaseless stream of information. Is this not an overwhelming condition? In *Understanding Media: The Extensions of Man*, Marshall McLuhan asserts that media function as extensions of human thinking and feeling and thus as a sort of defense mechanism that people use to cope with the increasing hostility and intensity of a world characterized by media saturation:

> Any invention or technology is an extension or self-amputation of our physical bodies, and such extension also demands new ratios or new equilibriums among the other organs and extensions of the body. . . . To behold, use or perceive any extension of ourselves in technological form is necessarily to embrace it. To listen to radio or to read the printed page is to accept these extensions of ourselves into our personal system and to undergo the "closure" of displacement that follows automatically. It is this continuous embrace of our own technology in daily use that puts us in the Narcissus role of subliminal awareness and numbness in relation to these images of ourselves. By continuously embracing technologies, we relate ourselves to them as servomechanisms.[30]

Through this idea of servomechanism, McLuhan posits that the developing relationship between media and humans continuously

Press photograph of Dematic's automated
storage and retrieval system (ASRS).
Courtesy of Dematic, Inc.

transforms both.[31] Writing a few years earlier, computer scientist J. C. R. Licklider anticipated McLuhan's argument in his assessment of the possibilities of new media technologies. Licklider's 1960 essay "Man–Computer Symbiosis" crystallized several ideas about the future of computing and offered a new understanding of the potential of interactive computing.[32] Licklider made the case for a closely linked relationship between humans and computers, where the two operate as a single entity with a seamlessly integrated interface that allows for faster and more effective decision making. He perceived humans and machines to be complementary in nature and argued that large organizations and companies were too reliant on labor-intensive calculations and time-consuming preparations. Predicting that "computing machines will do the routinizable work that must be done to prepare the way for insights and decisions in technical and scientific thinking," Licklider anticipated that in the same way industrial automation allowed for the routinization of manual labor, computers would enable new forms of management pertaining to information.[33]

For Licklider, the optimal human–computer interaction would be one in which the computer would do the labor and the human would do the "thinking." While this relationship animated much of the discourse around computing technology, the opposite scenario, where the roles are reversed, quickly provoked anxiety in the popular imagination, as is apparent in such 1960s films as *Fail Safe* (1964) and *2001: A Space Odyssey* (1968). In the case of Walmart, whose daily operations are characterized by an enormous amount of information management, the computer is actually performing many of the decision-making duties along with labor-intensive calculations. Because Walmart's supplies are so carefully calculated, the company makes decisions about where to route different goods based on inventory models developed by the retailer's extensive data-mining operations. What the computer cannot do is manage the physicality of the merchandise. It can locate the goods and determine where they should go, but it cannot execute the repetitive and labor-intensive tasks of selecting them and transporting them to the desired locations. It needs humans for this. Humans currently—and will for the foreseeable future—outdo computers in flexibility, agility, and economy.[34] This reliance on humans

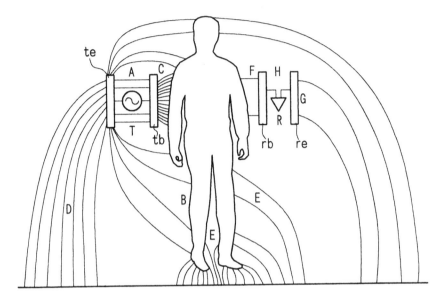

This illustration for a patent for the "Intrabody Information Transfer Device" shows how the human body relays signals with a communications network. Source: Nippon Telephone and Telegraph Company, "Intrabody Information Transfer Device which transfers a signal via a human body," U.S. Patent 6,223,018, 2001, 6.

by the computer to do the routinizable tasks that it is incapable of doing itself constitutes a reversal of the roles assigned by Licklider. Instead of the computer serving as the laboring "body" for the thinking human "head," the opposite is true. The servers in Bentonville are dependent on their organic counterparts to ensure that operations run smoothly. Combining McLuhan's version of extension and Licklider's symbiosis presents a new understanding of the inhabitants of these large distribution centers: they are not workers or decision makers or mechanically extended subjects but a collective servo-organism. If the machinic output in a servomechanism is disproportionately larger than the organic input, then in the case of the distribution center the machinic input is relatively small while the organic, human labor it prompts is extensive. In the same way that fixating on individual Walmart stores obscures the company's networked activities at a larger scale, focusing on a single worker and his or her augmenting technology obscures a much broader network of machinic logics acting in unison and governed by data generated by the mundane decisions of everyday life.

5 TERRITORY

Management City

IN 2005, THE NEW YORK PUBLIC LIBRARY sold the 1859 painting *Kindred Spirits,* by Asher B. Durand, to expand its endowment. New York's Metropolitan Museum of Art and the National Gallery of Art in Washington, D.C., in a joint effort, were the favored bidders going into the auction. To the surprise of many, they were outbid by a private party, Alice Walton, who purchased the painting for more than $35 million as part of her effort to develop one of the premier collections of Americana in the country. In commenting on the purchase, Rebecca Solnit referred to Durand's painting as "a touchstone for a set of American ideals that Wal-Mart has been savaging" and went on to suggest that Alice Walton was "turning hallowed American art into a fig leaf to paste over naked greed and raw exploitation."[1] Walton's collection is housed in Crystal Bridges Museum of American Art, a complex that opened near downtown Bentonville in 2011. Art historian Michael Leja, in a review of the museum and its collection, points to a range of "axes of political interest" running through the project, including wealth and its relationship to art patronage, the question of what constitutes "American" artwork, the "redistribution of national artistic patrimony," and the constitution of the museum's audiences. While supporting Solnit's position that the museum's connection to the Walmart corporation "renders impossible obliviousness to the paradox that the brilliant experiences of nature and culture provided by Crystal Bridges are made possible by unenlightened and deplorable business practices," Leja also observes that with its accessibility and lack of pretentiousness, the museum "offers itself as a place to feel at home with art." He suggests that Crystal Bridges could "contribute something toward easing the cultural divisions in the United States by making its national artistic culture more broadly shared."[2]

Leja points to the "domestic" as one of the features of the museum, one that resonates with larger tendencies of the region as it develops rapidly and as its population grows. However, Leja's comment that "profits from a dry goods enterprise" created Alice Walton's wealth might be better put as "profits from an international logistics operator." While logistics might not have any more to do with Walton's arts patronage than Carnegie's steel or Getty's oil did with theirs, the relationship between the company's headquarters and the nature of its operations is more direct. While Bentonville remains the site of Walmart headquarters, logistics, as area of work and habit of mind, decouples sites of management from sites of production. And Walmart's avowedly distant location, while not an uncommon feature of other industries, challenges the primacy of urban sites as centers of power. Moreover, the region is taking shape thanks to significant private investment, and, although it is still in formation, it is likely to develop not as an open urban system but rather as a hierarchical series of destinations that, like logistics itself, function to produce hyper-specified conditions through flexible, underspecified techniques. On one hand, Northwest Arkansas is a wealthy enclave that produces the image of the world imagined by its residents; on the other, the region's collision between deregulation and private interests has produced discontinuous pockets of cultural richness amid swaths of sprawling commercial and residential developments. What these two versions of Northwest Arkansas share is the fact that they are part of a kind of territorial form that is emerging, driven by private interests and detached from the historical form of the industrial city.

Walmart is a global company, yet its management operations remain concentrated in a relatively remote corner of the United States. Bentonville, however, demonstrates a diffuse set of urban conditions that are shaped by demographic shifts, cultural influx, infrastructural investment, burgeoning tourism, and elevated lifestyle expectations. The Northwest Arkansas Metropolitan Statistical Area (NWA MSA)—

Kindred Spirits as installed in Crystal Bridges Museum of American Art, 2015. Photograph by the author.

Aerial view of Crystal Bridges Museum of American Art with surrounding woods. Downtown Bentonville is out of frame, near the upper right portion of the image. Photograph by Timothy Hursley. Courtesy of Timothy Hursley.

or the Fayetteville–Rogers–Springdale Metropolitan Statistical Area, as the region is officially designated by the U.S. Census Bureau—is home to the highest concentration of management professionals in the United States.[3] This monoprofessional landscape is undergoing processes of diversification in order to be more resilient while at the same time it is changing the lifestyle expectations of residents of the historically rural region. As a result of increased demand, attention, and investment from people like Walton and organizations like the Walton Family Foundation, the region has seen an increase in access, transportation options, cultural offerings, luxury housing developments, and tourism levels, all catering to a generally affluent clientele. While such changes are familiar indicators of urban vitality, they have developed in Northwest Arkansas without reference to a historic urban center. Indeed, the region has few of the things often associated with the establishment of cities. There are no huge deposits of natural resources nearby, and while there is an available labor force, its size is not significant compared to the labor forces found in other sites of industrial concentration (e.g., Detroit, at one point). Nor does the region offer especially strategic location (like Chicago, for example). Walmart's managerial operations, of course, do not require a large concentration of labor, because most of the company's labor is distributed throughout its territorial and architectural holdings. Rather, Northwest Arkansas is reserved for the managerial elite of Walmart and hosts managers from its national and global operations.[4] In catering to this group, the region has generated discrete urban forms with specific cultural, culinary, entertainment, recreational, religious, commercial, and medical functions, but these are manifest as closed systems. This form of urbanism does not develop through the piecemeal infill of infrastructural zones; rather, it happens in large and specific chunks. Even the part of the city that gestures toward proto-urban conditions is itself a thematized version of the conditions it seeks to produce, emulating instead of generating. While the adjacencies and morphologies active in the NWA MSA could yield altogether new forms of aggregation, urban form, cultural production, and so on, they must remain vigilant if they do not want to be overwhelmed by the overdetermining tendencies of logistics to flatten, smooth, lubricate, and disperse.

Sam Walton was a systems builder, and his heirs, the current Walmart leadership, are continuing his efforts at a range of scales.[5] Thomas Hughes suggests that

> the systems builders, like Ford, led us to believe that we could rationally organize the second creation [of the world] to serve our ends. Only after World War II did a handful of philosophers and publicists whom we now associate with a counterculture raise doubts about the rationality and controllability of a nation organized into massive military, production, and communication systems. Their doubts increased as the nation's technological pre-eminence waned.[6]

However, in spite of the identification of changing attitudes about technological progress, this was exactly the period in which Walmart was ascending, buoyed by a faith in rational control. While Sam and Helen Walton were committed to working in small towns and rural communities, theirs was more of a regional attachment, and the arrival in Bentonville was a result of circumstance and opportunity. Walton opened Walton's 5–10 as a Ben Franklin franchise in Bentonville in 1950 and began working on plans for expansion. He then opened another store in Fayetteville, this time not as a franchise and also as one of the first self-service variety stores in the country.[7] A series of other variety stores followed before Walton shifted his focus to a discount retail model, which used lower margins and higher volumes. Through a risky self-financed venture, Sam Walton and his brother Bud opened the 16,000-square-foot Wal-Mart Discount City on July 2, 1962, in Rogers, Arkansas, a few miles from Bentonville. Walton continued to expand his operation, building eighteen Discount City stores in the region through the rest of the decade. In order to keep volume high and prices low, he had his own distribution facility and headquarters built south of downtown Bentonville in 1969. It comprised 60,000 square feet of distribution space and 12,000 square feet of office facilities.[8] Moreover, because the company had to rely on its own distribution network to serve the small towns and semirural locations within the region, Walmart grew concentrically, with each ring of growth reinforcing the centrality of Bentonville while further elaborating its logistics network. A map showing the retailer's locations is proudly displayed in each year's annual report, with Bentonville indicated prominently. With the absence of other forms of corporate legibility, the map itself becomes a kind of mascot for Walmart, in which the image of the corporation's territory is repeatedly broadcast as a way to cement imperatives of expansion and growth as part of the company's primary values and corporate imagination.

As Walmart eventually became a national and then international corporation, Sam Walton never indicated that the company would relocate its headquarters. Moreover, the location was well suited, according to most accounts of Walton's life, to the values that he espoused and the activities he enjoyed, including community service, hunting and being in the outdoors, religious observance, and the flying of small aircraft. Cultural patronage and appreciation appear to have interested Walton in only minor ways, if at all. Walton's philanthropy, such as it was, was mainly directed toward the promotion of Christianity and free enterprise. However, he shared with other industrialists such as Thomas Edison, Henry Ford, and Thomas J. Watson Sr. a commitment to organization and management in pursuit of growth and production. In contrast to the production systems of companies like Ford (and, to some extent, the communications systems of companies like IBM), the circulatory system of Walmart's logistical operations was diffuse and remote by nature, thereby distancing the firm's headquarters operation from the sites of its activities. Of course, as Ford's operations grew, satellite factories and towns followed, but the historical relationship between place and production connected the intellectual labor of management with the physical labor of production. Likewise, there is no small number of corporations overseeing global operations from remote sites. The difference in Walmart's case, as wrought by the logistical, is in part that its network is fundamentally physical. While other paradigmatic twentieth-century corporations tended to locate their primary operations based on opportunity or necessity, Walmart's location in Bentonville was the result of coincidence and reinforced by stubbornness. Logistical systems—systems of management and circulation of things in time and space—are fundamentally distributed, remote, externalized, and risk-averse enterprises. While manufacturing and production concerns exist with a logistical network, these might be

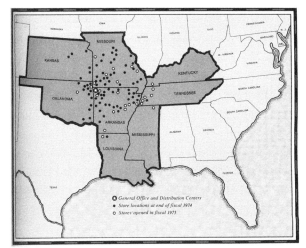

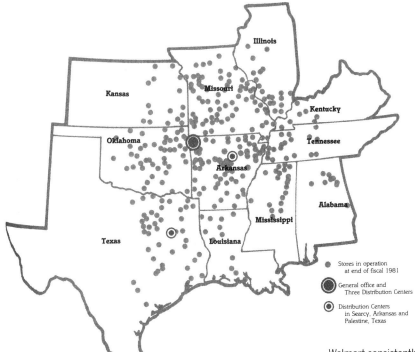

Walmart consistently includes maps in its annual reports that show its current store locations. These examples from 1975, 1979, and 1981 show the company's early growth within its home region. Sources: *Wal-Mart Stores, Inc. 1975 Annual Report,* 1975, 3; *Wal-Mart Stores, Inc. Annual Report 1979,* inside front cover; *Wal-Mart Annual Report 1981,* 25.

outsourced to suppliers, who would be more actively involved in sourcing and transforming raw materials and assembling them into finished products. This matters for questions of location because the headquarters of the firm need not be proximate to its sites of production in the way that Henry Ford found it necessary to combine managerial and productive locations in his River Rouge Plant. With a company like IBM, human rather than material resources were a significant factor in corporate locations.[9] In the case of Walmart, at least in its first few decades, the retailer preferred to hire managers locally and promote internally, and it relied on locally available personnel.

Bentonville is a symbolic site for Walmart's managerial elite (and probably for many of its 2.2 million employees) and a site of management at a distance. Over the years, Walmart headquarters has expanded to include a larger distribution center, additional office buildings for its various divisions (e.g., one building is dedicated to logistics and another to transportation), additional data centers, printing facilities, a fitness center, the Sam Walton Development Complex, and, of course, the Walmart home office, typically referred to without the definite article as simply "home office." Less than a mile south of the town's central square, the current headquarters building was built to include a large auditorium to accommodate the growing number of managers expected to attend Saturday meetings. The U.S. Census Bureau estimates that Bentonville's population in 2014 was 41,613, up from the 2006 population of 28,500.[10] As the town both grows in population and is increasingly cemented as the managerial and cultural center of the world's largest corporation and employer of two million people, this intersection produces different versions of the city itself.

To a Walmart supplier or manager from out of town, the experience of visiting Bentonville is something like entering a Walmart theme park, in which strings of meetings are punctuated with trips to the Walmart Museum, which features a re-created soda fountain and five-and-dime storefront selling nostalgic treats. A tourist's itinerary might include a trip to Crystal Bridges Museum of American Art, designed by Moshe Safdie, a stay at the Deborah Berke–designed 21c Museum

Hotel, and perhaps a meal at one of the new restaurants emphasizing seasonal and locally sourced ingredients. Walmart employees living in Bentonville are likely to be part of a managerial echelon, and some are among the many company executives to have benefited from the retailer's profit-sharing programs. They might live in one of the region's many gated communities and do their shopping at the experimental Walmart formats, including the retailer's forays into convenience stores (Walmart 2 Go) and "order and collect" locations, in which food orders can be placed online for in-store pickup. According to promotional literature from the Northwest Arkansas Council, residents of the region benefit from top-quality educational, cultural, recreational, and professional opportunities, all at affordable prices.[11] Employees of Walmart who live in the region might, as Sam Walton did, go to church with executives from J. B. Hunt, a leading logistics company, and from Tyson Foods, "the world's largest protein producer."[12] Suppliers and others affiliated with Walmart but not employed by the retailer directly might be settled more tentatively in the region. As perhaps the sole representatives of their respective companies, they likely have offices in one of the many "vendorvilles" in the region and spend their days there or meeting with Walmart buyers and negotiating ways to keep margins high while still satisfying the retailer's exacting demands and imperatives to constantly lower costs. These residents might also live in new developments, but perhaps not one of the more exclusive gated communities. If they are not likely to be staying permanently, they might choose to take up residence in one of Bentonville's many "extended stay" hotels. Whatever their circumstances in the region, Walmart suppliers and members of the company's new managerial classes have relocated from throughout the world, bringing with them specific sets of cultures, values, and lifestyle demands.[13]

Such growth is partly the result of long-term visions for infrastructural improvements that began in the 1990s. These include the development of the business-oriented and promotional Northwest Arkansas Council, a lobby to extend interstate highway connectivity, and a campaign to build a new regional airport. Sam Walton began some of these initiatives, and since his death in 1992 his children, especially Alice Walton, have continued many of them while adding their own.

The Walton Family Foundation, for example, includes "home region" as one of its three investment priorities, along with K–12 education and the environment. The mission of the foundation's Home Region Program is "to honor the Walton family's special and ongoing commitment to Northwest Arkansas where they launched an iconic American business success story by creating and sustaining long-term economic development for residents and businesses in the area; and, to enhance the educational and economic development opportunities in the Arkansas and Mississippi Delta Region."[14] As part of this goal, the foundation identifies four areas of strategic priority: education, arts and culture amenities, economic development, and "sense of place." While not defined explicitly, the last category involves attracting more residents to the region and includes initiatives related to expanding green space, recreation networks, public transportation, and active downtowns. In *The Image of the City*, Kevin Lynch suggests that "by appearing as a remarkable and well-knit *place*, the city could provide a ground for the clustering and organization of these meanings and associations." Thus, according to Lynch, a city that "appears" well organized and visually coherent "enhances every human activity that occurs there, and encourages the deposit of a memory trace."[15] While Walmart has been accused of undermining these aspects of some cities through its business practices, they remain active in Bentonville itself and are actively cultivated through the theming of the main downtown square. Fronting the side of the square opposite the courthouse, the original Walton's 5–10 houses the Walmart Museum, which includes "Mr. Sam's" meticulously preserved office. While most of the books visible in the office are popular business and management texts, tucked away on the third shelf is a copy of *The Image of the City*.

Northwest Arkansas Is an Urban Form in Its Adolescence

In June 2006, the Economics and Security Committee of the NATO Parliamentary Assembly visited Northwest Arkansas because the committee members saw it as a "positive example of local economic development through global business activity."[16] The delegates traveled to the region to gain a better understanding of how its combination of geographic isolation and global connectivity were producing and affecting the region's rapid growth—largely fueled by Walmart. According to the committee's report:

> Wal-Mart's extraordinary success has certainly been one of the most important catalysts for economic growth in North-West Arkansas. Not only has this high earning retail power pumped a tremendous amount of capital into the region, but it has also attracted representative offices of a range of supplier companies that simply cannot afford not to be present in the region due to the vital role Wal-Mart plays in getting their products to the market. . . .
>
> The region's growing population and the influx of Wal-Mart vendors has sparked a very dynamic local real estate market, and members reviewed plans for the construction of a large retail shopping centre close by the intersection of two important highway systems that link the region to the broader US economy and beyond. North-West Arkansas is also located near the centre of the United States and this has only facilitated the movement of people to the region and the flow of goods through and from it.[17]

The NATO visit is an indicator of the region's significant national and global position. However, this diffuse, remote, and, until recently, demographically homogeneous region shares few of the characteristics associated with urban areas, much less globally connected ones. For example, the population density of the NWA MSA is barely 150 people per square mile; compare that with Los Angeles's 7,500 or Chicago's almost 13,000 per square mile.[18] The region is neither typically suburban nor exurban, primarily because it has grown without a traditional urban center. Whereas earlier cities, based on aggregations of industry, eventually became legible urban entities, transforming from rural settlements to small towns to larger cities to major cities with exurban conditions, Northwest Arkansas grew from a series of small towns into a diffuse metropolitan region that continues not to be defined by a central city.[19]

It is significant that the NWA MSA has developed not around an urban core but around a cluster of corporations, Walmart being the most dominant. Scholars who have examined conditions associated with market-driven growth, frequently described with terms like *sprawl, suburbs,* and *exurbs,* often cast such conditions in relation to adjacent urban centers. Robert Lang develops this idea in his discussion of the distinction between "edge cities" and "edgeless cities" and in his work with Jennifer LeFurgy focusing on "boomburbs."[20] As Paul Knox notes, Lang and LeFurgy define "boomburbs" as "suburban jurisdictions with more than 100,000 residents that have maintained double-digit rates of population growth between 1970 and 2000."[21] These processes are evidence of shifting urban dynamics and highlight the speed with which some regions are growing, often driven by new economical engines around skilled technology-sector jobs. A Brookings Institution study categorizes an "exurb" as having at least 20 percent of workers commuting to an urbanized area, a growth rate that exceeds the average for the related metropolitan area, and housing density of 2.6 acres or more per unit.[22] Once again, the relationship to a metropolitan area is a defining feature of this kind of settlement pattern.[23] Anthony Flint suggests that exurban residents are "leading a self-contained life, with work at an office campus and big-box stores along a commercial strip all requiring lots of motoring."[24] However, the notion that the exurban conditions in Northwest Arkansas exist in isolation is complicated by the migration patterns catalyzed by Walmart. Marjorie Rosen describes how "in recent years Wal-Mart executives and suppliers have immigrated here from such big cities as Chicago, New York, and L.A., and from countries as far-flung as India, Mexico, and Peru" and goes on to point out the religious diversity of the region's population, which includes Jews, Hindus, Muslims, and Mormons. She also notes the area's significant Hispanic, Laotian, Marshallese, and African American populations, not to mention, of course, white Christians, the dominant demographic until recently.[25] And even though Rosen associates the area's physical traits with the conditions of sprawl cited above, she also suggests that "Bentonville may be in the process of learning."[26] While Bentonville and the NWA MSA seem to perpetuate the image of commercial-driven exurban sprawl, the area's social and cultural mix, its historical development, and the significant resources available to it all suggest a version of urbanization that merits some attention for the new configurations it might yet generate.[27] At the same time, the ways in which the region is developing tend to propagate discrete and closed urban systems that build in a range of barriers, thus impeding the congestion that often characterizes urban experience. The tendency of the logistical to deploy underdetermined forms in pursuit of overdetermined results is also active in the NWA MSA.

Northwest Arkansas remained primarily agricultural and rural until the economic shifts that occurred after World War II resulted in increased movement toward the region's small towns.[28] The conditions that arose reflect, in some ways, what Robert Fishman characterizes as a "technoburb," a new form of urbanization in which "residents look to their immediate surroundings rather than to the city for their jobs and other needs; and . . . industries find not only the employees they need but also the specialized services."[29] However, settlement patterns in Northwest Arkansas developed in relative isolation and often around shared values related to self-reliance. Moreover, as the closest large cities are Tulsa, Oklahoma City, and Little Rock (115, 220, and 214 miles away, respectively), there was never a major urban center to which Bentonville could be considered "sub" or "ex." In the case of technoburbs, in Fishman's characterization, even if they tend to develop some autonomy, they are still defined relative to some kind of preexisting dense urban center, especially an image of a distant "historic core."[30] The implication is that technoburbs, however opposed they might be to historic suburbs, remain subservient to the centralized concentrations of large U.S. cities. This is reiterated by Saskia Sassen in her essay "Why Cities Matter": "The more these [information] technologies enable global geographic dispersal of corporate activities, the more they produce density and centrality at the other end; the cities where their headquarter functions get done."[31] The NWA MSA frustrates some of these assessments because it performs as a technoburb in Fishman's formulation yet it is not defined in relationship to an existing city center, nor does it benefit from the kinds of incentives that Fishman and Sassen describe. In the case of Walmart, the world's largest company and a geographically dispersed corporation, its "other end"—while certainly a concentration of power and technology—is not part of a global city and shares few traits with historic and concentrated urban cores. When asked if the company would ever consider leaving Bentonville, Sam Walton responded:

> Move from Bentonville? That would be the last thing we [would] do unless they run us out. The best thing we ever did was to hide back there in the hills and eventually build a company that makes folks want to find us. They get there sometimes with a lot of trepidation and problems, but we like where we are. It's because of the work ethic, because of the chemistry of the people up there and the support we get. We're much better off than if we had gone to Chicago.[32]

While Walmart operates in the mainstream of the market, its geographical position is peripheral. However, with the completion of the Northwest Arkansas Regional Airport (which includes the Alice L. Walton Terminal Building), the extension of Interstate 41, and the opening of Crystal Bridges Museum, the NWA MSA is taking shape as an urban configuration of its own making and in its own image—that is, not in reference to a historic urban center, not because of a concentration of material or energy resources, and not because of a significantly strategic location. Logistics and the habits of mind formed around it, while not expressly responsible for Walmart's genesis in Northwest Arkansas, have allowed it to remain there and to thrive.

The circumstances that contribute to Walmart's home location and the reluctance of its executives to move run counter to many of the ways that economists and geographers identify or predict the logic of business location. As Paul Krugman writes, "Firms want to locate where market potential is high, that is, near large markets. But markets will tend to be large where lots of firms locate. So one is led naturally to a consideration of the possibility of self-reinforcing regional growth or decline."[33] In Walmart's case, Bentonville was one small-town option among many, and its remoteness was appealing to Sam Walton in a categorical way. It also allied Walmart with the kinds of towns that the company sought to create a presence in, especially in its first decades, when it was able to establish a market in rural areas of the United States where few thought it was possible. Transport has remained a significant part of the region's commercial history. Both John Tyson and Johnnie Bryan Hunt started here, the former going on to develop Tyson Foods and the latter to found J. B. Hunt.[34] The historical connections to transport align with Walmart's own emphasis on logistics and with its tendency to look to the logistics and transport division when promoting senior leadership. Transport is a peculiar kind of industry in that it is fundamentally nomadic and not bound to any center, instead remaining perpetually in between points.

Walmart is a regional thinker and actor, even if the NWA MSA scrambles relationships between region and building, town and infrastructure. Jane Jacobs quipped that "a region is an area safely larger than the last one to whose problems we found no solution."[35] The hint of isolationism identifiable in Walmart's attachment to Bentonville brings with it an air of entrenchment, perhaps in recognition of what David Harvey calls "territorial competition," which he asserts "plays a crucial role in the progress of capital accumulation."[36] In addition to a problem of scale (and of scalar categories), there is a problem of imagination. As Fishman has pointed out, as neither celebration of nor apology for sprawl conditions, the problem is that it remains in its adolescence: "The case for the techno-city can only be made hesitantly and conditionally. Nevertheless, we can hope that its deficiencies are in large part the early awkwardness of a new urban type. All new city forms appear in their early stages to be chaotic. . . . Sprawl has a functional logic that may not be apparent to those accustomed to more traditional cities. If that logic is understood imaginatively . . . then perhaps a matching aesthetic can be devised."[37] The NWA MSA offers a glimpse of future forms of urbanity wrought by logistics, sharing increasingly common traits with other territories but more advanced in its development. In the same way that other historical shifts in economic organization triggered transformation in territorial settlement and urban organization, the NWA MSA is demonstrative of a logistics economy changing urban patterns. The dynamics that Walmart's operations manage and the physical forms that result point to an increasingly common set of relationships enabled by the ability of logistics to untether, decouple, and smooth. To understand what is happening in the NWA MSA, one might bracket the idea of an imageable city (in spite of Bentonville's efforts to develop its scenographic town square) and instead develop an idea of a territorial form that is topological and elastic.

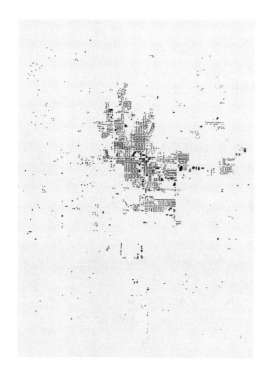

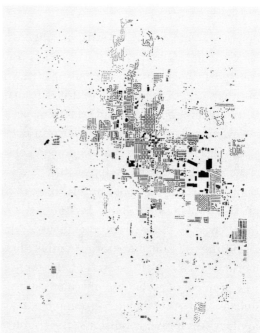

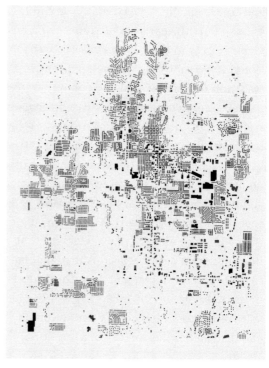

ABOVE LEFT: Bentonville, 1970. The lighter tones indicate buildings constructed in the previous decade (between 1960 and 1970). Illustration created by the author based on historical maps and aerial photographs.

ABOVE RIGHT: Bentonville, 1990. The large buildings at lower right are part of Walmart's headquarters complex. Illustration created by the author based on historical maps and aerial photographs.

BOTTOM: Bentonville, 2010. Illustration created by the author based on historical maps and aerial photographs.

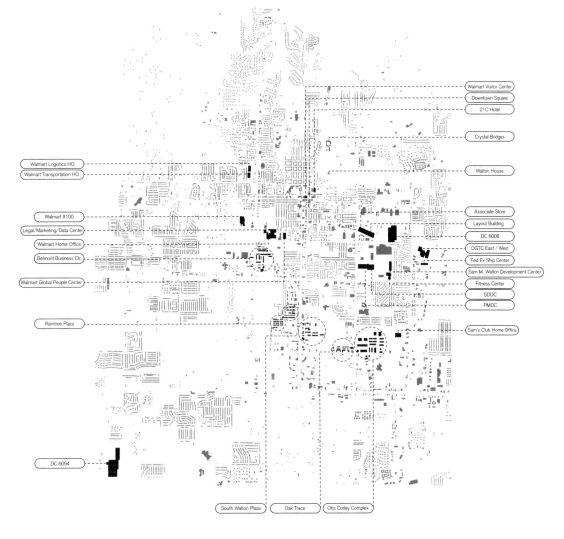

Walmart Visitor Center	
Downtown Square	
21C Hotel	
Crystal Bridges	
Walmart Logistics HQ	Walton House
Walmart Transportation HQ	
Walmart #100	Associate Store
Legal/Marketing/Data Center	Layout Building
Walmart Home Office	DC 6008
Belmont Business Ctr.	DGTC East / West
	Fed Ex Ship Center
	Sam M. Walton Development Center
Walmart Global People Center	Fitness Center
	SDDC
	PMDC
Raintree Plaza	Sam's Club Home Office
DC 6094	
South Walton Plaza	Oak Trace	Otis Corley Complex

Bentonville, 2015. Illustration created by the
author based on historical maps and aerial
photographs.

Vendorvilles Combine the Infrastructural and the Commercial with the Domestic

If Walmart's centrifugal growth patterns have prompted new ways of navigating larger territories, they have also produced a centripetal concentration of new commercial space in Bentonville itself. To help negotiate this ongoing pressure, suppliers have discovered the benefits of maintaining a physical presence near Walmart's home office.[38] Driving south from Walmart headquarters along Walton Boulevard, one sees clusters of low buildings with domestic appearances that disguise commercial contents. These developments, referred to locally as vendorvilles, serve as outposts for Walmart's numerous suppliers who have found it necessary to maintain a physical presence in Bentonville. The buildings borrow the idiom of inexpensive, rapidly produced housing stock, partly reflective of the transient nature of their tenants, subject as they are to the fluctuating demands Walmart places on them. Similarly, as these offices are rendered in a language of domestic architecture, they are camouflaged to some extent within their context of developer-driven subdivisions of single-family houses. These buildings are designed to suggest domesticity, or even simply to look like homes, but remain tentatively settled in the commercial landscape of Northwest Arkansas through unfamiliar sizes, proportions, and volumes. The vendorville complexes also maintain a low profile in the way they avoid broadcasting their presence. There is limited directional signage, and individual vendors are indicated, if at all, only by corporate logos on their doors; some prefer even more anonymity. The buildings absorb a changing mixture of suppliers who come from a range of places, including large cities. The vendors bring with them their own habits, desires, and needs, which in turn trigger social and cultural transformations in the area.

The vendorville developments share the architectural language of strip malls, but since these office spaces are densely packed with representatives from companies that supply merchandise to Walmart, the properties of their inhabitation are something like those of a collection of small consulates in a significant diplomatic capitol. Each of the vendor buildings typically includes a vestibule with a reception desk and

The architectural elements of "vendorville" office parks in Bentonville often gesture toward domestic imagery. Photographs by the author.

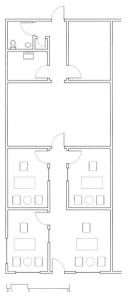

This typical plan of a unit at the Belmont Business Center includes a small reception area by the front entrance as well as small offices. The open space in the upper center of the plan is often used as a display space or showroom for the supplier's product line. Redrawn by the author.

occasional attendant. A small office for the corporate representative is usually adjacent to the entry space. Beyond the entry is a larger space that serves as both showroom and meeting room, where the representative hosts Walmart buyers and prices and contracts are negotiated.

The Belmont Business Center and Raintree Plaza are the vendorville complexes closest to Walmart's headquarters, directly across Sam Walton Boulevard. Further along the boulevard is Commerce Drive and another complex identified only by its address: 301 Southwest Eighteenth Street. Further south is South Walton Plaza, a complex designed to include small offices but also a few housing units. At the time of writing, these five linear office parks were home to 174 different businesses, each primarily concerned with attending to the needs of Walmart. Each of these developments has a single frontage and faces two or four rows of parking and another building opposite. The buildings at Raintree Plaza include colonnades protected by deep eaves and punctuated with vertical elements clad in faux cobblestone with a formal idiom derived, vaguely, from some distant chateau. If the buildings' precise stylistic source is elusive, their overall impression is one of accommodating domesticity. The design of these developments masks difference through repeated building forms, themselves internally repetitive and large enough to generate an impression of abundance and variety but without specificity. In a field dominated by intense competition among rivals for market share or share of shelf space, the long, low buildings of the vendorvilles absorb and neutralize these distinctions and enable individual suppliers, at the mercy of their largest account for most of the day, to at least return to the anonymity of their offices and to the implied solidarity of business partners in their complexes.

Awkward corporate domesticity is most apparent in the architecture and organization of South Walton Plaza, whose entry is marked with a ceremonial flagpole and obelisk. These offices, while similar in size and function to those in other complexes, are distributed throughout the development in smaller house-like units of four to eight companies, usually sharing a common entrance. The buildings' smaller footprints produce more interstitial space, which is covered with lawns and threaded with sidewalks. This results in a kind of "backyard urbanism" in which the casualness of that archetypal suburban space is inverted and thrust into the collective space of the development. The result is a continuous landscape of gas grills, air-conditioning units, lawns, driveways, and patios. If Raintree Plaza trades in distant palatial imagery, South Walton presents a domestic idiom that borrows from first-generation suburbs and antebellum plantations.

Companies with a substantial stake in Walmart have started to open larger offices in the region. For example, Procter & Gamble, whose largest client is Walmart, has opened a satellite headquarters in Bentonville. Similarly, Clorox, although smaller in operation, has opened a regional office in South Walton Plaza. The Clorox building's hybrid of institutional and residential architecture includes a back patio crowded with gas grills and a kitchen overflowing with only Clorox cleaning supplies. In Bentonville, since hospitality is part of the mission of companies like Clorox, vendor representatives work to cultivate stronger relationships with Walmart buyers. The vendors rely on Walmart as both host and guest. They know that the retailer will maintain the upper hand in negotiations, yet it also has a duty to its customers to provide the product mixture that its demographic profile–monitoring software suggests. Such corporate diplomacy unfolds in Walmart's sequestered supplier meeting rooms in the Sam Walton Development Complex, in vendorville showrooms, and over hot dogs in the front/backyards of these emerging spaces of corporate domesticity. The vendorvilles are a symptom of the logistical, manifesting its own logics of discontinuity. At the same time, Walmart's logistical expertise allows the retailer to operate at a distance and to set many of its own terms relative to price questions. Much of what the company sells is fungible, and the representatives in vendorville are in Northwest Arkansas to argue for the value of their products over those of others.

Crystal Bridges Is Cultural Infrastructure and Audience Maker

The activities of Walmart in Bentonville are the results of a confluence of a number of factors, including the continued success of Walmart, the company's sustained presence in and support of the region, the astonishing wealth of the Walton family, and the family's continued investment in Bentonville. At the same time, the transformations happening in Northwest Arkansas reflect the discontinuous nature of logistics. Because Walmart's entire operation is constituted as a far-flung network of distribution centers, retail outlets, highways, and so on, there is no actual "center" to it. Alice Walton, whose official residence is her ranch in Texas, has devoted significant time and financial resources to improving Walmart's home region. As part of the Northwest Arkansas Council (of which she was a founder), Walton was instrumental in developing the spur of Interstate 41 that connects the NWA MSA to Interstate 40, and she was so fundamental to the creation of the Northwest Arkansas Regional Airport that the airport's terminal is named in her honor.[39] Indeed, before the airport was built, visitors to Bentonville, including the thousands of suppliers and vendors traveling there annually from places like New York and Los Angeles, would fly to Little Rock and then to the very small Bentonville Municipal Airport. Having played crucial roles in terrestrial transport and aviation, Alice Walton took on a project, Crystal Bridges Museum of American Art, related more to cultural production than to infrastructure, even if the building she commissioned employs an idiom derived from large-scale projects like dams and bridges. When Walton was searching for an architect to design a facility to house her substantial collection of American art, a friend recommended that she visit the Skirball Cultural Center in Los Angeles, which was designed by Moshe Safdie. Walton did so and was immediately convinced; she began working with Safdie to develop a museum for her collection.

Crystal Bridges is part of an effort to develop downtown Bentonville as a place to live, do business, or visit, and the steady stream of managers, suppliers, and others involved with Walmart ensures a reliable flow of people to the area. The entrance to Crystal Bridges is a short walk from downtown Bentonville through a forest path studded with outdoor sculpture installations by artists such as James Turrell and Roxy Paine, as well as Frank Lloyd Wright's Bachman-Wilson House, relocated from New Jersey.[40] Through this entrance, the museum's extent gradually becomes clearer as one moves deeper into the complex. The institution's galleries, archives, library, education spaces,

Northwest Arkansas Regional Airport

*Over 50 round trip flights
daily to 15 destinations
on six airlines.*

- American/American Eagle to
  Dallas/Fort Worth, Chicago,
  New York and St. Louis
- Delta to Atlanta, Cincinnati,
  Memphis, Minneapolis
  and Detroit
- U.S. Airways to Charlotte, NC
- Continental to Houston
  and Newark
- United Express to Chicago
  and Denver
- Allegiant to Los Angeles,
  Las Vegas and Orlando

Alice L. Walton Terminal Building
One Airport Boulevard • Suite 100 • Bentonville, AR 72712
(479) 205-1000 • http://flyxna.com/

36° 16′ 31″ N / 94° 17′ 48″ W

northwest arkansas ozarks
where america does business with pleasure

Featuring > Bentonville > Eureka Springs > Fayetteville > Rogers > Siloam Springs > Springdale

if adventure is on your agenda, find it here:
> > > > > > nwatourism.org

relocation & relocation > shopping, dining & lodging > arts, attractions & entertainment > ozark
mountains & other recreation > romance & weddings > meetings, conventions & special events

Back and front covers of promotional
material highlighting airline connectivity
and the Alice L. Walton Terminal Building
at the Northwest Arkansas Regional Airport.
Source: Northwest Arkansas Tourism Association, *Northwest Arkansas Ozarks: Where
America Does Business with Pleasure*, 2008.
Collection of the author.

dining areas, public spaces, and event facilities are built into the sides of a small ravine and organized around a rechanneled portion of the creek that flows through the site.

Visitors enter through a corridor from the south entrance or from a courtyard connected to the main entrance and parking area. The entry lobby leads to galleries containing works from the colonial period to the nineteenth century; semicircular in plan, the galleries are built into the hill with an outdoor terrace at the center. The two "bridges" that give the museum its name span the reflecting pools formed by the rechanneled Crystal Creek. The upper bridge contains the restaurant, and the lower one houses two galleries featuring art from the early twentieth century. Concrete walls with exterior wood stripes define the galleries and support the roof assembly, which is made of laminated timber beams and finished with stripes of glass and copper cladding.[41] The two bridges employ an elaborate suspension system that supports large glue-laminated ribs, from which the lateral glass walls are hung. The resulting column-free spaces allow visitors views upstream and downstream, although the lower bridge also contains two large rectangular gallery volumes.

Crystal Bridges is infrastructural in ambition if not also in scale. The completed reflecting pool and mature vegetation disguise the infrastructural idiom of the project, something especially apparent during construction. The site work necessary to divert Crystal Creek and to situate the building's elements within the ravine required substantial feats of civil engineering, as did the construction of the weirs built to control water levels and the massive abutments for the project's eponymous gallery bridges. All these elements use thick walls, expressed cables, articulated hardware, and simple concrete geometry suggesting material efficiency, and together they conjure the charismatic forms of WPA-era infrastructure projects. Safdie, in describing the project, has suggested that "the dam is the floor and the bridge is a roof."[42] With Alice Walton's blessing, Safdie sought to embed the project into the landscape rather than crown one of the area's many ridges. In this sense, like infrastructure, Crystal Bridges is shielded in approach, and its size is revealed gradually and in different ways, depending on how one approaches it. While the bridges provide museumgoers with iconic

Under construction and with the creek diverted, the Crystal Bridges site could be mistaken for an infrastructure project. This view looks south to the restaurant bridge abutments. Photograph by the author.

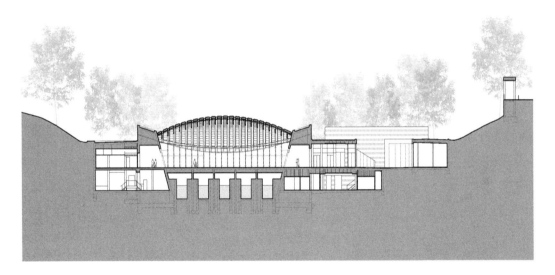

As Crystal Bridges is situated at the base of a ravine and over a creek, visitors descend into it. This transverse section through the valley, upper bridge, and weir illustrates the degree to which the building is embedded in its site. Courtesy of Safdie Architects.

forms, they are the only parts of the museum that are recognizable as discrete elements, as the rest is built into the ravine. Some critics have suggested that the bridges, while legible forms, are confused in terms of their purpose, citing the awkwardness of the two white boxes that needed to be built inside the lower bridge to house and display examples from the museum's early twentieth-century collection.[43] In terms of area, the galleries of the museum take up roughly half of the space. The rest of the building's functions include a restaurant, a café, event spaces, a children's space, a library, an art outreach space, a gift shop (designed by Marlon Blackwell), and an outdoor amphitheater. The Walton Family Foundation has endowed the museum with a grant of $800 million to support operations and acquisitions.

Close to downtown Bentonville and the Walmart Museum, Crystal Bridges is also located in Alice Walton's childhood backyard—and not just in the sense that she grew up in the area. Her family home (which Sam Walton commissioned from Fay Jones) spans the same creek as Crystal Bridges, just upstream and out of sight of the museum. This biographical fact helps to explain what might seem, at first glance, to be a counterintuitive location for a major art institution. The museum's location suggests that Walton's motives are personal as much as they are philanthropic. And while the museum attracts its share of visitors, one cannot but wonder if another location would more effectively fulfill the mission of the museum to provide a venue for art exposure to a constituency otherwise limited in access. In the same way that Sam Walton domesticated the personal aircraft by using it "pretty much like a station wagon," and the way that corporate office space is domesticated in the various vendorville complexes, Alice Walton has attempted to domesticate the art museum. Built in the woods in which she was raised and endowed to such an extent that admission will always be free, Crystal Bridges offers a utilitarian approach to artistic consumption in which it is presented as a resource available to all and as a potential part of everyday life.

If America's attenuated settlement patterns have been challenged for their dearth of cultural institutions, then Walton's creation of Crystal Bridges offers a potent counterexample.[44] The institutional patrons of the past were often located in cities, not just out of choice

While the water obscures the full extent of the
site work involved with Crystal Bridges, the
infrastructural idiom of the project remains
apparent in these views of the completed
upper bridge and restaurant, primary outdoor
gathering space, and water retention system.
Photographs by the author.

but also out of necessity. Furthermore, in the case of cultural institutions there is also the need for an audience, making urban concentrations desirable for museums because of the assured presence of visitors. While intense concentrations of wealth are able to override certain circumstantial constraints, the question of access remains. In its opening year, Crystal Bridges hosted 650,000 visitors; in 2013 and 2014, the numbers dipped slightly, to 506,000 and 533,000, respectively. By comparison, the J. Paul Getty Museum in Los Angeles, a similar institution in terms of patronage, received almost 1.8 million visitors in 2014. If one compares total visitors to estimated populations of the respective metropolitan statistical areas, the Getty has a visitation rate of 13.5 percent while Crystal Bridges has a rate of 108 percent, meaning more people visited the museum in 2014 than actually live in the region. In 2014, of the more than 500,000 visitors to Crystal Bridges, 36 percent hailed from the four counties surrounding Bentonville (which constitute a large part of the NWA MSA). While 28 percent of visitors came from bordering states, almost 19 percent came from elsewhere in the country.[45]

Crystal Bridges is part of a larger redevelopment effort that hopes to attract new tourists to the region, but there is a significant asymmetry between institutional scope and local constituencies. In this sense, Crystal Bridges is designed as much to attract audiences as to produce them, and its location in the dispersed metropolitan region of Northwest Arkansas, with its large regional population, seems well suited for such an institution. It privileges no group in particular yet is available to many. The museum is thus conceptualized as both a regional attraction and a growth catalyst that happens to be in Bentonville. Given Walmart's success at accommodating a "pull" economy in which consumer demand dictates growth decisions, it is surprising to see Crystal Bridges "pushing" its supply onto a public that may or may not be interested. However, in the same way that Walmart can effectively produce desire in its consumers, Alice Walton may succeed in creating new groups around her museum. Rather than the cultural institution being a product of urbanization, the institution comes first, with the hope that the city will follow. For example, in the 2014–15 season, Crystal Bridges hosted the exhibition *State of the Art: Discovering*

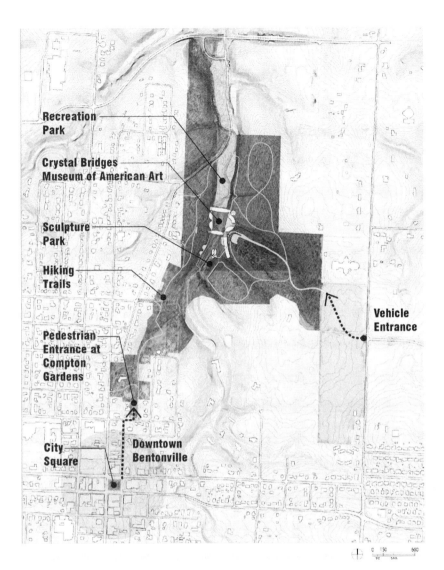

Recreation Park

Crystal Bridges Museum of American Art

Sculpture Park

Hiking Trails

Pedestrian Entrance at Compton Gardens

City Square

Downtown Bentonville

Vehicle Entrance

0 150 600

NEVER
A GENERAL ADMISSION FEE
THANKS TO

Walmart ☀

TOP: Site plan of Crystal Bridges, indicating the proximity of the museum to downtown Bentonville. Alice Walton's childhood home (designed by Fay Jones) is represented as the rotated L-shaped figure next to the pond upstream, just south of the museum. Courtesy of Safdie Architects.

LEFT: Wall display at Crystal Bridges acknowledging that admission to the museum is free because of a grant from Walmart Stores, Inc. Photograph by the author.

American Art Now in an effort to create an image of the museum as concerned with American art production throughout the country. As the nature of Walmart's operation is global and its sites of production are dispersed, there is no single community to which these resources might be directed. Instead, Crystal Bridges becomes a pilgrimage site and a potential growth catalyst, using Walton's patronage in an effort to attract a mobile cosmopolitan population. In downtown Bentonville, the former Walmart Visitor Center has been remodeled and redesigned as the Walmart Museum. Like the earlier version, it includes the restored storefront of Walton's 5–10, Sam Walton's pickup truck, and his office. The space includes a gallery that features streamlined and consistent corporate exhibitions that present the company's history and its work around the world in buoyant and confident tones. The Spark Café, attached to the museum and similar in ambition, attempts to conjure the historical moment in which Walton started his company through sanitized references and familiar, untroubled narratives. Visitors pour in to learn more about the company that has helped make the Walton family one of the world's wealthiest.[46]

The changing demographics of Northwest Arkansas are apparent in the area called Pinnacle Hills, home to a combination of shopping centers, housing developments, conference facilities, office spaces, discount retail, hotels, and megachurches. Situated along Interstate 540 on the way to the Walmart home office from the Northwest Arkansas Regional Airport, the Pinnacle Hills development contains a range of functions and services that offer discrete experiences. One can shop for groceries at the Walmart Neighborhood Market, be entertained at the Pinnacle Hills Promenade (an open-air shopping complex managed by General Growth Properties), worship at Cross Church, do business at one of the many office buildings, attend a conference at the Embassy Suites Convention Center, and receive medical treatment at the Mercy Medical Center. All the elements are clustered between two exits on I-540 and, though justified in terms of business traffic, primarily serve the region's local population. In spite of the area's dependence on personal automobiles to reach the various destinations, once there, many of these buildings and complexes support a high degree of activity and density of visitors.

TOP LEFT: Bentonville City Square, north side. Arvest Bank, of which Sam Walton's son Jim is chairman and CEO, is the largest bank in the state. Photograph by the author.

TOP RIGHT: Bentonville City Square, east side, location of the Benton County Courthouse. Photograph by the author.

BOTTOM LEFT: Bentonville City Square, south side. Photograph by the author.

BOTTOM RIGHT: Bentonville City Square, west side, including the Walmart Museum (at left) and reconstruction of the storefront of the original Walton's 5–10. Photograph by the author.

From the air, a lone Walmart Neighborhood Market is visible at the edge of the development. Constructed in anticipation of a sizable housing development known as The District at Pinnacle Hills, the store still sits alone because of a foreclosure suit filed against the developers in early 2010. The location of the Walmart is a reminder of the sequence in which these areas are produced: even before the infrastructure is installed for a housing development, a store is completed and opened nearby. The federal highway that splits the Pinnacle Hills project currently ends before crossing into Missouri and reverts to U.S. Route 71. Twenty miles later it beefs up again, only to die out at Joplin, Missouri. If this corridor were completed, there would be a continuous interstate connection between Kansas City and New Orleans. The central location of the area combined with the historically reliable success of Walmart was enough to convince powerful national developers such as John Q. Hammons and J. B. Hunt to invest in the Pinnacle Hills project. The W Hotel subsidiary chain Aloft opened an outpost in Pinnacle Hills in 2008 to cater to what the company saw as an underserved consumer group. As Walmart's merchandising increasingly influences other organs of popular culture, suppliers are obliged to forge ever-tighter relationships. Representatives from New York–based media groups like Nickelodeon and Comedy Central fly to Northwest Arkansas on a regular basis to discuss future cross-branding opportunities with Walmart executives. When they come to meet with Walmart, they stay at the Aloft hotel in Pinnacle Hills, where the bartenders know them by name.

The NWA MSA presents an emerging form of global urbanity that results from the numerous forces coalescing in Northwest Arkansas, largely due to Walmart's presence in the region. Although still in its adolescence, it is a form defined by logistics, by mercantilism, and by a commitment to promoting the value of the free market not just as a means to profit but also as a belief system and as a way of life. By taking advantage of the protocols and priorities required by its distribution network, Walmart has helped to establish an emerging territorial order whose settlement patterns and urban conditions are not defined in relation to a historically legible city. And while the forms that are emerging might not appear to be city-like, they are urban

The Walmart Museum and soda fountain in Bentonville City Square at night. Photograph by the author.

Sam Walton's office is preserved and on display in the Walmart Museum. Photograph by the author.

nonetheless. The concentration of corporate emissaries in the vendorville developments supports a mobile class of residents who bring with them new habits and desires. The production of new cultural infrastructure through largely private means provides leverage for a spate of new developments and strategic repositioning. The region is also a test bed for new Walmart formats such as Walmart Express and Walmart 2 Go. Buoyed by the managerial fervor that characterizes Walmart, the Bentonville Community and Economic Development Office, in conjunction with the Northwest Arkansas Council, has been involved in a series of urban planning initiatives, including "Bentonville Blueprint 2014" by Boyette Group, as well as a series of design proposals from Hight-Jackson Associates. While these diligent efforts to create a compact, walkable city proceed, an unimageable urbanism wrought by logistics—in which underspecified means produce overspecified conditions—circles around them. The region, for all its gestures toward publicness, is on the verge of becoming fully privatized at the hands of its patrons, a new citadel of logistics.

Aerial view of the Pinnacle Hills development, Rogers, Arkansas. The complex includes an outdoor shopping center, hospital, church (lower left), hotels, and convention facilities. A new Walmart, awaiting the completion of the adjacent housing development, is discernible in the upper right corner. Photograph by the author.

CONCLUSION

Form, Happiness, Infrastructure

THE INVESTIGATIONS INTO THE OPERATIONS of Walmart that led to this book have been part of an effort to understand more fully the general features of an emerging architecture of logistics. The industry, as both area of work and field of knowledge, has escaped the confines of its formally designated zones and is increasingly influencing the ways buildings are built, how maps are drawn, how urban sites grow, how cultural institutions are formed, and how subjects are constructed. While the focus here is a large and influential corporate entity, the intersections of architecture and urbanism with issues of control, measurement, prediction, risk, and privatization that a study of Walmart engages are increasingly common features of the globalized conditions of the early twenty-first century. This project developed through the conviction that research into contemporary aspects of architecture and the built environment can support formal and spatial invention while still probing assumptions about the capacities of architecture to provoke, enable, or participate in political, social, and cultural transformations.

Walmart, while the largest example of a retail logistics enterprise, remains one of many. The logistical techniques that Walmart uses mediate between the abstracting managerial protocols of calculation and the specific contingencies of locality. A growing range of technologies allows this, and these technologies are absorbed, collected, and deployed through a repertoire of intertwined built forms. All of this together contributes to the formation of what I have been calling the logistical. At the urban level, the logistical challenges the idea of an "image" of the "city" but allows understanding through form, territory, and topology. At the building level, the logistical privileges concerns of performance, transmission, and flexibility over form, content, and legibility. In terms of inhabitation, the logistical places the body between physical and informational systems. Taken together, the logistical and the conditions it creates mediate between the general protocols of management, control, and calculation and the contingencies of the specific, asking architecture to absorb risk. At the same time, these protocols, as they become increasingly linked to questions of automation and optimized locations and timing, begin to introduce a set of criteria not linked to the historical conditions under which urban spaces developed. In other words, with the emergence of data-driven decision making, the possibilities for counterintuitive results increase; the outcomes are at times surprising and thrilling and at times more disturbing. What is perhaps worth considering is the degree to which these conditions, although indirectly wrought by human agents, are increasingly illegible and undetectable. If we can no longer read what we have written, the questions might then concern some of the assumptions, consequences, risks, and opportunities that inhabiting this wilderness of our own making might offer.

One site of investigation involves the formal, spatial, and material aspects of architectural expression itself. The logistical repeatedly presents a version of architectural form that is both plastic and blank. Driven not by an overt tectonic expression of material or by pursuit of volumetric specificity, the logistical architecture looked at here engages questions of continuity and format that would not be out of place in debates around the nature of typology. The prototypes that Walmart deploys might be instructively decomposed as "proto-types" that occupy a space between the type and the model (or between "case study" and "precedent"), possessing aspects of each while still existing comfortably as their own category. Formal and formless, literal and abstract, the logistical proto-type does not necessarily possess charismatic formal qualities, yet its approach is potent and flexible.[1]

In the case of Walmart's buildings, speed and cost are determining factors, but the company's procedures, when translated into other contexts, could develop into a contingent and adaptable architecture of loose forms, attendant to specific means of realization but not insistent on their outcomes. An architecture of loose forms holds fast to certain relationships while allowing others to be reshaped. The same is true for sites themselves. Indeed, it is difficult to separate Walmart's buildings from their sites, connected as they are by the retailer's continuous and precise logistical operations. The prototype presents a nimble design approach but not an improvisational one. As with the rest of Walmart's operations, every move is calculated, only in different phases. The marketing, distribution, and replenishment demands of the stores require strict adherence to a prototypical floor plan. However, as each design can be completed only through its instantiation in a specific site, there is room to negotiate between the particulars of location and the requirements of Walmart's logistical operations. The prototype, in other words, provides the slack necessary to allow a rigid system to adapt to a range of unexpected situations while keeping the emphasis on performance.

As the prototype is just one piece of a system, it suggests ways of embedding architecture with certain biases that in turn could affect things beyond them. Through Walmart's logistical approach to architecture, the prototype takes on new potency and capacity because—through its incompleteness, slack, or looseness—it can mediate between the controlled aspirations of its sponsor and the contingent world of its surroundings. As opposed to more rigid proposals that could succeed only in their pure form, the prototype, by not insisting on the purity or specificity of its order, requires a certain amount of disorder. By definition it exists in compromised states; in fact, it seems to thrive in them. As architecture will increasingly be operating in such conditions, this model suggests a way to approach them that can adapt to the stresses of unexpected situations while preserving the internal aspirations of the designers. With an arsenal of loose forms, architecture might operate collectively rather than in a singular manner. Moreover, a prototype's encounter with specificity can often yield a product instead of just a sum as the interaction between site and format catalyzes unpredictable and hybridized outcomes. Architecture as a process of elaborating boundary conditions is supplanted by an infrastructural system of deployable prototypes imbued with geopolitical agency. The formats, not buildings, that Walmart's architects develop are further refined as the prototypes acquire specificity only through their instantiation. The retailer's hybrid approach to constructed environments—its deployment of buildings as fungible components of distribution networks—dissolves certain well-worn distinctions and results in buildings and landscapes that operate in both architectural and infrastructural registers. The company's pragmatic approach to territory—its use of buildings as political tools to circumvent narrow legislative constraints—suggests that architecture can acquire a new potency when coordinated skillfully and in sufficient quantity. The use of these elements is enabled by larger shifts in territorial perception as a result of logistical vision. As places—the objects of this vision—become increasingly rendered as statistics, the spaces they inhabit are also increasingly abstracted. Territory thus becomes a field of data to be manipulated, but the residue of these operations suggests other ways to occupy and develop the city in terms of mobility, settlement, and culture.

Walmart is a company that has defined itself through its expertise in logistics. It is a company that through a combination of ambition, determination, cruelty, and flexibility has become the largest on the planet and, in the words of Fredric Jameson, "the purest expression of that dynamic of capitalism which devours itself, which abolishes the market by means of the market itself."[2] Walmart has done this, in large part, through its command of logistics and its infusion of the logistical into all aspects of its operations. The logistical informs the way Walmart designs its buildings, the ways in which it draws maps to locate those buildings, and the ways in which it establishes control over those who work in them. The slippery qualities of the logistical are apparent even in Walmart's slogan/mission statement/mantra, "Saving people money so they can live better," a phrase that operates as both alibi and justification for the retailer's activities. The slogan is based on the (assumed to be self-evident) pro-market premise that having more money increases an individual's life quality, a correlation that scholars of happiness have not found to be especially consistent.[3]

As the spaces of distribution become more nimble and more flexible,

they increasingly offer a plausible glimpse into the spatial consequences of instant gratification. In fact, a materials handling company
formerly called Kiva Systems, now Amazon Robotics (since its purchase in 2012 by Amazon for $775 million), has even figured out a way
to arrange the floor of a distribution center around a similar ethic of
effortless acquisition—that is, to bring things to people, rather than
the other way around.[4] This approach replaces conveyors with small
robotic drive units (RDUs) that transport "inventory pods" to picking
stations, where workers take items from one rack and put them on
another for eventual packing and shipping. A series of algorithms control the robots, searching for the required inventory pods and directing
the nearest units to them. A grid of two-dimensional bar codes on the
warehouse floor provides checkpoints for the robots and controls their
movements to ensure a smooth flow of traffic to the picking stations.
As opposed to the conveyor-based model, in which inventory is hierar-
chically managed and placed in predictable locations, the robotic system does not require that objects be fixed in space. Because the RDUs
can reach any point in the warehouse, and because their movements
can be calibrated to eliminate traffic interference, the distribution of
goods in the warehouse is constantly changing based on what customers are ordering. The warehouses occupied by RDUs are immense
by human standards, but that size does not matter except in terms
of duration—the farther an inventory item is from a picker, the more
slowly the order is fulfilled. The algorithms governing the locations
of inventory items register desirability and frequency of requests and
keep the most wanted items close to the front; less desired items are
pushed out toward the edges. While these classification designations
and locations are understandable to the RDUs and the algorithms that
control them, the resulting environment is a homogeneous jumble to
human viewers.

The logistics paradigm of inventory systems based on conveyors
and regulated by bar codes like the UPC might be deemed notational
for these systems' control of the exact paths of things through space
and time. Notational logistics relies on routine: objects follow the
same paths over and over again. However, while no less concerned
with getting inventory from one place to another, the logistics of the

two-dimensional bar code is more algorithmic, because it controls operations through formulas contingent on the specific requirements at any given moment. Notational logistics follows a deductive, top-down route in which a plan is designed and executed repeatedly. With an algorithmic logistics, certain constraints are determined, but the process is allowed to unfold in unanticipated ways, perhaps even ways that exceed the intuition of the designers. In a warehouse using RDUs, for example, what seems like a muddle makes sense to the computer systems organizing it. However, for all the sophistication behind the design of such a responsive system, the form and performance of the distribution center floor are dependent on the fickle and often irrational desires of consumers. The fluid constitution and configuration of the inventory is a dynamic index of consumer demand mediated through the bar code and mapped onto space, all fueled by extensive transportation and information networks: the pursuit of better living through logistics.

But does the ability to obtain objects of desire quickly and easily actually generate happiness? In the emerging field of happiness studies, scholars divide measures of happiness into three basic categories: "momentary feelings of joy and pleasure, . . . overall contentment with life, . . . [and] the quality of life achieved by developing and fulfilling one's potential, which has been called *eudaimonia* or 'the good life.'"[5] While conclusions that "individuals tend to make systematic errors when choosing between alternatives" and that "happiness in the sense of subjective well-being doesn't seem to rise systematically with income" might not seem surprising, their emergence within institutional discourse is significant.[6] After all, the "pursuit of happiness" is inscribed as an inalienable right in the Declaration of Independence and forms a fundamental feature of economic identity in the United States. Even more, mainstream economics still largely assumes that consumers behave to "maximize utility, and that utility increases with the individual's consumption."[7] Such beliefs have allowed economic growth to become a major policy imperative—enabled and reinforced by the logistics systems discussed here. However, if the findings from happiness studies were to have some influence, these policies and their attendant logistics networks might change, triggering subsequent transformations in the ways consumable items are bought, sold, marketed, measured, and managed.

Contemporary algorithmic logistics orchestrates hedonic landscapes of desire as customers pursue happiness. Logistics could instead play a role in the development of a eudaemonistic landscape, a landscape of fulfillment, but this will not emerge through the current version of logistics as a military-industrial practice driven by measure, control, calculation, and prediction, because that version of the industry is too fundamentally conditioned by its sources. A great many people and organizations are invested in keeping the world's stuff flowing. These motives underpin much of what we have come to understand as globalization and what Cowen calls "neoliberal forms of bio-, necro-, and anti-political calculation where cost-benefit analysis and assumptions of market efficiency are embedded into its basic techniques."[8] These tendencies continue to exert influence in urban design with the emergence of data-driven decision-making processes, especially around discussions of big data and the industry involved in the development of "smart cities."[9] For its many accomplishments, data-driven planning and design, broadly speaking, is a goal-oriented pursuit intent on solving specific problems. As an approach to dealing with urban questions, it has generally not yet been able to furnish an adequate alternative to "efficiency" or "optimization." As is apparent in a number of "smart city" developments, the technological fantasies projected onto the built environment tend to reinforce many of the same kinds of impulses toward instant gratification and privatization evident in Walmart's logistical operations. Contemporary architectural research provides numerous examples of buildings and other built environments organized and deployed with aggressive geopolitical intent. Examples of similar means directed to different ends are more rare. If the logistical tends toward data-driven optimization and solving for efficiency of cost and speed, or if the capacity of logistical architecture to act beyond itself is most evident when that architecture colludes with efforts toward growth and dominance, other possibilities remain worth considering.

As only one thought among many alternatives, consider infrastructure as a way to advance the principles of logistics in pursuit of larger collective aims. As a site of common use, stewardship, and shared possibility, infrastructure is one of the few sites of collective investment in the United States. As discussed in this volume's introduction, infrastructure tends to be invisible and taken for granted. Its own design features and typologies also are, generally speaking, undertheorized and underdeveloped. Authorship of infrastructure has been historically diffuse, and its design is often a product of large bureaucratic conditions. As a result of this diffusion, infrastructural systems can quickly acquire aspects of permanence and perceived self-evidence. However, territorial organization, largely supported by infrastructural presence, is not a given; rather, it is something often imposed on inhabitants. Infrastructure conditions the sets of choices available, but its use is neither permanent nor self-evident. Often owing to historical circumstances, bureaucracies have installed large-scale infrastructural systems relatively quickly, only to discover that undoing their negative effects can be difficult. Such processes contribute to a world that is increasingly overdetermined, as do our own data-producing habits.

If options and alternatives are becoming more elusive, cultivating new forms of imagination is as important as ever. Infrastructures, and the logistical processes they support, are generally underspecified systems capable of being read, used, and appropriated in a range of ways. For example, before 1967 in Sweden, motorists used the left lane, as in England. For many Swedes, this condition raised a number of regulatory, safety, and commercial concerns. A governmental resolution initiated the process of change, and—after a gradually intensifying media-supported educational campaign, including a song contest, various logos, commemorative merchandise, and virtually nonstop television coverage leading up to the shift—the country's drivers, suddenly and all at once, switched to the other side of the road.[10] At 4:50 a.m. on September 3, 1967, everyone on the roads in the entire country stopped driving, quietly changed lanes, waited, and then, ten minutes later, started moving again.

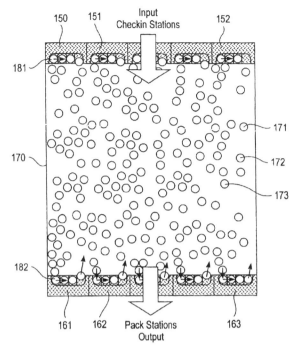

Input
Checkin Stations

150   151   152

181

170

171

172

173

182

161   162   Pack Stations   163
Output

Coordinating software determines the paths for robotic drive units used in distribution centers; RDUs do not follow fixed paths. Source: Distrobot Systems, "Material handling system and method using mobile autonomous inventory trays and peer-to-peer communications," U.S. Patent 6,950,722 B2, 2005, 8.

Kungsgatan in Stockholm, Sweden, on September 3, 1967, the day road traffic switched from the left lane to the right. Photograph by Jan Collsiöö.

ACKNOWLEDGMENTS

THIS BOOK HAS BENEFITED from the help and support of many people and institutions. I would like to thank the Graham Foundation for its assistance in funding the production of the book. The ETH Department of Architecture has also generously provided financial support.

Pieter Martin at the University of Minnesota Press has been incredibly helpful in shepherding the book through its development. I am tremendously grateful for his enthusiasm, support, and acuity. I also thank Kristian Tvedten for his tireless efforts in the preparation of the project and Judy Selhorst for her keen editorial eye. Thanks as well to Laura Westlund and Rachel Moeller at the Press and to Kitty Chibnik for the index. Jonathan Massey and an anonymous reader both offered excellent and demanding feedback during the review process, for which I am most appreciative.

I thank the outstanding students who helped with drawing production and illustration permissions: Jon Swendris and Rennie Jones at the University of Michigan and Eric Bieber, Frank DeBlasio, Kevin McIlmail, and Mila Popow at the School of Architecture at New Jersey Institute of Technology.

The book would not have been possible without the kindness of a number of people who contributed during the research, including Patrick Kennedy at the Troy Historical Society; Christopher Ratliff in Special Collections at the University of Memphis Library; Ed Stanesa at Safdie Architects; and Bill Selmeier, one of the inventors of the UPC. Bill Correll at Walmart deserves special thanks for his generous assistance.

The project began at the ETH Zurich under the professorship of Marc Angélil, who has my heartfelt thanks for his role as my adviser, for his support of the project, and for the opportunity he gave me to be part of the teaching team in Zurich. I cannot thank Keller Easterling enough for her generosity in supporting the project as a secondary adviser. Laurent Stalder at the ETH, the third reader, was amazingly helpful, thoughtful, and challenging in his appraisal of the project. My work improved thanks to friends and colleagues at the ETH: Zegeye Cherenet, Victoria Easton, Dirk Hebel, Rainer Hehl, Tanja Herdt, Jørg Himmelreich, Marion Kalmer, Bisrat Kifle, Lukas Küng, Forrest Meggers, Guillaume Mojon, Cary Siress, Katrina Stoll, Jörg Stollmann, and Benjamin Theiler. Navigating the university would not have been possible without the help of Zwi Kutner and Linda Christensen. Special thanks go to Reto Geiser, Annina Ludwig, and Deane Simpson. The completion of the dissertation on which this book is based was made possible by a grant from the Swiss National Science Foundation.

While I was a researcher at the ETH Future Cities Laboratory in Singapore, my work benefited from input and discussions with Stephen Cairns, Kees Christiaanse, Ludger Hovestadt, Ben Leclair-Paquet, Alex Lehnerer, and Milica Topalovic. I also conducted research as a visiting scholar at the Graduate School of Architecture, Planning, and Preservation at Columbia University through the support of Felicity Scott. Many thanks to her, Laurie Hawkinson, Reinhold Martin, Kazys Varnelis, and Mark Wasiuta.

As the Walter B. Sanders Fellow at the University of Michigan, I could not have asked for a more stimulating and engaging environment, largely due to the intellectual and personal generosity of McLain Clutter, Andrew Herscher, Irene Hwang, Nahyun Hwang, John McMorrough, Meredith Miller, Keith Mitnick, Monica Ponce de Leon, Rosalyne Shieh, Jason Young, Claire Zimmerman, and especially Thom Moran. In parallel, I participated in an experimental project called the Poiesis Fellowship, instigated by Richard Sennett and Craig Calhoun with the support of the BMW Foundation, the Herbert Quandt Foundation, and the Institute for Public Knowledge at New York University. I thank the organizers as well as Markus Hipp, Kerstin Meerwaldt, and the other advisers, Ash Amin, Peter Claussen, Gerald Frug, Birgit Meyer, and Saskia Sassen. Nerea Calvillo, Orit Halpern, and Wolfgang Pietsch were stimulating and challenging collaborators for whom I have much appreciation and gratitude. Thanks as well to Hillary Angelo, Naresh Fernandes, Monika Krause, Clapperton Mavhunga,

Michael McQuarrie, Harel Shapira, and Cassim Shepard, all of whom made for a lively set of interlocutors.

In my current position as assistant professor at the School of Architecture at New Jersey Institute of Technology, I have the good fortune to work with a number of outstanding colleagues, many of whom helped shape this project in significant ways. My thanks to Gabrielle Esperdy, Karen Franck, Richard Garber, Dean Urs Gauchat, Julianne Gola-Papa, María Hurtado de Mendoza, Keith Krumwiede, Michael Mostoller, Rhett Russo, Julia Sedlock, Jae Shin, Tony Schuman, Georgeen Theodore, and Steve Zdepski.

I had the opportunity to test different parts of this work in articles and presentations, and I am thankful for thoughts and feedback from Mathew Aitchison, Lucia Allais, Brennan Buck, Angela Co, Penelope Dean, Alexander Eisenschmidt, Daniela Fabricius, Salomon Frausto, Iker Gil, James Graham, Sarah Graham, Roger Horowitz, Ersela Kripa, Nancy Levinson, Clare Lyster, Stephen Mueller, Sina Najafi, Michael Osman, Michael Piper, Albert Pope, Jonathan Solomon, Richard Sommer, Bob Somol, Irene Sunwoo, Meredith TenHoor, Neyran Turan, Jesse Vogler, and Robert Wiesenberger. John Harwood deserves more thanks than I can give for his help at countless points along the way.

Without this project, I am not sure I would have met Tei Carpenter. In that sense, it has been life changing. My gratitude to her is inexpressible.

This book is dedicated to my parents, John and Rebecca LeCavalier.

NOTES

Introduction

1. International Council of Shopping Centers, "RECon: Poised for Progress—The Global Retail Real Estate Convention," official program, May 23–25, 2010, 172.

2. Ibid., 179.

3. Cass Gilbert, "The Financial Importance of Rapid Building," *Engineering Record* 41, no. 26 (1900): 624.

4. Ibid.

5. William Cronon, *Nature's Metropolis: Chicago and the Great West* (New York: W. W. Norton, 1992), 226.

6. "We Love Logistics" commercial for UPS, accessed May 28, 2014, http://youtu.be/VCh6HnXHKRc.

7. James A. Huston, *The Sinews of War: Army Logistics 1775–1953* (Washington, D.C.: Office of the Chief of Military History, U.S. Army, 1970), viii.

8. Deborah Cowen, "A Geography of Logistics: Market Authority and the Security of Supply Chains," *Annals of the Association of American Geographers* 100, no. 3 (2010): 600–620.

9. In her study of logistics and borders, Deborah Cowen notes: "If it is the security of efficient trade flows that animates maritime security today, then the interference that comes from 'inefficiencies' like democracy, and the actors that demand it, might themselves be construed as security threats." Ibid., 616.

10. For more on spaces of logistics, see Keller Easterling, "The New Orgman: Logistics as an Organizing Principle of Contemporary Cities," in *The Cybercities Reader,* ed. Stephen Graham (London: Routledge, 2004), 179–84. For further reading, see Clare Lyster, "Landscapes of Exchange: Re-articulating Site," in *The Landscape Urbanism Reader,* ed. Charles Waldheim (New York: Princeton Architectural Press, 2006), 219–38; Charles Waldheim and Alan Berger, "Logistics Landscape," *Landscape Journal* 27 (2008): 226; Jesse LeCavalier, "The Restlessness of Objects," *Cabinet,* no. 47, "Logistics" (Fall 2012): 90–97.

11. Zygmunt Bauman, *Liquid Modernity* (Cambridge: Polity Press, 2000), 13.

12. See, for example, Wiebe E. Bijker, Thomas Parke Hughes, and T. J. Pinch, eds., *The Social Construction of Technological Systems: New Directions in the Sociology and History of Technology* (Cambridge: MIT Press, 2012). See also Wiebe E. Bijker, *Of Bicycles, Bakelites, and Bulbs: Toward a Theory of Sociotechnical Change* (Cambridge: MIT Press, 1997); Thomas J. Misa, Philip Brey, and Andrew Feenberg, eds., *Modernity and Technology* (Cambridge: MIT Press, 2003).

13. As early as 1960, Reyner Banham warned: "The architect who proposes to run with technology knows now that he will be in fast company, and that, in order to keep up, he may have to emulate the Futurists and discard his whole cultural load, including the professional garments by which he is recognized as an architect. If, on the other hand, he decides not to do this, he may find that a technological culture has decided to go on without him." Reyner Banham, *Theory and Design in the First Machine Age* (Cambridge: MIT Press, 1960), 329–30.

14. Walmart, "Corporate and Financial Facts," accessed April 26, 2015, http://news.walmart.com.

15. "Global 500 2011," CNN Money, accessed October 29, 2012, http://money.cnn.com/magazines/fortune/global500/2011/full_list; Walmart, "Walmart Stores, Inc. Data Sheet—Worldwide Unit Details January 2012," accessed October 29, 2012, http://news.walmart.com/news-archive/2012/02/22/Walmart-stores-inc-data-sheet-worldwide-unit-details-january-2012. Global retail data from "2011 Top 250 Global Retails," Stores.org, online magazine of the National Retail Federation, accessed March 10, 2013, http://www.stores.org/2011/Top-250-List#.UUShHtGgk5d.

16. Quoted in Andrea Lillo, "Wal-Mart Gains Strength from Distribution Chain," *Home Textiles Today*, March 24, 2003.

17. Charles Fishman describes Walmart as "carefully disguised as something ordinary, familiar, even prosaic. . . . But, in fact, Wal-Mart is a completely new kind of institution: modern, advanced, potent in ways we've never seen before. . . . Wal-Mart has outgrown the rules—but no one noticed." Charles Fishman, *The Wal-Mart Effect: How the World's Most Powerful Company Really Works—and How It's Transforming the American Economy* (New York: Penguin Press, 2006), 221–22.

18. Sociologist and port labor expert Edna Bonacich points to a "major change that has been occurring over the last thirty years in the way goods are produced and delivered" and goes on to identify this change as "the logistics revolution, a revolution that has been led by Wal-Mart Stores Inc." Edna Bonacich with Khaleelah Hardie, "Wal-Mart and the Logistics Revolution," in *Wal-Mart: The Face of Twenty-First-Century Capitalism*, ed. Nelson Lichtenstein (New York: New Press, 2006), 163.

19. For detailed discussions of some of these issues, see Bob Ortega, *In Sam*

We Trust: The Untold Story of Sam Walton and Wal-Mart, the World's Most Powerful Retailer (New York: Times Business, 1998); Fishman, *The Wal-Mart Effect.*

20. As Sandra Vance and Roy Scott note: "By 1975 some 80 percent of all of Wal-Mart's merchandise flowed through its distribution facilities. The remaining 20 percent continued to go directly from suppliers to the individual stores. Because the distribution centers could handle large orders and make use of cheap modes of transportation, they created a sizable savings for the firm. . . . The centers also provided speedier and more certain deliveries to stores. By assuring individual stores of resupply from a central, company-owned facility, Wal-Mart could better control its inventory." Sandra S. Vance and Roy V. Scott, *Wal-Mart: A History of Sam Walton's Retail Phenomenon* (New York: Twayne, 1994), 71. For a discussion of Walmart's need to create its own distribution channels, in part because other transport companies were not interested in operating at the edges of town, see Natalie Berg and Bryan Roberts, *Walmart: Key Insights and Practical Lessons from the World's Largest Retailer* (London: Kogan Page, 2012).

21. This thinking is reflected in the quotations from company leaders displayed on the walls of the Walmart Visitor Center in Bentonville, Arkansas, when I visited there in July 2006. Former CEO David Glass: "Our distribution facilities are one of the keys to our success. If we do anything better than other folks, that's it." Then-current CEO Lee Scott: "From the time Sam Walton founded the company and established our first distribution center and our trucking fleet, he understood logistics as an integral part of Wal-Mart's success." In an interview, Walmart's chief architect, William Correll, stated, "Operational needs rule. . . . Productivity and efficiency are at the very center of what we're trying to accomplish." Jesse LeCavalier, "Interview with Bill Correll, Architect of Walmart," *archithese* (November/December 2007): 32–33 (this interview was conducted on July 31, 2006).

22. This is a common approach in retail, but Walmart's scale of operations sets it apart from competitors.

23. See, for example, Constance L. Hays, "What Wal-Mart Knows about Customers' Habits," *New York Times*, November 14, 2004, http://www.nytimes.com.

24. Sam Walton with John Huey, *Sam Walton: Made in America—My Story* (New York: Bantam, 1992), 272.

25. See, for example, Sanford Kwinter and Daniela Fabricius, "Generica," in *Mutations* (Barcelona: ACTAR, 2001).

26. *Walmart 2014 Annual Report,* http://stock.walmart.com.

27. For more on some aspects of Walmart's real estate approach, see Ellen Dunham-Jones, "Temporary Contracts: On the Economy of the Post-industrial Landscape," *Harvard Design Magazine*, no. 3 (Fall 1997).

28. Walmart Private Fleet, "Statistics," accessed March 22, 2015, http://walmartprivatefleet.com; Walmart, "Our Story," accessed January 12, 2016, http://corporate.walmart.com/our-story/our-business/logistics.

29. Floor manager of DC 6094, Bentonville, Arkansas, interview by author, January 2009.

30. "Distribution: Delivering Low Prices," in "Wal-Mart: Retailer of the Century," special issue, *Discount Store News*, October 1999, 115.

31. Jonathan Birchall, "Walmart Eyes Urban Expansion in US," *Financial Times*, November 1, 2009. According to Birchall, "Walmart has stepped up efforts to mobilize local political support for new store openings in US cities and urban areas" but has struggled for years to gain purchase in major metropolitan areas. For an account of Walmart's attempt to open a store in Los Angeles, see Abigail Goldman and Nancy Cleeland, "An Empire Built on Bargains Remakes the Working World," *Los Angeles Times*, November 23, 2003.

32. Gary Gereffi and Michelle Christian, "The Impacts of Wal-Mart: The Rise and Consequences of the World's Dominant Retailer," *Annual Review of Sociology* 35 (2009): 574.

33. In the range of publications on Walmart, the built environment is often addressed, but typically in the context of discussions about Walmart's efforts to establish new stores. Both *Wal-Mart World: The World's Biggest Corporation in the Global Economy*, edited by Stanley D. Brunn (New York: Routledge, 2006), and *Wal-Mart: The Face of Twenty-First-Century Capitalism*, edited by Nelson Lichtenstein (New York: New Press, 2006), are academic in nature and include chapters examining the built environment, if mostly collaterally. Lichtenstein's own book, *The Retail Revolution: How Wal-Mart Created a Brave New World of Business* (New York: Metropolitan Books, 2009), discusses the role of logistics in Walmart's operations, especially in chapter 2, titled "Supply and Command." Accounts from nonacademic presses include Fishman, *The Wal-Mart Effect*; Ortega, *In Sam We Trust*; and Anthony Bianco, *The Bully of Bentonville: How the High Cost of Wal-Mart's Everyday Low Prices Is Hurting America* (New York: Doubleday, 2006). Several volumes focus explicitly on the business history of Walmart, including Vance and Scott, *Wal-Mart*; and Berg and Roberts, *Walmart*, which includes chapters dedicated to logistics and information management. Spatial concerns are examined from perspectives of human geography and sociology in Paul Ingram, Lori Qingyuan Yue, and Hayagreeva Rao, "Trouble in Store: Probes, Protests, and Store Openings by Wal-Mart, 1998–2007," *American Journal of Sociology* 116, no. 1 (July 2010): 53–92; and from the perspective of economic geography in Thomas J. Holmes, "The Diffusion of Wal-Mart and Economies of Density," *Econometrica* 79, no. 1 (January 2011): 253–302.

34. Banham, *Theory and Design in the First Machine Age*, 330.

35. Daniel Bell, *The Coming of Post-industrial Society: A Venture in Social Forecasting* (New York: Basic Books, 1973), 26.

36. As noted in a 2005 *Fortune* magazine article, "Wal-Mart, America's biggest company, is many things to many people—discounter extraordinaire, union buster, guardian of small-town virtues, wrecker of small-town shops—but about

one thing there is no question: It is the repository of the nation's stuff." Devin Leonard, "The Only Lifeline Was the Walmart," *Fortune,* October 3, 2005, 74, http://fortune.com.

37. See, for example, Reinhold Martin, *The Organizational Complex: Architecture, Media, and Corporate Space* (Cambridge: MIT Press, 2003); John Harwood, *The Interface: IBM and the Transformation of Corporate Design 1945–1976* (Minneapolis: University of Minnesota Press, 2011); Louise A. Mozingo, *Pastoral Capitalism: A History of Suburban Corporate Landscapes* (Cambridge: MIT Press, 2011).

38. Compare the Spark to, for example, *Doonesbury* cartoonist Garry Trudeau's depiction of a certain U.S. president as only an asterisk.

39. Lee Scott, "Twenty First Century Leadership," Walmart, October 23, 2005, http://walmartstores.com.

40. Walmart has collaborated with Peterbilt, Great Dane Trailers, and Capstone Turbine to develop a high-efficiency prototype. Keith Barry, "A Fuel-Efficient Big Rig from Walmart That Looks Like a Smushed Corvette," *Wired,* March 5, 2014, http://www.wired.com.

41. Stephanie Rosenbloom, "Solution, or Mess? A Milk Jug for a Green Earth," *New York Times,* June 30, 2008, http://www.nytimes.com.

42. Don Moseley, director of sustainable facilities at Walmart, interview by author, July 31, 2006, Bentonville, Arkansas.

43. See, for example, Paul Nastu, "Wal-Mart Adding LEDs to 650 Stores," Environmental Leader, November 5, 2009, http://www.environmentalleader .com.

44. Michael Grunwald, "Warming to the Inconvenient Facts," *Washington Post,* July 23, 2006. See also Jared Diamond, "Will Big Business Save the Earth?," *New York Times,* December 5, 2009, http://www.nytimes.com.

45. Walmart, "Sustainability Index," accessed February 20, 2016, http: //corporate.walmart.com. For a website aimed more at Walmart suppliers, see Walmart, "Sustainability Hub," accessed February 20, 2016, http://www .walmartsustainabilityhub.com.

46. Walmart, "Walmart Announces Sustainable Product Index," press release, July 16, 2009, http://walmartstores.com.

47. In her study of the authority of nonstate actors, in reference to Walmart's sustainability efforts, Jessica Green writes, "Walmart has become, in effect, a global regulator of production practices." Jessica F. Green, *Rethinking Private Authority: Agents and Entrepreneurs in Global Environmental Governance* (Princeton, N.J.: Princeton University Press, 2014), 1.

48. Quoted in Michael Barbaro and Justin Gillis, "Wal-Mart at Forefront of Hurricane Relief," *Washington Post,* September 6, 2005, http://www.washington post.com.

49. Walmart, "Disaster Relief at Walmart," accessed November 6, 2009,

http://walmartstores.com/download/2304.pdf. See also Leonard, "The Only Lifeline Was the Walmart."

50. Ben Worthen, "How Wal-Mart Beat Feds to New Orleans," *CIO*, November 1, 2005, http://www.cio.com.

51. Claire Wilson, "Business Beats Feds in Disaster Response," *Arkansas Traveler* (University of Arkansas), October 21, 2005, http://www.uatrav.com /news; Greg Flakus, "Disaster Management Advances since Hurricane Katrina," Voice of America, October 30, 2012, http://www.voanews.com; Barbaro and Gillis, "Wal-Mart at Forefront of Hurricane Relief"; Buffy Rojas, "WalMart: Beyond Business Continuity Basics," *Continuity Insights*, February 28, 2006, http: //www.continuityinsights.com.

52. Quoted in Rojas "WalMart."

53. Ibid.

54. Ibid.

55. "Armed Forces: Engine Charlie," *Time*, October 6, 1961, http://www.time .com.

56. According to a report from the Urban Land Institute: "While a particular architectural style or extensively designed facade may please municipalities and first-generation users, . . . the extra investment may not add sustained value to the building or command a higher price on resale. Subsequent-generation users are likely to be more focused on functionality and cost containment than curb appeal." Luis A. Belmonte, "Implications for Building Demand, Design, and Location," in *Just-in-Time Real Estate: How Trends in Logistics Are Driving Industrial Development*, ed. Anne B. Frej (Washington, D.C.: Urban Land Institute, 2004), 74.

57. Roderick P. Neumann, "Political Ecology: Theorizing Scale," *Progress in Human Geography* 33, no. 3 (2009): 400.

58. Ibid., 404. Neumann, in a summary of a range of texts, writes: "Sayre uses ideas from ecology to critique the concept of scale in human geography. He suggests that much of the 'debate' on scale can be traced to the conflation of its meaning as size, level, and relation. Specifically, he argues that human geographers often conflate and confuse level and scale (as size) and consequently confuse epistemological moments with ontological moments" (400). See also Sallie A. Marston and Neil Smith, "States, Scales, and Households: Limits to Scale Thinking? A Response to Brenner," *Progress in Human Geography* 25, no. 4 (2001): 615–19.

59. Sallie A. Marston, "The Social Construction of Scale," *Progress in Human Geography* 24, no. 2 (2002): 221.

60. As David Harvey notes: "A hierarchy of scales (often depicted as local, regional, national and global, though these are arbitrary designations in themselves) exists through which the circulation of capital works at the same time as it produces its own distinctive scales of organization." David Harvey, *Spaces*

of Neoliberalization: Towards a Theory of Uneven Geographical Development (Stuttgart: Franz Steiner Verlag, 2005), 80.

61. Paul N. Edwards, "Infrastructure and Modernity: Force, Time, and Social Organization in the History of Sociotechnical Systems" in *Modernity and Technology,* ed. Thomas J. Misa, Philip Brey, and Andrew Feenberg (Cambridge: MIT Press, 2003), 186. Edwards goes on to make a plea for methodological inclusivity: when addressing large systems, he contends, one cannot address phenomena solely at either a micro or macro scale without omitting significant information and thereby operating in an overly reductive mode with resulting myopic views. Edwards acknowledges the difficulty of such an approach, however, and advises scholars to "focus on ever-smaller chunks of time and space. The discipline of history, for example, demands topics (and archival sources) that a historian can hope to master within a few years. . . . Historians are ill equipped to explore broad patterns and multiple scales. Similar points could be made about sociology, anthropology, and other empirical approaches to modernity. Today's scholars tend to sneer at genuinely macro-scale empirical studies, likely as they are to contain mistakes at the level of detail that occupies the forefront of the specialists' attention" (223).

62. Michel Foucault, "The Masked Philosopher," in *Essential Works of Foucault 1954–1984,* vol. 1, *Ethics,* ed. Paul Rabinow (New York: Penguin Press, 2000), 325.

63. This sentiment also owes a debt to the editorial statement of the journal *Cabinet,* which paraphrases Foucault's definition of curiosity as "the basis both for an ethical engagement with the world as it is and for imagining how it might be otherwise." "*Cabinet*: Mission Statement," *Cabinet,* accessed May 5, 2015, http://www.cabinetmagazine.org. See also "A Succinct Statement on Curiosity by Michel Foucault That Sums Up *Cabinet*'s Mission Better Than We Can," *Cabinet,* accessed May 5, 2015, http://www.cabinetmagazine.org.

64. Bruno Latour, *We Have Never Been Modern,* trans. Catherine Porter (Cambridge, Mass.: Harvard University Press, 1991), 47.

65. Foucault, "The Masked Philosopher," 323.

1. Logistics

1. For a comprehensive account of the transformation of logistics, see Deborah Cowen, *The Deadly Life of Logistics: Mapping Violence in Global Trade* (Minneapolis: University of Minnesota Press, 2014), esp. chap. 1. See also Edna Bonacich and Jake B. Wilson, *Getting the Goods: Ports, Labor, and the Logistics Revolution* (Ithaca, N.Y.: Cornell University Press, 2008). Although Bonacich and Wilson focus primarily on labor issues, they devote significant discussion to the sources and tendencies of logistics.

2. Charles B. Einstein, "Modeling the Wholesale Logistics Base," *Army Logistician* 15, no. 6 (November/December 1983): 17.

3. George C. Thorpe, "Logistics," *Scientific American*, September 16, 1916, 263. See also George C. Thorpe, *Pure Logistics: The Science of War Preparation* (Kansas City, Mo.: Franklin Hudson, 1917).

4. Huston, *The Sinews of War*, 424.

5. For a survey of some of the sources of managerial logistics, see Peter Klaus and Stefanie Müller, "Towards a Science of Logistics: Milestones along Converging Paths," in *The Roots of Logistics: A Reader of Classical Contributions to the History and Conceptual Foundations of the Science of Logistics*, ed. Peter Klaus and Stefanie Müller (Heidelberg: Springer, 2012).

6. Thorpe points to Napoleon's failed Russian Campaign as a primary example of this. Thorpe, *Pure Logistics*, 18–28.

7. Baron Antoine-Henri de Jomini, *The Art of War* (London: Greenhill Books, 2006), 252.

8. Ibid., 69.

9. Ibid., 253.

10. Ibid., 254.

11. For example: "9. Arranging and superintending the march of trains of baggage, munitions, provisions, and ambulances, both with the columns and in their rear, in such a manner that they will not interfere with the movements of the troops and will still be near at hand." Ibid., 255.

12. Jomini adds, "As the army advances and removes farther from its base, it comes the more necessary to have a good line of operations and of depots which may keep up the connection of the army with its base." Ibid., 262.

13. *Online Etymology Dictionary*, s.v. "logistics," accessed May 5, 2015, http://www.etymonline.com.

14. As John Harwood argues, "Even though [both management and logistics] are so directly concerned with spatial organization, their main representational tools are only rarely spatial in any conventional sense." He goes on to point out that "practitioners of management and logistics deploy diagrams . . . to model the space and time of the territory under their control. These models are topological, describing only those aspects of the objects represented that are relevant to the logistical process." Harwood, *The Interface*, 9.

15. See, for example, Vilém Flusser, *Into the Universe of Technical Images*, trans. Nancy Ann Roth (Minneapolis: University of Minnesota Press, 2011). In the opening section, "To Abstract," Flusser states: "The difference between traditional and technical images, then, would be this: the first are observations of objects, the second computations of concepts. The first arise through depiction, the second through a peculiar hallucinatory power that has lost its faith in rules" (10). See also John May, "Sensing: Preliminary Notes on the Emergence of Statistical-Mechanical Vision," *Perspecta: The Yale Architectural Journal*, no. 40, "Monster" (2008): 42–53.

16. Stuart Elden, *The Birth of Territory* (Chicago: University of Chicago Press, 2013), 322–23.

17. See, for example, Einstein, "Modeling the Wholesale Logistics Base," 17–19.

18. Ibid., 17–18.

19. Huston, *The Sinews of War,* viii. Matériel is the "equipment, apparatus, and supplies used by an organization or institution." *Merriam-Webster.com,* s.v. "matériel," accessed November 29, 2013, http://www.merriam-webster.com.

20. Ibid. Huston's reference is to the statement attributed to Otto von Bismarck that "politics is the art of the possible."

21. Carl von Clausewitz, *On War,* ed. and trans. Michael Howard and Peter Paret (Princeton, N.J.: Princeton University Press, 1976), 87.

22. Ibid., 339.

23. Manual DeLanda, *War in the Age of Intelligent Machines* (New York: Zone Books, 1991), 112.

24. Ibid., 108.

25. Cowen, *The Deadly Life of Logistics,* 30.

26. Huston, *The Sinews of War,* 656.

27. Ibid.

28. On this revolution, W. Bruce Allen writes: "Finally, the green-eye-shade mentality, along with the individual, was replaced by the computer. To the extent that institutional knowledge is valuable, it can be heavily captured by artificial intelligence. Routine, repetitive calculations can be handled rapidly. Deregulation's multitude of new rates can be analyzed easily. Models—routing, location, allocation—that had been developed by academics and that could be run only by a computer mainframe could now be run by a relative novice at a desktop computer." W. Bruce Allen, "The Logistics Revolution and Transportation," *Annals of the American Academy of Political and Social Science* 553 (September 1997): 108. In 1962, Peter F. Drucker pointed to logistics as an undeveloped sector in his article "The Economy's Dark Continent," *Fortune,* April 1962, 103–4.

29. Drucker, "The Economy's Dark Continent," 103; Peter F. Drucker, *Concept of the Corporation* (1946; repr., New Brunswick, N.J.: Transaction, 2006).

30. Drucker, "The Economy's Dark Continent," 103.

31. Cowen, *The Deadly Life of Logistics,* 36. Cowen lists these functions: "inventory carrying and obsolescence, warehousing, transportation, production alternatives, communications and data processing, customer service, alternative facilities use, channels of distribution and cost concessions" (36).

32. Ibid., 38.

33. Walmart, as I will describe below, concentrates its efforts at the end of the long production process encompassed by logistics. Thus, while Walmart is concerned with the production of the goods it sells, it does not concern itself

with the securing of raw material in a coordinated manner, say, in the way that a car manufacturer would.

34. Allen, "The Logistics Revolution and Transportation," 107.

35. Paul Schönsleben, *Integral Logistics Management: Operations and Supply Chain Management in Comprehensive Value-Added Networks,* 3rd ed. (Boca Raton, Fla.: CRC Press, 2010), 7.

36. Edward W. Smykay and Bernard J. La Londe, *Physical Distribution: The New and Profitable Science of Business Logistics* (Chicago: Dartnell, 1967), 5.

37. For a discussion of the trade-offs between the "lean" formation that is tightly coupled but more brittle and more robust or resilient modes that are less vulnerable to unexpected conditions, see Yossi Sheffi, *The Resilient Enterprise: Overcoming Vulnerability for Competitive Advantage* (Cambridge: MIT Press, 2005), 76–111. See also Karl E. Weick, "Educational Organizations as Loosely Coupled Systems," *Administrative Science Quarterly* 21, no. 1 (March 1976): 1–19.

38. For a more detailed examination of changing dynamics in manufacturing, especially related to the emergence of "lean production" and "pull" models, see James P. Womack, Daniel T. Jones, and Daniel Roos, *The Machine That Changed the World: The Story of Lean Production—Toyota's Secret Weapon in the Global Car Wars That Is Revolutionizing World Industry* (1990; repr., New York: Free Press, 2007). For further discussion of the industrial aspects of logistics, see, for example, Yossi Sheffi, *Logistics Cluster: Delivering Value and Driving Growth* (Cambridge: MIT Press, 2012).

39. Easterling suggests: "To truly exploit some of the intelligence related to network thinking, an alternative position might operate from the premise that the real power of many urban organizations lies within the relationships among multiple distributed sites that are both collectively and individually adjustable. This discussion transfers intelligence from many different models of active organization to an understanding of spatial environments. It pursues a fascination with simple components that gain complexity by their relative position to each other." Keller Easterling, *Organization Space: Landscapes, Highways, and Houses in America* (Cambridge: MIT Press, 1999), 2.

40. Noel P. Greis, "Integrated Infrastructures for Moving Goods in the Digital Age," in *Moving People, Goods, and Information in the 21st Century: The Cutting-Edge Infrastructures of Networked Cities,* ed. Richard E. Hanley (London: Routledge, 2004), 37.

41. Henri Lefebvre, *The Production of Space,* trans. Donald Nicholson-Smith (Oxford: Blackwell, 1991), 341–42. Lefebvre asserts: *"There is a violence intrinsic to abstraction,* and to abstraction's practical (social) use. Abstraction passes for an 'absence'—as distinct from the concrete 'presence' of objects, of things. Nothing could be more false. For abstraction's *modus operandi* is devastation, destruction (even if such destruction may sometimes herald creation)" (289).

42. This might serve as evidence in support of Easterling's assertion that "architecture, as it is used here, might describe the parameters or protocols for formatting space." Easterling, *Organization Space*, 2.

43. See James R. Beniger, *The Control Revolution: Technological and Economic Origins of the Information Society* (Cambridge, Mass.: Harvard University Press, 1986), 221.

44. Beniger identifies train conductors as "possibly the first persons in history to be used as programmable, distributed decision makers in the control of fast-moving flows through a system whose scale and speeds precluded control by more central structures." Ibid., 225.

45. My thanks to John Harwood for the reference to Ball and the Great Kipton Train Wreck.

46. Regarding the need for sustained communication, Armand Mattelart writes: "Globalization is above all a model of corporate management that, in response to the growing complexity of competitive environments, creates and promotes competencies on a global level with a view to maximizing profits and consolidating market shares. It is, in a sense, a framework for interpreting the world that is peculiar to management and marketing specialists. . . . The global firm is an organic structure in which each part is supposed to serve the whole. Any shortcoming in the interoperability between the parts, any lack of free interaction, is a threat to the system. Communication must therefore be omnipresent." Armand Mattelart, *Networking the World: 1794–2000*, trans. Liz Carey-Libbrecht and James A. Cohen (Minneapolis: University of Minnesota Press, 2000), 76–77. Elsewhere, Mattelart describes the railway as "the culmination of a rationality in which the ordering of time on a large scale is allied with the institution of security systems calling for the military mode of organization. Before designating applications of the new technologies, and even before the invention of the locomotive or the telegraph, the term 'line of communications' had been used in the treatises of the war academies. Its transfer to civilian vocabulary by no means took place metaphorically. It was the expression of a regime of organization." Armand Mattelart, *The Invention of Communication*, trans. Susan Emanuel (Minneapolis: University of Minnesota Press, 1996), 50.

47. Studies such as those published in Wiebe E. Bijker and John Law's edited volume *Shaping Technology/Building Society: Studies in Sociotechnical Change* (Cambridge: MIT Press, 1992) address these intertwined dynamics. Bijker's own *Of Bicycles, Bakelites, and Bulbs* further develops methods related to the study of large technical systems. See also Alfred Chandler Jr. and James Cortada, eds., *A Nation Transformed by Information: How Information Has Shaped the United States from Colonial Times to the Present* (London: Oxford University Press, 2003); as well as Edwards, "Infrastructure and Modernity," 185–226.

48. "The Most Tender, Fully-Meated Lobster You Will Find," Clearwater, accessed May 5, 2015, http://www.clearwater.ca/en/home/seafood-industry

/lobster/default.aspx. See also Nicki Holmyard, "Lobsters Alive!," IntraFish, August 21, 2008, http://www.intrafish.com.

49. "Just-in-Time Lobsters," in "The Physical Internet: A Survey of Logistics," *Economist*, June 17, 2006, 8. These dynamics illustrate, in David Harvey's words, "a basic law of capital accumulation" that enables "reduction in the cost and time of movement of commodities, people (labor power), money and information through what Marx called 'the annihilation of space through time.'" He goes on to point out that "since distance is measured in terms of time and cost of movement, there is also intense pressure to reduce the frictions of distance by innovations in transportation and communications." Harvey, *Spaces of Neoliberalization*, 76.

50. Giedion goes on: "The slow shaping of daily life is of equal importance to the explosions of history; for, in the anonymous life, the particles accumulate into an explosive force." Sigfried Giedion, *Mechanization Takes Command: A Contribution to Anonymous History* (New York: W. W. Norton, 1948), 3.

51. For a more detailed discussion of modules, see Harwood, *The Interface*, 109–11. Harwood writes, "Being a unit of serial delimitation, a module is necessarily both part and multiple" (109). He continues, "Modularity is the formal condition of architecture considered as a medium in the truest sense of McLuhan's 'law,' that it contains or is built up out of other media and may be contained by other media in turn" (111).

52. Alexander Klose, "Cells, Modules, Series: The Rationale of Space Processing in the Age of Containers" (paper presented to the German Department, Northwestern University, Chicago, February 13, 2006), 1. See also Alexander Klose, *The Container Principle: How a Box Changes the Way We Think*, trans. Charles Marcrum II (Cambridge: MIT Press, 2015). Klose examines the container as a fundamental, defining feature of modernity for its ability to universalize and connect modes and media.

53. For example, a 40 ISO container can hold twenty to twenty-one ISO 40-inch-by-48-inch pallets, depending on how they are arranged. For the International Organization for Standardization's standard description, see the ISO standards catalogue listing "Flat Pallets for Intercontinental Materials Handling—Principal Dimensions and Tolerances," accessed January 12, 2016, http://www.iso.org.

54. See Marc Levinson, *The Box: How the Shipping Container Made the World Smaller and the World Economy Bigger* (Princeton, N.J.: Princeton University Press, 2006). For a discussion dealing specifically with the shipping container, see Matthew Heins, "The Shipping Container and the Globalization of American Infrastructure" (PhD diss., University of Michigan, 2013). Heins focuses on the context of the container in the United States and uses the container to discuss changing ideas of infrastructure and place. The module of the container, and modularity more generally, allows for an abundance of interchangeability

between elements in space. Noticing a similar condition, Henri Lefebvre writes, "Space is thus produced and reproduced *as* reproducible." Lefebvre, *The Production of Space*, 337.

55. Levinson, *The Box*, 7.

56. Ibid., 6.

57. Klose, "Cells, Modules, Series."

58. Edwards, "Infrastructure and Modernity," 185.

59. Susan Leigh Star and Karen Ruhleder, "Steps toward an Ecology of Infrastructure: Design and Access for Large Information Spaces," *Information Systems Research* 7, no. 1 (March 1996): 111–34.

60. Edwards, "Infrastructure and Modernity," 191. Edwards writes: "Infrastructures act like laws. . . . They create both opportunities and limits; they promote some interests at the expense of others. To live within the multiple, interlocking infrastructures of modern societies is to know one's place in gigantic systems that both enable and constrain us" (191). Edwards is drawing from Langdon Winner, *The Whale and the Reactor: A Search for Limits in an Age of High Technology* (Chicago: University of Chicago Press, 1986), particularly the chapter "Do Artifacts Have Politics?"

61. As Edwards notes: "If we look at function rather than at the particular technology or infrastructure that fulfills it, we see not disappearance but growth. Gas lighting may be dead, but artificial light illuminates the world; the telegraph is gone, but far more intricate and capable long-distance communication systems have replaced it." Edwards, "Infrastructure and Modernity," 205.

62. Lewis Mumford singles out mechanization and regimentation as two particularly acute historical phenomena related to this issue, saying that while they are not new, "what is new is the fact that these functions have been projected and embodied in organized forms which dominate every aspect of our existence." Lewis Mumford, *Technics and Civilization* (New York: Harcourt Brace, 1934), 4.

63. Bell, *The Coming of Post-industrial Society*, 29.

64. Edwards extends this notion to ideas of infrastructure as well: "As historians, sociologists, and anthropologists of technology increasingly recognize, all infrastructures (indeed, all 'technologies') are in fact *sociotechnical* in nature. Not only hardware but organizations, socially communicated background knowledge, general acceptance and reliance, and near-ubiquitous accessibility are required for a system to be an infrastructure." Edwards, "Infrastructure and Modernity," 188.

65. Stephen Graham and Simon Marvin, *Splintering Urbanism: Networked Infrastructures, Technological Mobilities and the Urban Condition* (London: Routledge, 2001), 191.

66. Deborah Cowen, "Containing Insecurity: Logistic Space, U.S. Port Cities, and the 'War on Terror,'" in *Disrupted Cities: When Infrastructure Fails*, ed. Stephen Graham (London: Routledge, 2009), 69–84.

67. Graham and Marvin, *Splintering Urbanism*, 192.

68. As Zygmunt Bauman observes, "Modernity is, apart from anything else, perhaps even more than anything else, *the history of time*: modernity is the time when time has a history." Bauman, *Liquid Modernity*, 110.

69. For further discussion of the development of standard time, see, for example, Lawrence Busch, *Standards: Recipes for Reality* (Cambridge: MIT Press, 2011), particularly the chapter "Standardizing the World," 77–150. See also Michael O'Malley, *Keeping Watch: A History of American Time* (Washington, D.C.: Smithsonian Institution Press, 1990).

70. For an introduction to the development of probability theory, see Ian Hacking, *The Taming of Chance* (Cambridge: Cambridge University Press, 1990). In the context of economics, Frank Knight had already identified, in 1921, the important distinction between risk and uncertainty. Knight's writing became influential after World War II with the rise of Chicago School economics, including the influence of Knight's student Milton Friedman. See Frank H. Knight, *Risk, Uncertainty, and Profit* (Boston: Houghton Mifflin, 1921), available on the Library of Economics and Liberty website, http://www.econlib.org. For further discussion in the context of contemporary finance, see Arjun Appadurai, "The Ghost in the Financial Machine," *Public Culture* 23, no. 3 (Fall 2011): 517–40.

71. Arthur C. Clarke, "Extra-terrestrial Relays: Can Rocket Stations Give World-wide Radio Coverage?," *Wireless World,* October 1945, 305.

72. Ibid., 306.

73. Manuel Castells, "Space of Flows, Space of Places: Material for a Theory of Urbanism in the Information Age," in Graham, *The Cybercities Reader,* 85. This essay touches some of the major points of Castells's three-volume *The Information Age: Economy, Society, and Culture* (Oxford: Blackwell, 1996). Volume 1 of that series, *The Rise of Network Society,* includes the chapter "The Space of Flows" (376–428), in which Castells relates the challenge of information logics to cities of the Industrial Revolution. His distinction between the "space of flows" and the "space of places" establishes these as the two poles of the spectrum of transformation wrought by globalization.

74. According to Snyder and Wall, "Distribution and consumption are altering traditional urban form in four ways: at street scale, by filling our roads with trucks working via electronic control on schedules that lead to intense traffic volume and accidents disrupting the daily urban system of every large city; at an urban scale, by transforming the front- and back-stage areas of cities; at a regional scale, by creating new urban structures that will provide the armature for the growth of new communities; and at a continental scale by re-ordering the hierarchy of cities in a country's commerce." Susan Nigra Snyder and Alex Wall, "Emerging Landscapes of Movement and Logistics," *Architectural Design* 68 (July/August 1998): 20. These authors also define the distribution landscape as "the domain of the logistics industry . . . where information and technology

intervene with the physical bulk of goods at ports, rail yards, air cargo and truck depots" (16).

75. Lyster, "Landscapes of Exchange," 230.

76. Easterling describes this logistical urbanism as "a live three-dimensional enactment of the orgman's data-tracking software. It is an urbanism of the work addict, of stacking and sorting behaviors necessary to move containers from ships and pallets from warehouses with increasingly high expectations of efficiency." Easterling, "The New Orgman," 182. Regarding the aspirations of their project, Snyder and Wall write, "Beyond understanding the locational logic of these new urban developments, we believe the distribution landscape is a testing ground for new kinds of settlement, spatial patterns and possibly an architecture where the shape of urban life is free to take on a new form." Snyder and Wall, "Emerging Landscapes of Movement and Logistics," 21.

77. See Jesse LeCavalier, John Harwood, and Guillame Mojon, *This Will _ This* (Basel: Standpunkte Press, 2009), 21–23.

78. Harwood, *The Interface*, 128.

79. Ibid., 131.

80. See Easterling, *Organization Space*; Mark Wigley, "Network Fever," *Grey Room*, no. 4 (Summer 2001): 82–122.

81. Peter Galison uses Baran's research to show how civilian officials in the government were asked to assess their own towns' vulnerability to nuclear attack and subsequently to develop plans to decentralize industry and protect such systems with spatial strategies. He argues that the process of the officials assessing their own settlements was key because "they began, quite explicitly, to see themselves, to see America, through the bombardier's eye . . . each community, each industry, each factory was pressed into service this way, pressed to see itself this way, rather than simply receiving a designated perimeter line drawn by the federal government." Peter Galison, "War against the Center," *Grey Room*, no. 4 (Summer 2001): 29. In developing his argument, Galison discusses research conducted at the RAND Corporation at the time that was concerned not just with the physical installations of U.S. industries but also with their telecommunications systems.

82. Jon Goss, "The Built Environment and Social Theory: Towards an Architectural Geography," *Professional Geographer* 40, no. 4 (1988): 394.

83. For example, see John Agnew, "Global Political Geography beyond Geopolitics," *International Studies Review* 2, no. 1 (Spring 2000): 91–99. In this review essay, Agnew examines three volumes that address the changing dynamics of political geography after the binaries of the Cold War and with increased globalization. He also briskly traces the fraught intellectual history of geopolitics and champions efforts to recover it as a field of inquiry dissociated from certain midcentury attachments.

84. David Gissen notes the emergence of "a select number of architects [who]

attempt to rebuild geography with architecture—a project in which buildings bring their own territorial concerns into focus." David Gissen, "The Architectural Reconstruction of Geography," in *Coupling: Strategies for Infrastructural Opportunism,* ed. Mason White and Lola Sheppard (Princeton, N.J.: Princeton Architectural Press, 2011), 42.

85. The use of architecture specifically to abet or instigate political maneuvering has been documented in works such as Eyal Weizman's *Hollow Land: Israel's Architecture of Occupation* (London: Verso, 2007); and Keller Easterling's *Enduring Innocence: Global Architecture and Its Political Masquerades* (Cambridge: MIT Press, 2007); as well as in journals like *New Geographies.*

86. Paul Krugman, for example, writes, "Firms tend, other things equal, to choose locations of maximum 'market potential,' where the market potential of a site was defined as some index of its access to markets, involving both the purchasing power of all the markets to which it might sell and the distance to those markets." Paul Krugman, *Development, Geography, and Economic Theory* (Cambridge: MIT Press, 1995), 44.

87. Roy E. H. Mellor, *Nation, State, and Territory: A Political Geography* (London: Routledge, 1989), 1.

88. See Orit Halpern, Jesse LeCavalier, Nerea Calvillo, and Wolfgang Pietsch, "Test-Bed Urbanism," *Public Culture* 25, no. 2 (Spring 2013): 272–306.

89. Stuart Elden, "Governmentality, Calculation, Territory," *Environment and Planning D: Society and Space* 25 (2007): 578.

90. For a discussion of political plastic, see Weizman, *Hollow Land.*

91. Elden, *The Birth of Territory,* 322.

92. Kevin Lynch, *The Image of the City* (Cambridge: MIT Press, 1960), 13.

2. Buildings

1. Susan Hartley, "Happy Birthday No. 30," *Troy Daily News,* June 26, 2004.

2. Walton describes how he "read an article about these two Ben Franklin stores up in Minnesota that had gone to self-service—a brand-new concept at the time. I rode the bus all night long to two little towns up there—Pipestone and Worthington. They had shelves on the side and two island counters all the way back. No clerks with cash registers around the store. Just checkout registers up front. I liked it. So I did that too." Walton, *Sam Walton,* 42.

3. For a thorough account of the development of mass merchandising and discount retail, see Vance and Scott, *Wal-Mart,* 16–38. For an overview of the transformation of business structures in the nineteenth century, a transformation that laid much of the groundwork for the supply chain networks utilized by Walmart, see Alfred Chandler Jr., *The Visible Hand: The Managerial Revolution*

(Cambridge, Mass.: Harvard University Press, 1977). James Beniger refers to the new retail outlets of the 1930s as "new supermarket buildings *qua* material processors." Beniger, *The Control Revolution,* 341.

4. In the June 1, 1918, issue of the internal publication *Whats and What Nots of Piggly Wiggly System,* Saunders noted, "After any and all merchandise has been placed on display, it is there for the customer alone to select with his or her own hands and without physical assistance from a store employee." Mississippi Valley Collection, University of Memphis Library, 438-03-16.

5. Vance and Scott, *Wal-Mart,* 12.

6. C. Saunders, "Self Serving Store," U.S. Patent 1,397,824 (filed June 20, 1917, and issued November 22, 1921), 3.

7. *Whats and What Nots of Piggly Wiggly System,* June 1, 1918.

8. The astonishing history of Saunders and Piggly Wiggly includes a dramatic effort on Saunders's part to corner the market in 1922, only to be thwarted by the intervention of the U.S. Securities and Exchange Commission. For a detailed history, see John Brooks, "Annals of Finance: A Corner in Piggly Wiggly," *New Yorker,* June 6, 1959, 128–50. For more on the architecture of Saunders's subsequent experiments in networked and automated retail, see Jesse LeCavalier, "Networks of Architecture: Keedoozle and Walmart," *MAS Context,* no. 9, "Network" (Spring 2011).

9. *Whats and What Nots of Piggly Wiggly System,* June 1, 1918.

10. Stephen A. Brown, *Revolution at the Checkout Counter: The Explosion of the Bar Code* (Cambridge: Wertheim Publications in Industrial Relations, 1997), 5.

11. Information on the development of the UPC comes from Harry E. Burke, *Automating Management Information Systems,* vols. 1–2 (New York: Van Nostrand Reinhold, 1990); Lawrence E. Hicks, *The Universal Product Code* (New York: American Management Association, 1975); and "UPC—The History of the UPC and Item Identification," ID History Museum, accessed January 13, 2016, http://www.idhistory.com. See also George Lauer, *Engineering Was Fun! An Autobiography* (self-published, 2007); Bill Selmeier, *Spreading the Barcode* (self-published, 2008). John Dunlop and Jan Rivkin offer this description: "When a consumer purchases an item, say a man's shirt at one of Federated's department stores, the bar code scanner at the checkout register reads the UPC symbol on the item. The point-of-sale register uses the Code to look up the item's current price from a database in an on-site or central computer. At nearly the same time, the information that the shirt has been sold is relayed to Federated's buyers. There, the information is used in two ways. First, it provides Federated with immediate and precise knowledge of what is selling and what is not. Buyers can use this knowledge to adjust their purchases from vendors. Second, it triggers a process of replenishing the stock of a particular fabric, size, color, and style of the shirt at the store." John T. Dunlop and Jan W. Rivkin, "Introduction," in Brown, *Revolution at the Checkout Counter,* 10.

12. In recent years, radio-frequency identification (RFID) has been positioned as the heir to the UPC as the primary mode of inventory monitoring and managing. As RFID "tags" (each consisting of a transmitter and antenna) continuously broadcast their locations in space, the parties monitoring them can maintain close watch over their entire journey. This is different from the current mode of the UPC, which can account only for products' locations at the checkpoints along their paths. The promise of RFID is ultimately to automate the process of shopping almost entirely. If all the items in a shopper's cart have RFID tags, then the consumer can pass through an electronic gate and the system will instantly and automatically deduct the amount of the total sale from the customer's account.

13. Logistics operations became increasingly technological with the implementation of semiautomated inventory management, but these developments were not unidirectional. For example, the retail industry led the charge on bar code implementation, which, in turn, influenced military operations. Ten years after the bar code was first used, the journal *Army Logistician* made its case for bar code implementation by pointing out that "techniques similar to those used in BARCIS [Bar Code Inventory System] are widely used in civilian industry. Once LOGMARS [Logistics Application of Marking and Reading Symbols] is fully instituted, bar coding will become a way of life for DOD [Department of Defense] logisticians, from the wholesale level to the using unit." The report also noted that "tests conducted by ERADCOM [Electronics Research & Development Command] indicated that the bar code system of inventorying reduced the time spent on manual inventories by 68 percent. Equipment is managed more efficiently, since items are easier to identify. Accountability also has improved, and hand receipt holders have accepted and learned to use the system." John H. Kern, "Bar Coding: A Better Way to Manage Property Books," *Army Logistician*, March/April 1983, 5. The choice of language here is instructive when considering the ways in which logistics and semiautomated data management have become insinuated into daily life. Once people have "accepted" the system, they can make it part of their "way of life." This is exactly the means by which Walmart approaches its own culture, cultivating habits of thought and action in pursuit of cost savings and efficiency.

14. According to Dunlop and Rivkin: "The retailer's purpose in employing this suite of technologies is straightforward. Thanks to the U.P.C., bar code scanners, low cost microprocessors, and low cost electronic communications, the retailers can collect and process information concerning consumer demand, as expressed in thousands of transactions, inexpensively. The retailer can then use this information to reduce its exposure to market demand risk. It does so both by adjusting its orders quickly in response to shifts in demand and by minimizing the amount of inventory it holds." Dunlop and Rivkin, "Introduction," 11.

15. "Seen in this light, a significant feature of the U.P.C., EDI, and associated innovations is their *non-specific* character. Thanks to the setting of industry-level standards, firms can invest in these technologies, and engage in pseudo-integration with partners, without exposing themselves as much to the hazards of relationship-specific assets." Ibid., 31.

16. William Correll, the head of Walmart's architecture division, described one duty of his department by stating, "We put together, if you will, the vehicles of choice. I wouldn't look at it as cookie cutters of building layouts, but as base formats that one might take and apply while coming up with new concept stores. The prototypes are designed to be starting points—kind of like springboards." LeCavalier, "Interview with Bill Correll," 35.

17. *Random House Dictionary,* s.v. "format," accessed February 27, 2011, http://dictionary.reference.com.

18. According to Weick: "If all of the elements in a large system are loosely coupled to one another, then any one element can adjust to and modify local unique contingency without affecting the whole system. These local adaptations can be swift, relatively economical and substantial." Weick, "Educational Organizations as Loosely Coupled Systems," 7.

19. Ibid.

20. Ibid.

21. Walton, *Sam Walton,* 142–43.

22. Lisa Selin Davis, "Trying to Fit In: The Look of Wal-Mart Stores in the Suburbs," *Plenty,* November/December 2005, 69.

23. Ibid., 67.

24. LeCavalier, "Interview with Bill Correll," 33.

25. Ibid.

26. "Correll's team met with a coalition of civic groups in a Fort Worth neighborhood and asked them about their favorite buildings in the area and the characteristics 'they would like to see reflected' in the future store. A number of people cited a 1930s high school as a favorite. 'So,' Correll says, 'we took many of the elements—including some arched windows, clay tile roofs, brick, and other material—and put these colors and materials together as part of the design of the Wal-Mart Supercenter. Does this defuse public opposition? I'm sure it does. But the real drive for us is to be good neighbors.'" Karrie Jacobs, "Massive Markets," *Metropolis,* June 1, 2004, http://www.metropolismag.com.

27. Walmart is also constantly developing new prototypes, including an "urban" prototype and a "lifestyle" prototype. See Davis, "Trying to Fit In," 66–69; Rachel Lianna Davis, "Wal-Mart Stores Change, Steer Clear of Compact Design," *Northwest Arkansas News,* June 2, 2006; Chuck Bartels, "New Wal-Mart Style Unifies Stores," *USA Today,* October 29, 2008, http://www.usatoday.com; Anne D'Innocenzio, "Wal-Mart Unveils Tiny Walmart Express in Gentry," NWA Online, June 3, 2011, http://www.nwaonline.com.

28. For additional information on Lippincott's rebranding campaign for Walmart, see Lippincott, "Walmart," accessed February 19, 2016, http://www.lippincott.com/en/work/walmart.

29. Quoted in James Bickers, "GlobalShop: Walmart on the Return of Retail Architecture," RetailCustomerExperience.com, March 16, 2010, http://www.retailcustomerexperience.com.

30. Ibid.

31. Robert Venturi, Denise Scott Brown, and Steven Izenour, *Learning from Las Vegas: The Forgotten Symbolism of Architectural Form*, rev. ed. (Cambridge: MIT Press, 1977), 87.

32. Julia Christensen, in *Big Box Reuse* (Cambridge: MIT Press, 2008), focuses on the capacity of retailer warehouse buildings to support transformation by social entrepreneurial efforts. Alejandro Zaera Polo, in "The Politics of the Envelope: A Political Critique of Materialism," *Volume*, no. 17, "Content Management" (2008): 76–105, works to locate architectural agency within the building skin and cites the increasing operational specificity that comes with buildings. Alexander d'Hooghe, in "The Case for the Big Box: Joys of a Non-expressionist Architecture," *Volume*, no. 19, "Architecture of Hope" (2009): 34–38, shares some of Christensen's views, especially in terms of the possibilities for large-format discount stores to become hubs.

33. It is also worth noting the change in overall floor area, from 29,345 square feet in 1955 to 155,230 in 2007.

34. Max McCoy, "Wal-Mart's Data Center Remains a Mystery," *Joplin Globe*, May 28, 2006, http://www.joplinglobe.com.

35. Information on property tax rates comes from Benton County Assessor's Office, accessed May 5, 2015, http://bentoncountyar.gov; and "Missouri: McDonald County," LowTaxRate.com, accessed May 5, 2015, http://www.lowtaxrate.com. Aside from property tax savings, a Community Development Block Grant was established to help with the construction of the data center, resulting in six hundred new jobs. See McDonald County Commission minutes, November 14, 2012, http://www.mcdonaldcountygov.com/notices/11-14-2012%20Minutes.pdf.

36. This description is based on what I observed on Sunday, January 20, 2008, as I was trying to photograph the center. At that time I was questioned by one plainclothes deputy and then subsequently by a uniformed officer.

37. Google Data Centers, "The Dalles, Oregon," accessed March 20, 2013, http://www.google.com/about/datacenters. See also John Markoff and Saul Hansell, "Hiding in Plain Sight, Google Seeks More Power," *New York Times*, June 14, 2006; Andrew Blum, *Tubes: Behind the Scenes at the Internet* (New York: Ecco, 2012), 227–62.

38. Martin Pawley argues, in *Terminal Architecture* (London: Reaktion Books, 1998), for an expanded idea of what constitutes architectural design. The

book examines architecture related to transit and material flows but also suggests that architecture's days might be numbered.

39. Luiz André Barroso and Urs Hölzle, "Handheld + Landheld = Cloud Computing," *CLOG*, "Data Space" (2012): 18–19.

40. In a 2012 interview with the editors of *CLOG*, Joseph Lauro of Gensler stated: "When we are designing a data center, we're designing a space or a container to house technology in three years. It's impossible to predict what that technology will be in three years. . . . So the systems that are updated the most are the software and applications, then the physical hardware, and lastly, the architecture." "An Interview with Gensler," *CLOG*, "Data Space" (2012): 123.

41. Walmart uses a range of distribution types. For simplicity's sake, I am using the term *distribution center* to refer to what is more precisely a "general merchandise distribution center," or GMDC. For other types of distribution facilities within Walmart's operations, see MWPVL International, "The Walmart Distribution Center in the United States," accessed February 21, 2016, http://www.mwpvl.com/html/walmart.html.

42. Don Soderquist, *The Wal-Mart Way: The Inside Story of the Success of the World's Largest Company* (Nashville: Thomas Nelson, 2005), 154.

43. Ibid, 160–61.

44. Ibid., 161.

45. Ibid., 159.

46. Remarks made in *The Age of Walmart*, documentary film, CNBC, first aired May 20, 2007.

47. Dunham-Jones, "Temporary Contracts," 3. Freed from the burden of permanence and longer-term aspirational branding by the corporation, these installations present a version of temporary architecture capable of adapting to changing circumstances. The disincentive to stay in a place if the market turns further reinforces the temporal nature of Walmart's built work.

3. Locations

1. For example, Walmart leadership was instrumental in the operations of the organization Students in Free Enterprise (SIFE), including Sam and Helen Walton, Don Soderquist, and Jack Shewmaker, Walmart's former president and chief operating officer. Shewmaker was one of the Walmart executives most adamant about developing the company's communications system and one of the key figures responsible for implementing its satellite network. He was especially devout in his belief in the principles and virtues of a free market system (Milton Friedman's *Capitalism and Freedom* was first published in 1962, the year Walmart was founded). These convictions prompted Shewmaker to play a prominent role in SIFE, which aims to "bring together a diverse network of university

students, academic professionals and industry leaders around the shared mission of creating a better, more sustainable world through the positive power of business." SIFE, "The Change You Want to See," accessed January 22, 2016, http://sifethechangeyouwanttosee.blogspot.com. The organization, which has more than 42,000 members in forty countries, oversees a range of development projects organized and run by students.

2. The evidence to support the claims in this chapter is assembled from a range of material. Many of the historical data related to Walmart's early formation and growth are drawn from the memoirs of company executives and employees. Two examples are Walton, *Sam Walton*; and Soderquist, *The Wal-Mart Way*. Additional material comes from Walmart documents such as annual reports and fact sheets, site visits, and material from third-party literature such as that published by software suppliers and trade organizations.

3. "This was at a time [1966] when quite a few people were beginning to go into computerization. I had read a lot about that, and I was curious. I made up my mind I was going to learn something about IBM computers. So I enrolled in an IBM school for retailers in Poughkeepsie, New York." Walton, *Sam Walton*, 107.

4. Ibid., 109.

5. Quoted in ibid., 110–11.

6. Retail Leaders Industry Association, "Who We Are," accessed November 4, 2014, http://www.rila.org/about/bod/Pages/default.aspx.

7. According to Reinhold Martin: "As IBM's mainframes took on the organization with the help of so-called modern design, color-coded modular components made it possible to recognize this line of computers as an integrated system. Modular compatibility thus became the basis of the 360's logical and visual organization alike." Martin, *The Organizational Complex*, 178.

8. Quoted in ibid., 177.

9. For an in-depth discussion of these relationships, see Bethany Moreton, *To Serve God and Wal-Mart: The Making of Christian Free Enterprise* (Cambridge, Mass.: Harvard University Press, 2009), esp. chaps. 3, 9, and 10.

10. Bob Ortega, for example, has written thorough accounts of Walmart's aggressive location strategies. See Ortega, *In Sam We Trust*, esp. chaps. 11 and 18.

11. Vance and Scott, *Wal-Mart*, 58.

12. Soderquist, *The Wal-Mart Way*, 179.

13. See, for example, Thomas O. Z Graff and Dub Ashton, "Spatial Diffusion of Wal-Mart: Contagious and Reverse Hierarchical Elements," *Professional Geographer* 46, no. 1 (1994): 19–29; Marlon G. Boarnet, Randall Crane, Daniel G. Chatman, and Michael Manville, "Emerging Planning Challenges in Retail: The Case of Wal-Mart," *Journal of the American Planning Association* 71, no. 4 (Autumn 2005): 433–49; Emek Basker, "The Causes and Consequences of Wal-Mart's Growth," *Journal of Economic Perspectives* 21, no. 3 (Summer 2007): 177–98.

14. Walton, *Sam Walton*, 141.

15. "It became increasingly apparent that Walton's small-town strategy had been sound and farsighted. While large metropolitan areas began to suffer from too much retail competition during the 1970s, Wal-Mart was virtually unchallenged in the small-town markets in its territory. In most instances a Wal-Mart store was 'the biggest thing around,' making it the dominant nonfood retailer in the small communities it served. As such, it was capable of drawing customers not only from the town itself but also from a sizable surrounding area. Placing stores in small towns and cities afforded other advantages as well. The cost of land, buildings, and other operating expenses was lower, and the dedication of the workforce was higher." Vance and Scott, *Wal-Mart*, 69.

16. Quoted in Robert Slater, *The Wal-Mart Decade: How a New Generation of Leaders Turned Sam Walton's Legacy into the World's #1 Company* (New York: Portfolio, 2003), 92.

17. Quoted in ibid., 94.

18. Ortega, *In Sam We Trust*, 76.

19. Walton, *Sam Walton*, 25–26.

20. Ibid., 52.

21. Ibid., 143–44. Don Soderquist reinforces this: "We started by looking in a general area on a map and identifying potential towns. A real-estate associate then visited all of the sites and recommended a few possibilities. We considered the demographics involved, and then senior leadership flew out to look at the potential locations from the air—Sam liked to look at the road systems and traffic flow from that vantage—before driving around the area to take an up close look." Soderquist, *The Wal-Mart Way*, 156.

22. John Huey, remarks in "Sam Walton—Bargain Billionaire," *A&E Biography* (A&E DVD Archives, 2004).

23. Walton, *Sam Walton*, 143.

24. *Wal-Mart 1988 Annual Report*, 2, http://stock.walmart.com.

25. Soderquist, *The Wal-Mart Way*, 179.

26. "My appreciation for numbers has kept me close to our operational statements, and to all the other information we have pouring in from so many different places. . . . I found out early that one of my talents is remembering numbers. I can't recall names and a lot of other things as well as I would like to. But numbers just stick with me, and always have. That's why I come in every Saturday morning usually around two or three, and go through all the weekly numbers." Walton, *Sam Walton*, 147.

27. James Martin clarifies the performance of satellite communication networks: "For all these signals it should be regarded as a broadcasting medium accessible from anywhere beneath it, not as a set of cables in the sky." James Martin, *Communications Satellite Systems* (Englewood Cliffs, N.J.: Prentice Hall, 1978), 9.

28. Arthur Markowitz, "Wal-Mart Launches World's Largest Private Satellite Communication System," *Discount Store News*, February 1, 1988.

29. Once Walmart shifted to bar code use, a product's status could be registered and updated through the company's computer systems at all stages of its journey. "Wal-Mart Tests UPC," in "Wal-Mart: Retailer of the Century," special issue, *Discount Store News*, October 1999, 37.

30. Quoted in Walton, *Sam Walton*, 270–71.

31. Markowitz, "Wal-Mart Launches."

32. David W. Rees, *Satellite Communications: The First Quarter Century of Service* (New York: John Wiley, 1990).

33. Walton, *Sam Walton*, 271, emphasis added.

34. Ibid., 272.

35. Ibid., 272–73.

36. Martin, *Communications Satellite Systems*, 4.

37. Rees, *Satellite Communications*, 22.

38. Lyndon B. Johnson, "Remarks at a Ceremony Marking the First Commercial Communication Satellite Service," June 28, 1965, http://www.presidency .ucsb.edu. The satellite whose launch the ceremony was celebrating also broadcast Johnson's speech.

39. Quoted in Markowitz, "Wal-Mart Launches."

40. Flusser's concept of "anonymous apparatus-operator complex" is illuminating in this instance: "The crowd does not dialogue with itself in the classical Greek sense, because it is continually exposed to discourses and therefore it only has control of information which is sent to everyone and everyone receives." Vilém Flusser, quoted in Andreas Ströhl, "Introduction," in Vilém Flusser, *Writings*, ed. Andreas Ströhl, trans. Erik Eisel (Minneapolis: University of Minnesota Press, 2002), xvii.

41. Walmart real estate division employee, interview by author, January 2009, Bentonville, Arkansas, emphasis added.

42. For discussions of retail site selection, see Peter R. Attwood, *Logistics of a Distribution System* (Aldershot, England: Gower, 1992); Dov Izraeli, *Franchising and the Total Distribution System* (London: Longman, 1972); John U. Marshall, *The Location of Service Towns: An Approach to the Analysis of Central Place Systems* (Toronto: University of Toronto Press, 1969); Richard L. Nelson, *The Selection of Retail Locations* (New York: F. W. Dodge, 1958); Peter Scott, *Geography and Retailing* (London: Hutchinson, 1970).

43. Nielsen, "Nielsen Signs US Cooperation Agreement with Walmart, World's Largest Retailer," press release, July 21, 2011, http://www.nielsen.com.

44. Nielsen, "Celebrating 90 Years of Innovation," accessed May 11, 2015, http://sites.nielsen.com/90years.

45. Regarding statistical primacy in regional science and the work of Walter Isard, Paul Krugman writes, "Isard's conclusion . . . was that one could therefore

simply view location as another choice variable in a general equilibrium competitive model, of the kind that was coming to dominate economic analysis. And this was simply wrong: to make any sense of the various approaches to location that he surveyed, one must take account of increasing returns and hence of imperfect competition." Krugman, *Development, Geography, and Economic Theory*, 56. For more on regional science, see Walter Isard, *Introduction to Regional Science* (Englewood Cliffs, N.J.: Prentice Hall, 1975).

46. For example, Walmart relies on a company called Weather Trends International (http://www.weathertrends360.com) for long-term weather predictions on which to base sales projections.

47. Nielsen, "Market and Site Analysis," accessed May 19, 2010, http://www.nielsen.com.

48. For more information on Esri's demographics categories, see Esri, "Esri Demographics: Tapestry Segmentation," accessed February 20, 2016, http://doc.arcgis.com/en/esri-demographics.

49. Simon Thompson, "The Future of Retail: Understanding the Geography of the Marketplace Helps Businesses Thrive," Esri, 2010, http://www.esri.com.

50. Simon Thompson, "Geo Means Business! GIS to Dashboards: For Everyone in the Enterprise," *LBx Journal* 1, no. 1 (Spring/Summer 2009), excerpted at Esri, http://www.esri.com.

51. One article describes how Esri's engine can "run in reverse": it can collect "ideal store profile data" and "plug all this into the ArcGIS system and tell it to go find locations." Michael Pickes, "Re-tooling Real Estate: How Are Cutting-Edge Real Estate Tools Being Enhanced to Meet New Challenges?," *Chain Store Age*, May 2007, 166–67.

52. These articles include Frederic M. Biddle, "Battle of Vermont: Wal-Mart Plots Its Assault on Last Unconquered State," *Boston Globe*, July 18, 1993; Malcolm Gladwell, "Wal-Mart Encounters a Wall of Resistance in Vermont," *Washington Post*, July 27, 1994; John Greenwald, "Up against the Wal-Mart," *Time*, August 22, 1994: Ross Sneyd, "Wal-Mart Lost Battles, Won the War: Vermont Store Opens," *St. Paul Pioneer Press*, September 20, 1995; Pam Belluck, "Preservationists Call Vermont Endangered, by Wal-Mart," *New York Times*, May 25, 2004; George F. Will, "Waging War on Wal-Mart," *Newsweek*, July 05, 2004; Alex Beam, "Wal-Mart and the Battle of Vermont," *Boston Globe*, September 12, 2007.

53. Walton, *Sam Walton*, 141.

54. Matthew Zook and Mark Graham, "Wal-Mart Nation: Mapping the Reach of a Retail Colossus," in Brunn, *Wal-Mart World*, 20.

55. For example, see Ingram et al., "Trouble in Store." These researchers' findings indicate that Walmart assesses the likelihood of protests first, in order to determine whether a location is worth pursuing. The more likely the company is to face resistance, the less likely it is to move forward.

56. The other entries in the 2004 list of endangered places were as follows: 2 Columbus Circle, New York; Bethlehem Steel Plant, Pennsylvania; Elkmont Historic District, Tennessee; George Kraigher House, Texas; Gullah/Geechee Coast, South Carolina; Historic Cook County Hospital, Illinois; Madison-Lenox Hotel, Michigan; Nine Mile Canyon, Utah; Ridgewood Ranch, Home of Seabiscuit, California; and Tobacco Barns of Southern Maryland, Maryland. The 1993 list comprised, in addition to the state of Vermont, Brandy Station Battlefield, Virginia; Downtown New Orleans, Louisiana; Eight Historic Dallas Neighborhoods, Texas; Prehistoric Serpent Mound, Ohio; Schooner C.A. Thayer, California; South Pasadena/El Sereno, California; Sweetgrass Hills, Montana; Thomas Edison's Invention Factory, New Jersey; Town of Ste. Genevieve, Missouri; and Virginia City, Montana. National Trust for Historic Preservation, "11 Most Endangered," accessed January 14, 2016, http://www.preservationnation .org.

57. Biddle, "Battle of Vermont." Perhaps it is worth noting that the comparison, however evocative, is misleading because the Maginot Line of bunkers and fortifications was designed to serve protective and preventive purposes.

58. The Walmart location in Canada that is closest to the Vermont border is Store 5839 in Cowansville, Quebec. Walmart entered Canada in 1994 and by 2015 had 281 supercenters and 114 discount stores there. Store 5839 is not included in this count of stores near the Vermont border because, even if the store is geographically proximate, the national border remains less elastic than U.S. state borders.

59. In a 2007 story for WCAX in Williston, Andy Potter described the town a decade after the Walmart store opened. Andy Potter, "A Decade of Wal-Mart," WCAX.com, January 29, 2007, http://www.wcax.com.

60. Quoted in Sally Johnson, "Vermonters Are Up against the Wal-Mart— Effort to Stop Retail Chain from Entering Vermont," *Insight on the News,* January 10, 1994.

61. This is based on David Glass's description of using a hundred-mile radius to locate new distribution centers. Walton, *Sam Walton,* 94.

62. City of Merced, California, "Wal-Mart Distribution Center and Environmental Impact Report," accessed February 12, 2011, http://www.cityofmerced .org.

63. Thaddeus Miller, "Wal-Mart Likely to Delay Merced Distribution Center," *Merced Sun Star,* December 10, 2013, http://www.mercedsunstar.com. As of February 2015, the project remained on hold. "Fitch Affirms Merced City School District, CA GOs at 'AA–'; Outlook Stable," Business Wire, February 26, 2015, http://www.businesswire.com. For information about the Supreme Court ruling, see City of Merced, "Wal-Mart Distribution Center and Environmental Impact Report: Supreme Court Ruling Favors City," March 13, 2013, https: //www.cityofmerced.org.

64. Quoted in Ameera Butt, "Judge Hears Wal-Mart Distribution Center Arguments," *Modesto Bee*, September 4, 2010, http://www.modbee.com.

65. Quoted in Jonah Owen Lamb, "Wal-Mart Wants Time to Determine If Competitors Might Be Supporting Lawsuits," *Modesto Bee*, June 26, 2010, emphasis added, http://www.modbee.com.

66. For an assessment of local protests regarding the locations of new Walmart stores, see Ingram et al., "Trouble in Store."

67. The first phase of the Campus Parkway Project is complete. Funding for phases 2 and 3 is under consideration by the California State Assembly. According to the proposed legislation (designated ABX1-11), "This bill would appropriate $97,600,000 from the General Fund to the Merced County Association of Governments for construction of phases 2 and 3 of the Campus Parkway Project, a planned road project to connect the University of California, Merced to State Highway 99, in the County of Merced." California Legislative Information, accessed February 20, 2016, https://leginfo.legislature.ca.gov.

68. Merced itself is strategically located to serve California's growing Central Valley region. Not only is it positioned along the heavily trafficked Highway 99 corridor, but it is also a planned stop along the state's proposed high-speed rail line. While Walmart's distribution network relies primarily on its fleet of semitrucks, it is currently trying to curtail its fuel consumption. As large as its operations are, small reductions in costs can have significant impacts when distributed across the entire network.

69. John Austin, *Lectures on Jurisprudence 1832* (1879), II.xlvi.807, in OED Online, http://dictionary.oed.com.

70. Quoted in John M. Broder, "Voters in Los Angeles Suburb Say No to a Big Wal-Mart," *New York Times*, April 8, 2004, http://www.nytimes.com.

71. Marc Augé, *Non-places: Introduction to an Anthropology of Supermodernity*, 2nd ed. (London: Verso, 2008).

72. Elden, *The Birth of Territory*, 292. He also notes, "Descartes's view of space outlined in the *Discours*, and elaborated in the *Geometry* as measurable, mappable, strictly demarcated, and thereby controllable, is precisely that which underpins the modern notion of political rather than solely geographical borders, the boundaries of states" (291).

73. Belmonte, "Implications for Building Demand," 74.

4. Bodies

1. "Oriental Trading Company," *Undercover Boss*, CBS, season 3, episode 7, March 9, 2012.

2. Another category of building devoted to inventory processing is the fulfillment center. Such buildings are common in e-commerce applications

like Amazon's. For example, see Sarah O'Connor, "Amazon Unpacked," *Financial Times*, February 8, 2013, http://www.ft.com. While the term *fulfillment* is closely associated with e-commerce, it is also applicable to other forms of retail distribution.

3. "Taylor's stopwatch time studies were the basis of finding an optimal and standardizable method of production and of designing appropriate tools. Once this one best way was found, it became the performance standard and the basis of the reward and payment system." Hugo Kijne and J.-C. Spender, "Introduction," in *Scientific Management: Frederick Winslow Taylor's Gift to the World?*, ed. J.-C. Spender and Hugo Kijne (London: Kluwer Academic, 1996), xii.

4. Geoffrey W. Clark, "Machine-Shop Engineering Roots of Taylorism: The Efficiency of Machine-Tools and Machinists, 1865–1884," in Spender and Kijne, *Scientific Management*, 47. These issues have been the subject of much academic scrutiny, including, for example, Anson Rabinbach, *The Human Motor: Energy, Fatigue, and the Origins of Modernity* (Berkeley: University of California Press, 1992); Beniger, *The Control Revolution*; and, of course, works that address larger questions about labor and power, including Michel Foucault, *Discipline and Punish: The Birth of the Prison*, trans. Alan Sheridan (New York: Penguin Press, 1977).

5. David E. Wellbery, foreword to Friedrich A. Kittler, *Discourse Networks 1800/1900* (Stanford, Calif.: Stanford University Press, 1990), xv. Wellbery positions Kittler as a synthesizer of various dimensions of the work of Lacan, Derrida, and Foucault, three of poststructuralism's protagonists. He does so partly in an effort to recover aspects of poststructuralism but also to provide more precise means to engage Kittler's text.

6. O'Connor, "Amazon Unpacked."

7. The "robot company" that Amazon acquired is called Kiva Systems. For further discussion of this topic, see Jesse LeCavalier, "Logistics Makes the World," *Art Papers,* January/February 2015.

8. John McPhee, "Out in the Sort," in *Uncommon Carriers* (New York: Farrar, Straus and Giroux, 2006), 176.

9. Ibid., 164.

10. Marquard Smith and Joanne Morra assert their concern with "how the material and metaphorical figurations of prosthesis initiate considerations of the historical and conceptual edges between 'the human' and the posthuman, the organic and the machinic, the evolutionary and the postevolutionary, and flesh and its accompanying technologies." Marquard Smith and Joanne Morra, "Introduction," in *The Prosthetic Impulse: From a Posthuman Present to a Biocultural Future*, ed. Marquard Smith and Joanne Morra (Cambridge: MIT Press, 2007), 3. This connects to a broader discourse around humans, control, and technology, including works by Norbert Wiener, Marshall McLuhan, Georges Canguilhem, Ian Hacking, Donna Haraway, and others.

11. Misha Petrovic and Gary G. Hamilton, "Making Global Markets: Wal-Mart and Its Suppliers," in Lichtenstein, *Wal-Mart*, 133.

12. Andrew McAfee and Erik Brynjolfsson, "Big Data: The Management Revolution," *Harvard Business Review*, October 2012, 61–68. The authors write that 2.5 exabytes of data are created each day and that Walmart collects 2.5 petabytes of data per hour. The percentage figure is arrived at as follows: 1 exabyte = 1,000 petabytes (1 petabyte = 1,000,000 gigabytes) and 2.5 exabytes = 2,500 petabytes, thus 2.5 petabytes/hour × 24 hours = 60 petabytes/day; 60/2,500 = 0.024, or 2.4 percent.

13. Marshall McLuhan described this condition as being related to the "new electric Age of Information and programmed production," in which "commodities themselves assume more and more the character of information." Marshall McLuhan, *Understanding Media: The Extensions of Man* (Cambridge: MIT Press, 1964), 102.

14. The image is a promotion for the Walmart credit card, not to be confused with a loyalty card. For much of its history, Walmart did not have a loyalty or rewards program. In 2014, the company began testing a pilot venture called Savings Catcher. Al Urbanski, "Walmart to Roll Loyalty Program Nationwide," *Direct Marketing News*, June 9, 2014, http://www.dmnews.com.

15. *The Age of Walmart.*

16. *Wal-Mart 1997Annual Report*, 12, http://stock.walmart.com.

17. Data Performance, Inc., accessed August 12, 2010, http://www.dp400.com/SYM_mobilecomputers.html. Symbol Technologies was acquired by Motorola, whose "Enterprise Division" was, in turn, acquired by Zebra Technologies. For more on Symbol's original catalog, see "Symbol Scanner and Mobile Computer," accessed May 12, 2015, http://www.barcodesinc.com/symbol. For more on Zebra Technologies' series of wearable computers, see "Mobile Computers: Wearable Computers," accessed May 12, 2015, https://portal.motorolasolutions.com.

18. Soderquist, *The Wal-Mart Way*, 159.

19. According to users of such systems, they make the work of picking easier, faster, and more accurate. They also demonstrate the disciplining of the body as identified by Foucault, "the formation of a relation that in the mechanism itself makes it more obedient as it becomes more useful." Foucault describes how a "'political anatomy,' which was also a 'mechanics of power,' was being born; it defined how one may have a hold over others' bodies, not only so that they may do what one wishes, but so that they may operate as one wishes, with the techniques, the speed, and the efficiency that one determines." Foucault, *Discipline and Punish*, 138. Regarding new forms of monitoring, "it implies an uninterrupted, constant coercion, supervising the process of the activity rather than its result and it is exercised according to a codification that partitions as closely as possible time, space, movement. These methods, which made possible the

meticulous control of the operations of the body, which assured the constant subjection of its forces and imposed upon them a relation of docility-utility, might be called 'disciplines.'" Ibid., 137.

20. Dematic, "Voice-Directed Picking," promotional video, accessed May 12, 2015, https://youtu.be/quAqpmDNgGQ. See also Dematic, "Pick-to-Voice," accessed May 12, 2015, http://www.dematic.com.

21. Dematic, "Voice-Directed Picking."

22. Jennifer by Lucas, "Voice Picking at Do It Best with Jennifer and Motorola MC9000," promotional video, accessed May 12, 2015, https://youtu.be/t7-Vlf47raA.

23. Ibid.

24. Jennifer by Lucas, "Voice Picking at the Container Store—B2C Fulfillment," promotional video, accessed May 12, 2015, youtu.be/alsdUOsR8jQ.

25. On feedback, Foucault writes: "The training of schoolchildren was to be carried out in the same way: few words, no explanation, a total silence interrupted only by signals—bells, clapping of hands, gestures, a mere glance from the teacher, or that little wooden apparatus used by the Brothers of the Christian Schools; it was called *par excellence* the 'Signal' and it contained in its mechanical brevity both the technique of command and the morality of obedience." Foucault, *Discipline and Punish*, 166. Norbert Wiener notes: "In this conversation between the parts of the machine, it is often necessary to take cognizance of what the machine has already said. Here there enters the principle of feedback, which we have already discussed, and which is older than its exemplification in the ship's steering engine, and is at least as old, in fact, as the governor which regulates the speed of Watt's steam engine." Norbert Wiener, *The Human Use of Human Beings: Cybernetics and Society*, 2nd ed. (Boston: Da Capo Press, 1954), 151–52.

26. BaxTek, "Southeast Frozen Foods Vocollect Voice Warehouse Solution," promotional video, accessed August 12, 2010, http://www.youtube.com/watch?v=nHUT6Tqc4-Y.

27. Quoted in Maida Napolitano, "Three Voices, Three Solutions," *Logistics Management,* July 2010, 42.

28. Marc Levinson's book *The Box* provides a detailed account of the development of the shipping container. In 1956 the trade magazine *Modern Materials Handling* published Herbert Hall's three-part article "We're Ready NOW to Standardize Shipping Containers," which developed a comprehensive case for intermodal transit enabled by a standard shipping unit. See *Modern Materials Handling,* October 1956, 89–93; November 1956, 104–11; December 1956, 97–103.

29. J. C. R. Licklider, "Man–Computer Symbiosis," *IRE Transactions on Human Factors in Electronics,* no. 1 (March 1960): 6, available at http://groups.csail.mit.edu/medg/people/psz/Licklider.html.

30. McLuhan, *Understanding Media*, 45–46.

31. Elaborating on this notion, McLuhan writes, "The effects of technology do not occur at the level of opinions or concepts, but alter sense ratios or patterns of perception steadily and without any resistance. . . . We become what we behold." Ibid., 18.

32. Licklider, "Man–Computer Symbiosis." According to Paul Edwards, Licklider's essay "rapidly achieved the kind of status as a unifying reference point in computer science. . . . It became the universally cited founding articulation of the movement to establish a time-sharing, interactive computing regime." Paul N. Edwards, *The Closed World: Computers and the Politics of Discourse in Cold War America* (Cambridge: MIT Press, 1996), 266.

33. Licklider, "Man–Computer Symbiosis," 4.

34. According to distribution expert Jolyon Drury, "The final picking of discrete articles generally has to be done manually." Jolyon Drury and Peter Falconer, *Building and Planning for Industrial Storage and Distribution*, 2nd ed. (London: Architectural Press, 2003), 204.

5. Territory

1. Rebecca Solnit, "Alice Walton's Fig Leaf," *The Nation*, February 21, 2006, http://www.thenation.com.

2. Michael Leja, "Crystal Bridges Museum of American Art, Bentonville, Ark.," *Art Bulletin* 94, no. 4 (December 2012): 652–55.

3. Northwest Arkansas Council, "Greater Northwest Arkansas Development Strategy," executive summary, January 2011, 4, http://www.greaternorthwestar kansas.com.

4. Whereas, for example, Robert Lang and Joel Garreau identify these new conditions in terms of their relationship to a metropolitan center, Northwest Arkansas has no such reference point. For a discussion of the distinction between "edge cities" and "edgeless cities," see Robert E. Lang, *Edgeless Cities: Exploring the Elusive Metropolis* (Washington, D.C.: Brookings Institution Press, 2003). Additionally, Lang and Jennifer LeFurgy, in *Boomburbs: The Rise of American Accidental Cities* (Washington, D.C.: Brookings Institution Press, 2007), further elaborate this work, although they continue to focus on development in reference to existing urban centers. Lang and LeFurgy align their "boomburb" with Robert Fishman's "technoburb," but Fishman's point seems to be that it is difficult to continue using terms like *suburb* or *boomburb* to refer to conditions that have little to no relationship to adjacent urban concentrations. Although he does not celebrate this condition, he does point out that it is still in its adolescence. Robert Fishman, *Bourgeois Utopias: The Rise and Fall of Suburbia* (New York: Basic Books, 1987), 204.

5. For a discussion of systems building in the technological development of the United States, see Thomas P. Hughes, *American Genesis: A Century of Invention and Technological Enthusiasm* (Chicago: University of Chicago Press, 1989), esp. 1–12 and 184–248.

6. Ibid., 3. In a chapter titled "The System Must Be First" (184–248), Hughes offers a further elaboration and fuller engagement of systems building by focusing on Ford and Samuel Insull.

7. Vance and Scott, *Wal-Mart*, 12. According to Vance and Scott: "Walton was becoming increasingly convinced that for operators of large stores, small towns were an untapped market that offered certain unique advantages. First, existing competition was limited. Major retail chains such as Sears and J. C. Penney were ignoring their outlets in country towns, preferring instead to concentrate their efforts in their new giant stores in shopping centers near major cities, and local merchants would not be able to compete with a large store in price or selection. Second, if a store were large enough to dominate business in a town and its surrounding area, other retailers would be discouraged from entering the market" (41).

8. Ibid., 51.

9. See Mozingo, *Pastoral Capitalism*; Harwood, *The Interface*.

10. U.S. Census Bureau, "Bentonville, Arkansas," accessed February 20, 2016, http://quickfacts.census.gov.

11. Northwest Arkansas Council, *Northwest Arkansas: Great for Business. Great for Life*, brochure, 2012, author's collection.

12. Ibid.

13. For accounts of some of the cultural transformations occurring in Northwest Arkansas, see Marjorie Rosen, *Boom Town: How Wal-Mart Transformed an All-American Town into an International Community* (Chicago: Chicago Review Press, 2009); Michael Barbaro, "In Wal-Mart's Home, Synagogue Signals Growth," *New York Times*, June 20, 2006.

14. Walton Family Foundation, "Home Region," accessed April 29, 2015, http://www.waltonfamilyfoundation.org.

15. Lynch, *The Image of the City*, 119.

16. Marcus Kabel, "NATO Group Tours Arkansas Wal-Mart Boom," Associated Press, June 27, 2006.

17. NATO Parliamentary Assembly, "26–30 June 2006—Visit to Arkansas and San Francisco by the Economics and Security Committee," mission report, paras. 5–6, http://www.nato-pa.int/default.asp?SHORTCUT=1008.

18. Paul Lewis, citing Lewis Mumford and Manuel Castells, writes, "Urbanization is a social and geographic process whereby human settlements acquire great size and high levels of density, heterogeneity, specialization, and interdependence." Paul G. Lewis, *Shaping Suburbia: How Political Institutions Organize Urban Development* (Pittsburgh: University of Pittsburgh Press, 1996), 3.

19.	The NWA MSA comprises Benton, Madison, Washington, and McDonald Counties and has a population of almost 425,000. According to the U.S. Office of Management and Budget, a Metropolitan Statistical Area is "one or more adjacent counties or county equivalents that have at least one urban core area of at least 50,000 population, plus adjacent territory that has a high degree of social and economic integration with the core as measured by commuting ties." U.S. Office of Management and Budget, "Update of Statistical Area Definitions and Guidance on Their Uses," OMB Bulletin No. 10-02, December 1, 2009, http://www.whitehouse.gov/omb. There are currently 366 MSAs that the government uses for statistical purposes. Of these, the NWA MSA is ranked 108th in terms of estimated population but 12th in terms of its growth rate. The area also straddles state boundaries, including Missouri's McDonald County. While the MSA classification has no inherent jurisdictional implications, it does acquire political significance through its use as a regional identifier. It is also significant that each of the three "cores" that define the NWA MSA (i.e., Fayetteville, Springdale, and Rogers) is only marginally above the cutoff population of 50,000. The three cities' combined population remains less than half of the entire MSA.

20.	Lang, *Edgeless Cities*; Lang and LeFurgy, *Boomburbs*. Paul Knox notes that "boomburbs are a new and distinctive kind of place, and they are stealthily eclipsing many traditional cities in terms of economic and demographic vitality." Paul L. Knox, *Metroburbia USA* (New Brunswick, N.J.: Rutgers University Press, 2008), 47. See also Joel Garreau, *Edge City: Life on the New Frontier* (New York: Anchor Books, 1991).

21.	Knox, *Metroburbia USA*, 46.

22.	Cited in ibid., 48.

23.	Robert Bruegmann reinforces the idea that settlements that evince proto-urban, suburban, or exurban forms are, understandably, necessarily defined vis-à-vis the urban: "Because I believe that every part of the urban system is intimately connected to the rest of the system, I have tried to treat sprawl as something that happens not just at the edge but as a process that affects every part of the metropolitan area." Robert Bruegmann, *Sprawl: A Compact History* (Chicago: University of Chicago Press, 2005), 9.

24.	Quoted in Knox, *Metroburbia USA*, 47.

25.	Rosen, *Boom Town*, 2.

26.	Ibid., 6.

27.	See Dolores Hayden, *A Field Guide to Sprawl* (New York: W. W. Norton, 2004); Ellen Dunham-Jones and June Williamson, *Retrofitting Suburbia: Urban Design Solutions for Redesigning Suburbs*, updated ed. (Hoboken, N.J.: John Wiley, 2011); Melvin Webber "The Joys of Spread City," *Urban Design International* 3, no. 4 (1998): 201–6.

28.	For a thorough account of this phenomenon, see Moreton, *To Serve God and Wal-Mart*, chaps. 1–2.

29. Fishman, *Bourgeois Utopias*, 184. Fishman also notes: "The massive rebuilding that began in 1945 represents not the culmination of the 200 year history of suburbia but rather its end. Indeed, this massive change is not suburbanization at all but the creation of a new kind of city, with principles that are directly opposed to the true suburb" (183).

30. "Large and powerful organizations still seek out a central location that validates their importance, and the historic core of great cities still meets that need better than the office complexes on the outskirts. Moreover, the corporate and government headquarters in the core still attract a wide variety of specialized support services . . . that continue to make the center cities viable." Ibid., 197–98.

31. Saskia Sassen, "Why Cities Matter," in *Cities: Architecture and Society*, exhibition catalog, 10th Architecture Biennale, Venice (Venice: Marsilio, 2006), 38.

32. Quoted in Vance and Scott, *Wal-Mart*, 51, brackets in original.

33. Krugman, *Development, Geography, and Economic Theory*, 46.

34. Rosen, *Boom Town*, 173.

35. Jane Jacobs, *The Death and Life of Great American Cities* (New York: Random House, 1961), 146. Robert Fishman writes of Jacobs: "Yet, for all her enthusiasm for cities, Jacobs's message is an essentially negative one. Her faith in individual action is more than counterbalanced by an overwhelming skepticism about what people can accomplish together. To go from Howard to Jacobs is to go from a world that can still be radically re-formed to one whose physical and social foundations cannot be moved. For Jacobs, the cities are already built. The can be renovated but never transformed. . . . The logic of her argument calls for even greater freedom for the capitalist entrepreneur." Robert Fishman, *Urban Utopias in the Twentieth Century: Ebenezer Howard, Frank Lloyd Wright, Le Corbusier* (Cambridge: MIT Press, 1977), 271.

36. Harvey, *Spaces of Neoliberalization*, 65.

37. Fishman, *Bourgeois Utopias*, 204.

38. These developments are described in the NATO Parliamentary Assembly's report, as noted previously. NATO Parliamentary Assembly, "26–30 June 2006," para. 5.

39. Northwest Arkansas Regional Airport, "History," accessed April 30, 2015, http://www.flyxna.com.

40. Jonathan Birchall, "The Town That Wal-Mart Built," *Financial Times*, July 10, 2009, http://www.ft.com. See also Jeffrey Goldberg, "Wal-Mart Heiress's Art Museum a Moral Blight," Bloomberg View, December 12, 2011, http://mobile.bloomberg.com; Rebecca Mead, "Alice's Wonderland: A Walmart Heiress Builds a Museum in the Ozarks," *New Yorker*, June 27, 2011.

41. Philip Kennicott, "Crystal Bridges Art Museum Wows—and Also Confuses," *Washington Post*, September 30, 2011, http://www.washingtonpost.com.

42. Remarks made in *The Art of Crystal Bridges: From Vision to Reality*, documentary film, written and produced by Larry Foley, Crystal Bridges Museum of American Art, 2012.

43. James Russell, "Wal-Mart Heiress's $1.2 Billion Castle Has Warhol, Glass Bridge," Bloomberg Business, October 24, 2011, http://www.bloomberg.com.

44. Robert Fishman addresses the gap in cultural production: "In dealing with these concerns, we must acknowledge the essential truth that the new city will probably never be able to compete culturally with the old centers. There will be for the foreseeable future a division founded on choice between those who seek out even at great cost the kind of cultural excitement that can only be found in the center, and those who choose the family centered life of the outer city. Yet the issue still remains undecided, whether it is possible to create a truly decentralized culture, one in which the family centered life is compatible with a fair degree of choice. There is the irony that American society, which can find in these decentralized regions more than enough specialists in the most arcane engineering specialties, cannot hope to attract a large enough audience to support a chamber music concert." Fishman, *Bourgeois Utopias*, 202.

45. James Cuno, "2014 by the Numbers," Getty Iris, December 15, 2014, http://blogs.getty.edu; Diane Carroll, director of communications, Crystal Bridges Museum of American Art, personal correspondence with author, April 8, 2015.

46. According to the 2015 *Forbes* list of the world's billionaires, Alice Walton's fortune is worth $38 billion, making her the eleventh-richest person in the world; her rank falls between those of her two brothers, Jim ($39.2 billion) and Rob ($37.6 billion). Her sister-in-law Christy Walton, widow of Alice's late brother John, is ranked ninth, with an estimated worth of $40.5 billion. "The World's Billionaires," *Forbes*, accessed March 31, 2015, http://www.forbes.com.

Conclusion

1. The discussion and debate around type in architecture is extensive. In the nineteenth century, Quatremère de Quincy asserted: "'Type' presents less the image of a thing to copy or imitate completely than the idea of an element which ought itself to serve as a rule for the model. . . . The model, as understood in the practical execution of the art, is an object that should be repeated as is; the type, on the contrary, is an object after which each [artist] can conceive works of art that may have no resemblance." Quatremère de Quincy, "Type," in *Oppositions Reader*, ed. K. Michael Hays (New York: Princeton Architectural Press, 1998), 618, brackets in original. Anthony Vidler elaborates on the concept in his essay "The Idea of Type: The Transformation of an Academic Ideal, 1750–1830," in Hays, *Oppositions Reader*. Rafael Moneo's "On Typology" looks at type in

terms of continuity and collectivity, while Alan Colquhoun, in "Form and Figure," attempts to develop more precise definitions of the terms. Rafael Moneo, "On Typology," *Oppositions* 13 (Summer 1978): 22–45; Alan Colquhoun, "Form and Figure," *Oppositions* 12 (Spring 1978): 28–37. Robert Somol addresses similar questions in an effort to examine the sources of postmodern historicism in architecture and what he refers to as "the constructive swerves, or misreadings, of the neo–avant-garde." He states that this form of postwar repetition "sets in motion divergent series and exists as a continual process of differentiating. One points back to a static moment of being, while the other advances through modes of becoming." Robert E. Somol, "Dummy Text, or The Diagrammatic Basis of Contemporary Architecture," in Peter Eisenman, *Diagram Diaries* (New York: Universe, 1999), 9. He goes on to characterize a "diagrammatic practice" as one "flowing around obstacles yet resisting nothing" and opposes it to "the tectonic vision of architecture as the legible sign of construction (which is intended to resist its potential status as either commodity or cultural speculation)." Such an approach "multiplies signifying processes (technological as well as linguistic) within a plenum of matter, recognizing signs as complicit in the construction of specific social machines" (24).

2. Fredric Jameson, "Utopia as Method, or the Uses of the Future," in *Utopia /Dystopia: Conditions of Historical Possibility*, ed. Michael D. Gordin, Helen Tilley, and Gyan Prakash (Princeton, N.J.: Princeton University Press, 2010), 30. Jameson goes on to identify "the shape of a utopian future looming through the mist, which we must seize as an opportunity to exercise the utopian imagination more fully, rather than as an occasion for moralizing judgments or regressive nostalgia" (32). In regard to Walmart, he asserts, "Anyone who does not appreciate this historic originality of Wal-Mart and its strengths and accomplishments is really not up to the discussion . . . but such admiration and positive judgment must be accomplished by the absolute condemnation that completes the dialectical ambivalence we bring to this historical phenomenon" (32).

3. See Bruno S. Frey, *Happiness: A Revolution in Economics* (Cambridge: MIT Press, 2008).

4. Evelyn M. Rusli, "Amazon.com to Acquire Manufacturer of Robotics," *New York Times*, March 20, 2012, http://www.nytimes.com. E. M. Forster anticipated this development in his 1909 short story "The Machine Stops," which describes a world in which inhabitants of automated megacities, freed from the demands of physical labor, are able to devote their energy to the life of the mind. Residents share ideas through sophisticated interfaces and rarely leave their individual living chambers underground because, from their point of view, they have little need to do so. Early in the story, speaking of the mother of the protagonist, who has temporarily escaped the Machine, the third-person narrator derisively acknowledges, "Of course she had studied the civilization that had immediately preceded her own—the civilization that had mistaken the function

of the system, and had used it for bringing people to things, instead of for bringing things to people." E. M. Forster, "The Machine Stops" (1909), in *The Science Fiction Century*, vol. 1, ed. David G. Hartwell (New York: Tim Doherty Associates, 1997), 137. Residents come to deify the Machine even as it breaks down, and, although they could seek an alternative life on the surface of the planet, they are helpless to escape, too seduced by their own techno-utopia.

5. Daniel Nettle, quoted in Frey, *Happiness*, 5.

6. Ibid., x; Amitava Krishna Dutt and Benjamin Radcliff, "Introduction: Happiness, Economics and Politics," in *Happiness, Economics and Politics: Towards a Multi-disciplinary Approach*, ed. Amitava Krishna Dutt and Benjamin Radcliff (Cheltenham, England: Edward Elgar, 2009), 9.

7. Dutt and Radcliff, "Introduction," 8.

8. Cowen, *The Deadly Life of Logistics*, 231.

9. There are extensive literatures on both big data and smart cities. On big data in business, see, for example, McAfee and Brynjolfsson, "Big Data"; Erik Brynjolfsson and Andrew McAfee, *The Second Machine Age: Work, Progress, and Prosperity in a Time of Brilliant Technologies* (New York: W. W. Norton, 2014). For a more historical approach, see Orit Halpern, *Beautiful Data: A History of Reason and Vision since 1945* (Durham, N.C.: Duke University Press, 2014). For an examination of the term *smart city*, see Robert G. Hollands, "Will the Real Smart City Please Stand Up? Intelligent, Progressive or Entrepreneurial?," *City* 12, no. 3 (2008): 303–20.

10. "Sweden: Switch to the Right," *Time*, September 15, 1967, http://www.time.com. See also Volvo Owners' Club, "History of the Volvo Car: September 3 1967. 40 Years of Driving on the Right Side in Sweden," accessed May 29, 2015, https://www.volvoclub.org.uk.

INDEX

Page numbers in italic refer to illustrations

116, 180, 181, 182–84, 186–88,
191, *193*, *194*, *195*, 200, *207*, *209*,
248n35; demographics, 182, 186;
extended stay hotels, 187; gated
communities, 187; redevelopment
of, 192, 200, *201*, 206, 212;
remoteness of, 192; suppliers'
offices/commercial spaces, 187,
196, *197*, 198–99, 212, 262n38
"Bentonville Blueprint 2014," 212
Bentonville City Square, *209, 211*
Bentonville Community and
Economic Development Office, 212
Berger, Alan, 56
Berke, Deborah, 186
Birchall, Jonathan, 232n31
Bismarck, Otto von, 237n20
Blackwell, Marlon, 204
bodies, 154, 216, 256n10; disciplining
of, 167, 257n19
Bonacich, Edna, 230n18
books, 76
boomburbs, 190, 259n4
borders, 4, 51, 136, 229n9, 255n72;
national, 125, 254n58; state, 136,
137, 138, 140, *141*, 142, 145, 261n19,
Plate 10
Box, The (Levinson), 49, 258n28
Boyette Group, 212
branding, 19, *21*, 66, 82, 233n38
Brooklyn Army Terminal, New York,
54, *55*
Bruegmann, Robert, 261n23
buildings: high-rise, 3; value of, 3–4,
170, 234n56
built environment, 7, 8, 10, 31–32, 49,
54, 58, 60, 218, 221, 242nn73–74,
243n76
business continuity, 20, 22

Cabinet, 235n63
California Environmental Quality Act,
144
Campus Parkway Project, Merced,
146, 255n67
Canada, 254n58
cannibalization, 131
capitalism, 51, 107, 193, 218, 249n1
Capstone Turbine, 233n40
cashiers, *67*
Castells, Manuel, 54, 242n73
catchment areas, 140
Central Valley, California, 142, 255n68
chess, 32–33
chewing gum, 63, *65*
Christensen, Julie, 248n32
cities, 61–62, 180, 182, 188, 216,
263n44; development of, 7, 56, 61–
62, 180, 182, 190, 218, 242nn73–
74, 243n76, 259n4, 262nn29–30,
262n36; evaluation of, 2, 243n81;
smart, 221; thematized, 182, 186,
188, 208, *209, 210*
Clarke, Arthur C., 52
Clausewtiz, Carl von, 33; *On War*, 36
Clearwater, 44, 46
Clorox, 199
Colquhoun, Alan, 264n1
Commerce Drive, Bentonville, 198
communications, 52, 58, 125; human-
network, *177*; long-distance, 50,
241n61; networks, 58; satellite,
52, *53*, 88, 108, 120–22, *123*,
124–26, 249n1, 251n27, 252n38;
television, 125–26; wireless, 52
computerization, 39, 176, 178,
237n28; anxiety about, 176;
container ships and, 49;
interactive, 176, 259n32
computers: handheld, 160, *161*, 164,
169; IBM, 110, *111*, 130, 250n7
concreteness, 42–46, 48, 51

consumers and consumer behavior, 64, 66, 68, 74, 219, 220; data collection and, 7–8, 41, 63, 70, 74, 129–30, 246n14; surveys of, 130
container principle, 49
corporations: international, 230n46; paradigmatic, 10
Correll, William, 80, 231n21, 247n16, 247n26
cost analysis, 40, 41, 237n31
Council of Logistics Management, 40
Cowen, Deborah, 38, 40, 51, 221, 229n9
Cree, 20
CRISP program, 82
Cronon, William, 3
cross-docking, 98
Crown, 170, 172
Crystal Bridges Museum of American Art, Bentonville, 179–80, *181*, 186, 192, 199–200, 202, *203*, 204, *205*, 206, 208; admission to, 204, *207*; infrastructure and, 202, *203*, *205*; site plan, *207*; visitation rate, 206
Crystal Creek, Bentonville, 202
cultural institutions, 179–80, 204, 206, 208, 212, 263n44
curiosity, 30, 235n63

data: big, 221; consumer, 7–8, 41, 63, 121, 126, 130–31, 246n14; demographic, 129–30, 131, 132; encryption of, 48; point of sale (POS), 16; public sector, 129; sources of, 129–31; storage of, 76; weather, 157, 253n46
data centers, 94, 249n40; invisibility of, 90, 92. *See also* Google data center, The Dalles, Oregon; Walmart data center, McDonald County, Missouri

DC 6094, Arkansas, 96, 100
Dean, Howard, 107, 140
decision-making: data-driven, 216, 221
decorated shed, 84
DeLanda, Manuel, 36, 38
Dematic, Inc., 101, *103*, 164, *165*, 172, *175*
de-skilling, 156
dexterity, 156
diagrammatic practice, 264n1
diagrams, 34–35, *37*, 46, 49, 58, *59*, 72, 109, 236nn14–15, 264n1, *Plate 1*
Discount Store News, 121, 122
Discourse Networks 1800/1900 (Kittler), 154, 256n5
distance: measured in time, 43, 44, 47
distribution centers (DCs), 15, *99*, *103*, 153–54, 156, *Plate 6*; conveyors within, *103*; employee monitoring/management, 156, 159, 162, *163*, 164, *165*, 166–68, 257n19, 258n25; human labor and, 156, 174, 176, 178, 219; interiors of, 170, *171*, 219, *223*; loading docks and, 170, *171*; location of goods within, 168, 170, 219; order processing and, 158–59, 166; robotic drive units (RDUs) and, 219, 220, *223*; space of, 162, *163*, 168, 170, *171*, 172, 219, *223*; technology-human relationships and, 151–60, *161*, 162–76, *177*, 178, 219, 257n19, 258n25
District at Pinnacle Hills, Rogers, Arkansas, 210
driving: right lane, 222, *223*
Drucker, Peter F., 39, 40, 237n28
Drury, Jolyon, 259n34
Duke, Mike, 20
Dunlop, John, 74, 245n11, 246n14
Durand, Asher B.: *Kindred Spirits*, 179, *181*

Easterling, Keller, 238n39, 239n42, 243n76
economics, 220, 252n45; capitalist, 51, 107, 193, 218, 249n1; risk and uncertainty factors, 74–75, 242n70, 246n14
Edwards, Paul, 25, 50; "Infrastructure and Modernity," 235n61, 241nn60–61, 241n64
efficiency: industrial, 154, 158
Einstein, Charles B.: "Modeling the Wholesale Logistics Base," 31, 32, 49, *Plate 1*
Elden, Stuart, 35, 60–61, 149, 255n72
environments: logistical, 168, 170, *171*, 172, *173*, 174, 176, *177*, 178
Esri, 132, 253n51; market assessment map by, *133*
eudaimonia, 220, 221
exchangeability, 42–43
exurbs, 190

Fail Safe (movie), 176
Fayetteville, Arkansas, 183
Fayetteville-Rogers-Springdale Metropolitan Statistical Area. *See* Northwest Arkansas Metropolitan Statistical Area (NWA MSA)
Federated Stores, 245n11
feedback, 166–67, 168, 258n25
Fishman, Charles, 230n17
Fishman, Robert, 191, 193, 259n4, 262nn29–30, 262n35, 263n44
Flex-Sort Sliding Shoe Sorter, *103*
Flint, Anthony, 190
Flusser, Vilém, 236n15, 252n40
Ford, 184
Ford, Henry, 183, 186, 260n6
Ford, Rollin, 101, 102
formats, 76
Forster, E. M.: "The Machine Stops," 264n4

Fort Worth, Texas, 247n26
Foucault, Michel, 30, 257n19, 258n25
franchising, 64, 66, 68
free market trading, 107, 112, 114–15, 210, 249n1
fuel, 38
fulfillment centers. *See* distribution centers (DCs)
fungibility, 146, 148–50

Galison, Peter, 243n81
Garreau, Joel, 259n4
General Motors, 24–25, *Plate 3*
geography: architectural, 58, 60, 243n84, 244n85; political (*see* geopolitics)
geopolitics, 58, 60, 218, 221, 243n83, 244n85
Giedion, Sigfried, 48, 240n50
Gilbert, Cass, 3, 54
GIS, 132
Glass, David, 117, 126, *127*, 140, 231n21, 243n84, 254n61
globalization, 7, 28, 51, 150, 188–89, 215, 221, 239n46, 242nn73–74; regulation and, 20, 233n47
GM. *See* General Motors
goods: exchange of, 3–4, 6–7, 18, 28, 232n36; forecasting and, 41, 157–58; identified as data and information, 71–72, 157; packing and picking of, 48, 151–78, 240n52, 255n2; production and distribution of, 7, 18, 28, 38–42, 44, 46, 48, 49, 57, 68, 71–72, 74, 98, 100–102, 230n18, 232n36, 237n31, 237n33, 238n38, 240n49, 242n74, 243n76, 244n86; space of, 42–43
Google data center, The Dalles, Oregon, 92, *93*
Goss, Jon, 58

Graham, Stephen, 51
Great Dane trailers, 233n40
Green, Jessica, 233n47

Habern, Glenn, 122
Hall, Herbert: "We're Ready NOW to
    Standardize Shipping Containers,"
    258n28
happiness, 218, 220–21
Harvey, David, 193, 234n60, 240n49
Harwood, John: *The Interface*, 57,
    236n14, 240n51
Heath, Brenda, *139*
Heins, Matthew: *The Shipping
    Container and the Globalization
    of American Infrastructure*,
    240n54
Hercules, California, 77, 78
Hight-Jackson Associates, 212
highways, 58, 117, 142, *141*, 146, 210,
    255n67, *Plate 9*
Hilton, Conrad, 38
Hinsdale, New Hampshire, 141, 142
history (discipline), 235n61
Hölzle, Urs, 94
Hooghe, Alexander d', 248n32
horizontality, 75, 88
Huey, John, 119
Hughes, Thomas, 183, 260n6
Hughes Network Systems, 122
human-tool relationships. *See*
    technology-human relationships
Hunt, Johnnie Bryan, 192
Hurricane Katrina, 20, 22, 23, 24
Huston, James, 32, 36, 37, 38, 39,
    237nn19–20

IBM, 24, 110, 184, 186, 250n7, *Plate 3*
IBM Corporate Headquarters,
    Armonk, 57, *Plate 3*
ICSC. *See* International Council of
    Shopping Centers (ICSC)

imageability, 61, 216
Image of the City, The (Lynch), 61, 188
infrastructure, 8, 25–26, 38, 49–52,
    218, 221–22, 240n54; goals and,
    51; invisibility of, 50–51, 84, 222
"Infrastructure and Modernity"
    (Edwards), 235n61, 241nn60–61,
    241n64
Inglewood, California, 148
Inglewood City Council, 148
instant gratification, 219, 221
Insull, Samuel, 260n6
Integral Logistics Management
    (Schönsleben), 40
Interface, The (Harwood), 236n14,
    240n51
interfaces: computerized, 151–52,
    159–60, 162
International Council of Shopping
    Centers (ICSC), 1, 135
Internet, 156, 257n12
Interstate 40, 200
Interstate 41, 192, 200
Interstate 94, 117
Intrabody Information Transfer
    Device, *177*
inventory management, 11, 13, 14,
    15, 16, 20, 46, 52, 63–64, 70, 71,
    88–89, 94, 108–9, 121, 152–54,
    155, 156–78, 231n20, 246nn13–
    14, 252n29, 255n2. *See also*
    distribution centers (DCs); goods:
    production and distribution of
Isard, Walter, 252n45
isolationism, 192, 193

Jackson, Jason, 22
Jacobs, Jane, 193, 262n36
Jameson, Frederic, 218, 264n2
J. B. Hunt, 187, 192, 210
Jennifer VoicePlus, 151–52, 166–67
John Q. Hammons, 210

"Machine Stops, The" (Forster), 264n4
Macom & Hughes Corporation, 122
Maginot Line, 138, 254n57
"Man-Computing Symbiosis" (Licklider), 176, 259n32
Manhattan, 13, *Plate 4*
marketing, 41, 66
market segments, 132
market share, 130
market site analysis, 131–32
Marks, Abe, 108–9
Marsh Supermarkets, 63
Martin, James, 125, 251n27
Martin, Reinhold, 250n7
Marvin, Simon, 51
mass merchandising, 64, 68
matériel, 170, 237n19
Mattelart, Armand, 239n46
McAdams, Bob, 148
McDonald County, Missouri, 90, 248n35
McLuhan, Marshall, 257n13; *Understanding Media*, 174
McPhee, John, 156
mechanization, 241n62
media, 174, 259n31
Mellor, Roy, 60
Merced, California, *141*, 142, *143*, 144–46, 255n68
Merced Alliance for Responsible Growth (MARG), 144
Metropolitan Statistical Areas (MSAs), 261n19
military: logistics, 31, 32, 33–36, *37*, 38–39, 108–9, 170, 221, 239n46, 246n13; supply movements, 33–36, *37*, 38–39, 46; warehouses, 35, 54, *55*
mobility, 168, 170, *171*, 172, *173*
"Modeling the Wholesale Logistics Base" (Einstein), 31, 49, *Plate 1*

modernity, 149, 242n68
modularity, 46, 48–49, 240n51, 240n54, 250n7
Moneo, Rafael, 264n1
Morra, Joanne, 256n10
Motorola, 160, 166, 257n17
Mumford, Lewis, 241n62
Murrieta, California, 2

Napoleon, 38, 236n6
National Mass Retailers' Institute (NMRI), 108
National Trust for Historic Preservation, 138
nations, 60
NATO Parliamentary Assembly, Economics and Security Committee, 188–89, 262n38
networks: distributed, 58, *59*; friction and, 36, 38, 46, 240n49; logistical, 32–33, 43, 51–52, *59*, 109, 184, 238n38
Neumann, Roderick P., 25, 234n58
New York Public Library, 179
Nielsen, Arthur, 129–30
Nielsen Corporation, 129–30
NMRI. *See* National Mass Retailers' Institute (NMRI)
non-places, 149
North Dakota, 117
Northwest Arkansas Council, 187, 200, 212
Northwest Arkansas Metropolitan Statistical Area (NWA MSA), 180, 182, 187, 206, 261n19; demographics, 189, 190, 208, 210, 261n19; growth, 189–93, 261n19; infrastructure improvements, 187–88; privatization of, 212; redevelopment of, 192, 200, *201*, 206
Northwest Arkansas Regional Airport, 192, 200, *201*

Noyes, Eliot, 110, 112
NWA MSA. *See* Northwest Arkansas Metropolitan Statistical Area (NWA MSA)

objects, 48, 71–72, 220, 240n50; rendering of, 32–33, *37*, 46, 49, 63, *Plate 1*
office parks. *See* vendorvilles
On War (Clausewitz), 36
orders: assembling of (*see* picking); processing, 159, 162, 164, 166
Oriental Trade Company, 151
Ortega, Bob, 117, 250n10
Owen, Robert, 167

packet switching, 49
Paine, Roxy, 200
pallet jacks, 170, *171*
pallets, 48, 170, 240n53
pallet trucks. *See* pallet jacks
Pawley, Martin, 248n38
perceptions, 259n31
Peterbilt, 233n40
Phoenix, Arizona, *79*
pickers, 159, 162, 259n34. *See also* distribution centers (DCs): employee monitoring/ management; picking systems: employees and
picking systems, 156, 159, 219, 259n34; break-pack, *155*; employees and, 167–68; put-to-light, *155*; voice-directed, 151–52, 162, 164, *165*, 166–68, *169*, 257n19
Piggly Wiggly, 64, 66–68, 70, 245n8
pigs, 3
Pinnacle Hills, Rogers, Arkansas, 208, 210, *213*
places, 149, 218; endangered, 138, 254n56
Pop-Tarts, 157, *Plate 11*

postwar historicism, 264n1
Potter, Andy, 254n59
power, 58, 243n84, 244n85
privatization, 212, 221
Proctor & Gamble, 199
profit margins, 11, 12, 19
prostheses, 256n10
public policy, 24, 233n47
push-pull supply chain strategy, 41

quartermasters, 34, 36
Quatremère de Quincy, Antoine-Chrysostome, 263n1

radio-frequency identification (RFID). *See* RFID
railroads. *See* trains
Raintree Plaza, Bentonville, 198
Ramirez, John, 144
RAND Corporation, 109, 243n81
RDUs. *See* robotic drive units (RDUs)
real estate, 1–2, 38, 150; regulation and, 137; value of, 3–4, 170, 234n56. *See also* site selection
RECon, Las Vegas, 1–3, *5*
Rees, David, 125
regimentation, 241n62
regional science, 130, 149, 252n45
regions, 192, 193
REgis, 132, *133*
replenishment, 159
Retail Industry Leaders Association (RILA), *59*, 109
Retail Real Estate Convention (RECon), Las Vegas. *See* RECon, Las Vegas
RFID, 246n12
RILA. *See* Retail Industry Leaders Association (RILA)
River Rouge Plant, Michigan, 186
Rivkin, Jan, 74, 245n11, 246n14
robotic drive units (RDUs), 219, 220, *223*

robots, 156, 219, *223*, 256n7

Rosen, Marjorie, 190

Ruhleder, Karen, 50

Rutland, Vermont, *139*, 140

Safdie, Moshe, 186, 200, 202

sales volume, 11, 12

Sam M. Walton Development Complex, Bentonville, *29*

Sam's Clubs, 13

Sassen, Saskia: "Why Cities Matter," 191

Satellite Business Systems (SBS)-4 satellite, 122, *123*, 124

satellites: communication, 52, *53*, 88, 108, 120–22, *123*, 124–25, 249n1, 251n27, 252n38; regulation of, 125

Saunders, Clarence, 64, 66–68, 245n4, 245n8; *The Turnstile, 69; Whats and What Nots of Piggly Wiggly System*, 68, 70

scale, 25, 234n58, 234n60, 235n61

scan guns. *See* bar code scanners

Schönsleben, Paul: *Integral Logistics Management*, 40

scientific management, 153, 154

Scott, Lee, 10, 19, 231n21

Scott, Roy V., 114, 260n7

Scott Brown, Denise, 84

Scribner, Gail, *139*

security: national, 51; Walmart data centers and, 90, *91, 92, 93,* 94, *95*, 96

self-service, 63–64, 66, *67*, 68–70, 183, 245n4

senses, 259n31

servomechanisms, 174, 178, 259n31

Sheffi, Yossi, 41

shelves: high-density storage, 172, *173, 175*

Shewmaker, Jack, 112, 115, *115*, 122, 249n1

Shipping Container and the Globalization of American Infrastructure, The (Heins), 240n54

shipping containers, 16, 48–49, 240n53

ships, 49

shopping: automation of, 246n12

shopping centers, 1–2

simulations, 32, *37*; computerized, 39, 237n28

site selection, 130, 131–32, *133*, 134–37, 253n51; location software, 128–37; prospecting software, 134, 136

Sites USA, 132; market visualization by, *133*

Skidmore, Owings & Merrill (SOM), 56–57

Skirball Cultural Center, Los Angeles, 200

SKUs. *See* stock keeping units (SKUs)

Smith, Marquand, 256n10

Smykay, Edward, 41

Snyder, Susan Nigra, 56, 242n74, 243n76

Soderquist, Don, 98, 116, 121, 249n1, 251n15

Solnit, Rebecca, 179

SOM. *See* Skidmore, Owings & Merrill (SOM)

Somol, Robert, 264n1

sortation, 156

Southeast Frozen Foods, 167

South Walton Plaza, Bentonville, 198–99

spaces, 149, 218, 255n72

Spark (logo), 19, *21*, 233n38, *Plate 3*

Spark Café, Bentonville, 208

spatiality, 32, 34–35, *37*, 40–43, 51, 60–61, 218–19, 236n12, 236nn14–15, 238n39, 240n49

Spinks, Lisa, 82
Star, Susan Leigh, 50
State Highway 99, California, *141*, 146, 255n67
State of the Art: American Art Now (exhibition), 206, 208
states, 60
stock keeping units (SKUs), 46
stockpickers, 172
stores, 6, 11, 89, 131; discount, 64, 66, 68, 108, 183; pathways within, 67, 89
storms, 157
Students in Free Enterprise (SIFE), 249n1
subject (concept), 154
suburban sprawl, 30, 140, 180, 190–93, 261n23
suburbs, 190, 198–99, 259n4, 262nn29–30, 263n44
Supercenter Prototype 143, *81*, 84, 88
supermarkets, *65*, 70, 88–89, 245n3, 248n33
supermodernity, 149
supplies: military's movement of, 33–36, *37*, 38–39, 46; terminals for, 54
supply chains, 32–33
sustainability, 20, 233n47
Sustainable Product Index, 20
Sweden: switch to right lane driving, 222, *223*
Symbol Technologies, 159, *163*, 257n17
systems: builders of, 183, 184; loosely coupled, 74, 89, 247n15, 247n18; sociotechnical, 50–51, 241n64

Taylor, Frederick Winslow, 153, 154
technoburbs, 191, 193, 259n4, 262n30
technology, 10, 25, 38, 50, 158–59, 230n13; interactions with humans, 151–60, *161*, 162–76, *177*, 178, 257n19, 258n25
technology-human relationships, 151–60, *161*, 162–76, *177*, 178, 257n19, 258n25, 259n32
television: consumers' viewing habits, 129, 131; live via satellite, 125, 252n38
temporality, 8, 14, 18, 34, 35, 43, 51, 240n49
territories, 35, 56, 58–62, 108, 132, 180, 222, 236n15, 242nn73–74, 243n76, 244n86; cartographic control over, 58, 60–61, 84, 116, 131–32, 134, 136, 137–38, *139*, 140–46, 148–50, 193, 218, 221, 222, 244n85, *Plate 10*; data and, 132; fungibility and, 146, 148–50; logistical, 108, 146, 148–50, 191, 210
TEUs. *See* twenty-foot equivalent units (TEUs)
Theory and Design in the First Machine Age (Banham), 17–18, 230n13
Thorpe, George, 236n6
301 Southwest Eighteenth Street, Bentonville, 198
throughput, 153
time: standardization of, 51; zones, 43, 51. *See also* temporality
time-and-motion studies, 154
tool-human relationships. *See* technology-human relationships
trade areas, *133*, 134
trailers, *21*, *23*, 170, *171*
train conductors, 44, 239n44
trains, 43, 239n46; collisions, 43; schedule synchronization of, 43–44; travel rates, 43, 47
transport, 192–93

12, 19–20, 187, 196, 198–99, 210,
230n20; target markets, 11, 132,
137, 138; television network, 120,
121, 124–25, 126, *127*; territory
and, 114, *115*, 116, 119–20, 121, 126,
128, 137–38, *139*, 140–42, 145,
184, 210, *Plate 9, Plate 10*; trucks,
trailers and trucking, 14, 18–19,
21, 23, 98, 100, 102, 146, 158, *171*,
255n68; Vermont and, 137–38,
139, 140–42, 254n59, *Plate 10*
Walmart data center, McDonald
County, Missouri, 90, *91*, 92, *93*,
94, *95*, 96
Wal-Mart Discount City, Rogers,
Arkansas, 183
Walmart Distribution Center,
Bentonville, 14, *15*, 16, 183
Walmart Express, 212
Walmart 5861, Warrenton, Oregon,
82, *83, 85, 86, 87*
Walmart Museum, Bentonville, *15*,
186, 188, 208, *209, 211*, 231n21
Walmart Neighborhood Market,
Rogers, Arkansas, 210, *213*
Walmart Stores, Inc. *See* Walmart
Walmart 2 Go, 212
Walmart Visitor Center, Bentonville.
See Walmart Museum, Bentonville
Walton, Alice, 179, 187, 200, 206,
263n46; childhood home, 204,
207
Walton, Bud, 118, 119, 183
Walton, Christy, 263n46
Walton, Helen, 249n1
Walton, Jim, 117–18, 209, 263n46
Walton, John, 263n46
Walton, Rob, 263n46
Walton, Sam, 11, 64, 120, *127*, 182,
184, 187, 192, 204, 244n2,
249n1, 260n7; interest in
computerization, 107, 108–9,

124, 250n3; military aspirations
of, 118; obsession with aerial
reconnaissance and flying, 109,
118–20; obsession with stores'
performance data, 12, 112, 121,
124, 251n26; office, 188, 208, *211*;
pickup truck, 208; satellites and,
122, 124, 126; on site selection,
116, 117, 118, 119, 120, 137, 251n21;
on store architecture, 78; values
of, 184, 192
Walton family: wealth of, 208,
263n46
Walton Family Foundation, 182, 188,
204; Home Region Program, 188
Walton's 5-10 (Five and Dime), 11, 64,
183, 188, 208, *209, 211*
warehouses: military, 35, 54, *55*
warfare, 32, 33–34, 36, 38
watches, 44, *45*
weather, 157, 253n46
Weather Trends International, 253n46
Weick, Karl, 74, 77, 247n18
Wellbery, David, 154, 256n5
Wennberg, Jeff, *139*
"We're Ready NOW to Standardize
Shipping Containers (Hall),"
258n28
Western Railroad, 43
*Whats and What Nots of Piggly
Wiggly System* (Saunders), 68, 70
"Why Cities Matter" (Sassen), 191
Wiener, Norbert, 167, 258n25
Williston, Vermont, 254n59
Wilson, Charles Erwin, 24
Wireless World, 52
Wright, Frank Lloyd, 200

Zaera Polo, Alejandro, 248n32
Zebra Technologies, 257n17

JESSE LECAVALIER is assistant professor of architecture at the
New Jersey Institute of Technology.